"A lover of books, ideas, book clubs, libraries and reading, Donna Diamond has taken her years of experience creating book groups, selecting titles and leading discussions to write the ultimate primer on how to make reading a fundamental pursuit of community life and a path to personal enrichment. Donna Diamond is a beautiful writer. More than a how-to, her book is a what-if of ideas, a compilation of great books, personally curated and described, designed to bring people together, spur discussions and encourage readers to apply big ideas and imaginative thought to their own lives. Magnificent!"

~ *Adriana Trigiani, New York Times bestselling author of eighteen books including Tony's Wife, Kiss Carlo, The Shoemaker's Wife, Big Stone Gap series and Valentine trilogy.*

***

Donna, you are a "cheerleader for literature!"

~ *Meg Wolitzer, Bestselling author of THE INTERESTINGS, THE TEN YEAR NAP, THE POSITION, SAG and Hollywood Foreign Press winner for Glenn Close's portrayal - THE WIFE, THE FEMALE PERSUASION*

***

"Donna, Happy Holidays to you and all of the amazing readers who follow you. YOU are a book goddess!"

~ Chris Bohjalian, author of 19 books including the bestsellers MIDWIVES and THE SANDCASTLE GIRLS

***

"Donna Diamond has lived a life immersed in books and stories and to be asked to speak to her group is to be allowed into "the club" where one gets to watch a master at work with literature. Donna enriches everyone's lives with her love of books and her own story will enrich yours."

~ Lee Woodruff, New York Times Bestselling author, journalist, essayist, media consultant and co-founder with her husband, Bob Woodruff, of the Bob Woodruff Foundation, #Stand4Heroes to support our men and women war veterans

BOOK CLUB

How I Became the Ultimate Hard-core, High-handed, Card-carrying Bibliophilist

DONNA J. DIAMOND

"To my husband, Ted, my Theo, my love, my rock. Thank you for always showing me what it means "in sickness and in health," and "for better or for worse."

"Je t'aime, plus qu'hier, moins que demain. A nous deux pour toujours."

AND

"To my beloved children, Dani(elle) and Brett, my forever loves, the lights of my life. You are the absolute BEST of your Dad and me and I couldn't be prouder of the woman and man, the Mom and Dad, you have become. Thank you for always championing me on our life journey together and for remembering our nightly anthem, "Bonsoir poupee, A demain, Je t'aime". Now it's my turn to

"Grab a piece of the world and make it ours!"

Table of Contents

Useful Definitions: 19

PREFACE...20

Chapter 1 23

The Beginning of My Book Life... With Several Hiccups Along the Way to Becoming the Ultimate Hard-core, High-Handed, Card-carrying Bibliophilist (May – December 1996)...23

MAY 1996: Snow Falling On Cedars by David Guterson...................................25

JUNE 1996: Primary Colors by Anonymous...31

JULY 1996: The Runaway Jury by John Grisham...31

AUGUST 1996: I Was Amelia Earhart by Jane Mendelsohn 38

SEPTEMBER 1996: The Fourth Estate by Jeffrey Archer and The Deep End of The Ocean by Jacquelyn Mitchard 48

OCTOBER 1996: The Last Don by Mario Puzo 53

NOVEMBER 1996: The Deep End of the Ocean by Jacquelyn Mitchard..........57

DECEMBER 1996..60

Chapter 2 63

CRASH! BOOM! BANG! – Feeling My Way Through Books and Life (1997 and 1998) 63

JANUARY 1997: The Horse Whisperer by Nicholas Evans 64

FEBRUARY 1997: The Third Twin by Ken Follett...66

MARCH 1997: The Shipping News by E. Annie Proulx....................................67

APRIL 1997: Angela's Ashes by Frank McCourt 69

MAY 1997: Midnight in the Garden of Good and Evil by John Berendt 71

JUNE 1997: All the Pretty Horses by Cormac McCarthy.................................73

JULY 1997: Plum Island by Nelson DeMille 75

SEPTEMBER 1997: Songs in Ordinary Time by Mary McGarry Morris.............77

OCTOBER 1997: The Reef by Edith Wharton...78

NOVEMBER 1997: Up Island by Anne Rivers Siddons 79

DECEMBER 1997: A Civil Action by Jonathan Harr 80

JANUARY - DECEMBER 1998...83

JANUARY 1998: Larry's Party by Carol Shields 84

FEBRUARY 1998: Cold Mountain by Charles Frazier 85

MARCH 1998: The Color of Water: A Black Man's Tribute to His White
Mother by James McBride 86

APRIL 1998: A Certain Justice by P.D. James 88

MAY 1998: At Home in Mitford (The Mitford Series) by Jan Karon 89

JUNE 1998: Memoirs of a Geisha by Arthur Golden 90

JULY 1998: A Widow For One Year by John Irving..92

AUGUST 1998: Wait Till Next Year by Doris Kearns Goodwin 93

AUGUST 1998: Colony by Anne Rivers Siddons..94

SEPTEMBER 1998: Philistines at the Hedgerow: Passion and Property in the
Hamptons by Stephen Gaines 95

OCTOBER 1998: She's Come Undone by Wally Lamb 96

DECEMBER 1998: For Kings and Planets by Ethan Canin 98

Chapter 3 99

Turning the Page on the Book and the 20th Century (1999) Author Friends
and Invited Guests...99

Chapter 4 113

When One Door Closes Another Door Opens (2000)...........................113

JANUARY 2000: 'Tis by Frank McCourt...116

FEBRUARY 2000: The Weight of Water by Anita Shreve..............................118

MARCH 2000: A Gesture Life by Chang-Rae Lee 120

APRIL 2000: The Hours by Michael Cunningham 121

MAY 2000: Alias Grace by Margaret Atwood................................122

JUNE 2000: Tuesdays With Morrie: An old man, a young man, and life's
greatest lesson by Mitch Albom..126

JULY 2000: Horse Heaven by Jane Smiley 128

AUGUST 2000: Half a Heart by Rosellen Brown 129

SEPTEMBER 2000: Flags of Our Fathers by James Bradley............................130

OCTOBER 2000: Winter Solstice by Rosamunde Pilcher 134

NOVEMBER 2000: Corelli's Mandolin by Louis de Bernieres 136

DECEMBER 2000: The Samurai's Garden by Gail Tsukiyama 138

Chapter 5 141

The End of Camelot (2001)...141

JANUARY 2001: Tyrannosaurus Sue: The Extraordinary Saga of the Largest, Most Sought Over T. Rex Ever Found by Steve Fiffer 142

FEBRUARY 2001: Morgan's Run by Colleen McCullough 143

MARCH 2001: Plainsong by Kent Haruf...144

APRIL 2001: Drowning Ruth by Christina Schwarz 145

MAY 2001: Girl with A Pearl Earring by Tracy Chevalier 146

JUNE 2001: House of Sand and Fog by Andre Dubus III 148

JULY 2001: Scarlet Feather by Maeve Binchy...............................153

AUGUST 2001: Salem Falls by Jodi Picoult 155

SEPTEMBER 2001: The Gates of the Alamo by Stephen Harrigan.................158

SEPTEMBER 11, 2001 163

OCTOBER 2001: While I Was Gone by Sue Miller............................164

NOVEMBER 2001: Waiting by Ha Jin 165

DECEMBER 2001: John Adams by David McCullough 166

Chapter 6 181

"Il n'y a pas de roses sans épines." ~ Every Rose Has Its Thorns, But Chocolate Cream Pie In The Face Can Make It Better (2002).......................181

JANUARY 2002: In the Heart of the Sea: The Tragedy of the Whaleship Essex by Nathaniel Philbrick 184

FEBRUARY 2002: The Bee Season by Myla Goldberg 187

MARCH 2002: The Amazing Adventures of Kavalier and Clay by Michael Chabon 189

APRIL 2002: Hateship, Friendship, Loveship, Courtship, Marriage by Alice Munro...190

MAY 2002: The Heart is a Lonely Hunter by Carson McCullers....................191

JUNE 2002: Plain Truth by Jodi Picoult 193

JULY 2002: Women of the Silk by Gail Tsukiyama 195

AUGUST 2002 196

SEPTEMBER 2002: Nine Parts of Desire: The Hidden World of Islamic Women by Geraldine Brooks 197

OCTOBER 2002: The True Sources of the Nile by Sarah Stone 199

NOVEMBER 2002: Empire Falls by Richard Russo 203

DECEMBER 2002: Peace Like a River by Leif Enger 205

1977, 1979, 1981, 1983, 1988 206

1981 209

1983 211

1988 213

Chapter 7 218

Donna's Big Gaff! (Among Other Things) 2003 218

THE YEAR 2003 221

JANUARY 2003: Standing in the Rainbow by Fannie Flagg 222

FEBRUARY 2003: The Lovely Bones by Alice Sebold 223

MARCH 2003: The Piano Tuner by Daniel Mason 226

APRIL 2003: How the Garcia Girls Lost Their Accents by Julia Alvarez 227

MAY 2003: Seabiscuit: An American Legend by Laura Hillenbrand 228

JUNE 2003: Five Quarters of the Orange by Joanne Harris 230

JULY 2003: A String of Pearls: From Infamy to Victory, a WWII Series – Book One by Benedict Baglio 231

AUGUST 2003: Bel Canto by Ann Patchett 232

SEPTEMBER 2003: The Vineyard: The Pleasures and Perils of Creating an American Family Winery by Louisa Thomas Hargrave 233

OCTOBER 2003: The Da Vinci Code by Dan Brown 235

NOVEMBER 2003: Atonement by Ian McEwan 238

DECEMBER 2003: The Secret Life of Bees by Sue Monk Kidd 239

Chapter 8 241

Why Thaddeus Named Me the Ultimate Hard-core, High-handed, Card-carrying Bibliophilist (2004) 241

JANUARY 2004: The Eyre Affair by Jasper Fforde and Jane Eyre by Charlotte Bronte 243

FEBRUARY 2004: The Passion of Artemisia by Susan Vreeland....................245

MARCH 2004: Benjamin Franklin by Walter Isaacson 246

APRIL 2004: Snow in August by Pete Hamill..247

MAY 2004: The Amateur Marriage by Anne Tyler...249

JUNE 2004: Aloft by Chang-Rae Lee 258

JULY 2004: Angle of Repose by Wallace Stegner 259

AUGUST 2004: Pompeii by Robert Harris...260

SEPTEMBER 2004: The Other Boleyn Girl by Philippa Gregory 262

OCTOBER 2004: The Namesake by Jhumpa Lahiri 263

NOVEMBER 2004: The Good German by Joseph Kanon 264

DECEMBER 2004: Before You Know Kindness by Chris Bohjalian 266

Chapter 9 268

Of Kites and Plots and Crows and Devils (2005)..268

JANUARY 2005: The Kite Runner by Khaled Hosseini....................................268

FEBRUARY 2005: The Plot Against America by Phillip Roth 270

MARCH 2005: Crow Lake by Mary Lawson 272

APRIL 2005: Travels with Charley: In Search of America by John Steinbeck
(* A Long Island Reads Selection)..273

MAY 2005: The Devil in the White City: Murder, Magic, and Madness at the
Fair That Changed America by Erik Larson...274

JUNE 2005: Paradise Alley by Kevin Baker 276

JULY 2005: Vanishing Act by Jodi Picoult..278

AUGUST 2005: Nightfall by Nelson DeMille 279

SEPTEMBER 2005: McNally's Bluff by Vince Lardo *(Guest Author) 281

OCTOBER 2005: The Historian by Elizabeth Kostova....................................282

NOVEMBER 2005: The Cruelest Miles: The Heroic Story of Dogs and Men
in a Race Against an Epidemic by Gay and Laney Salisbury 284

DECEMBER 2005: 1776 by David McCullough..285

Chapter 10 286

Jump Start Your Book Club & Literary Terms, Nancy Pearl's 'RULE OF 50', A
Few of My Favorite Books 286

The Year I Became Mimi (2006) 286

JANUARY 2006: Sweetwater Creek by Anne Rivers Siddons 291

MARCH 2006: The March by E. L. Doctorow 292

APRIL 2006: Amagansett by Mark Mills *(A Long Island Reads Selection 2006) 293

MAY 2006: Snow Flower and the Secret Fan by Lisa See 294

JUNE 2006: Lucia, Lucia by Adriana Trigiani 295

'RULE OF 50' 298

JULY 2006: The Birth of Venus by Sarah Dunant 299

AUGUST 2006: The Tender Bar by J.R. Moehringer 300

SEPTEMBER 2006: Time and Again by Jack Finney 302

OCTOBER 2006: Fate and MS Fortune by Saralee Rosenberg *(Guest Author) 303

NOVEMBER 2006: Krakatoa: The Day the World Exploded by Simon Winchester 305

DECEMBER 2006: Water for Elephants by Sara Gruen 307

Chapter 11 313

Back by Popular Demand (2007) 313

JANUARY 2007: For One More Day by Mitch Albom 314

FEBRUARY 2007: The Memory Keeper's Daughter by Kim Edwards 315

MARCH 2007: The Double Bind by Chris Bohjalian 316

APRIL 2007: Striver's Row by Kevin Baker 317

MAY 2007: The Georgetown Ladies' Social Club: Power, Passion, and Politics in the Nation's Capital by C. David Heymann 318

JUNE 2007: The Glass Castle by Jeannette Walls 319

JULY 2007: The Last Van Gogh by Alyson Richman 320

AUGUST 2007: One Thousand White Women: The Journals of May Dodd by Jim Fergus 321

SEPTEMBER 2007: The Gods of Newport by John Jakes 322

OCTOBER 2007: Nineteen Minutes by Jodi Picoult 323

NOVEMBER 2007: A Thousand Splendid Suns by Khaled Hosseini 325

DECEMBER 2007: Mayflower: A Story of Courage, Community, and War by Nathaniel Philbrick 326

Chapter 12 328

Authors, Fraternities, Sororities, and a Wedding at the Plaza (2008) 328

JANUARY 2008: Loving Frank by Nancy Horan 329

FEBRUARY 2008: Bridge of Sighs by Richard Russo 331

MARCH 2008: When Crickets Cry by Charles Martin 332

APRIL 2008: Native Speaker by Chang-Rae Lee 334

MAY 2008: The Camel Bookmobile by Masha Hamilton 336

JUNE 2008: Eat, Pray, Love: One Woman's Search for Everything Across Italy, India & Indonesia by Elizabeth Gilbert 339

JULY 2008: The Pillars of the Earth by Ken Follett 340

AUGUST 2008: The Appeal by John Grisham 342

SEPTEMBER 2008: The Ten Year Nap by Meg Wolitzer 344

NOVEMBER 2008: Dear Neighbor, Drop Dead by Saralee Rosenberg 349

DECEMBER 2008: More Than It Hurts You by Darin Strauss 350

Chapter 13 352

Playing Tennis, (or not) (2009) 352

JANUARY 2009: Suite Francaise by Irene Nemirovsky 353

FEBRUARY 2009: The Guernsey Literary and Potato Peel Pie Society by Mary Ann Schaffer and Annie Barrows 353

MARCH 2009: Very Valentine by Adriana Trigiani.....................................355

APRIL 2009: Wait Till Next Year by Doris Kearns Goodwin 357

MAY 2009: Revolutionary Road by Richard Yates 359

JUNE 2009: The Story of Edgar Sawtelle by David Wroblewski....................360

JULY 2009: Paths of Glory by Jeffrey Archer 360

AUGUST 2009: Heart and Soul by Maeve Binchy 362

SEPTEMBER 2009: Shanghai Girls by Lisa See 362

OCTOBER 2009: People of the Book by Geraldine Brooks 364

NOVEMBER 2009: Olive Kitteridge by Elizabeth Strout...............................365

DECEMBER 2009: The Lost Symbol by Dan Brown.....................................366

11

A BOOK LOVER'S CHRISTMAS 367

Chapter 14 368

On Breaking the Bank, Chasing Lincoln's Killer and Meeting a Girl with a Dragon Tattoo and a Girl in a Blue Dress (2010) 368

JANUARY 2010: Breaking the Bank by Yona Zeldis McDonough 370

FEBRUARY 2010: Manhunt: The 12 Day Chase for Lincoln's Killer by James Swanson 371

MARCH 2010: Brava Valentine by Adriana Trigiani 372

APRIL 2010: The River of Doubt: Theodore Roosevelt's Darkest Journey by Candice Millard 374

MAY 2010: The Help by Kathryn Stockett 375

JUNE 2010: A Reliable Wife by Robert Goolrick 376

JULY 2010: Secrets of Eden by Chris Bohjalian 377

AUGUST 2010: A Silent Ocean Away: Colette's Dominion – The Colette Trilogy (Book One) by DeVa Gantt 378

SEPTEMBER 2010: Girl in a Blue Dress: A Novel Inspired by the Life and Marriage of Charles Dickens by Gaynor Arnold 379

OCTOBER 2010: The Surrendered by Chang-Rae Lee....................................380

NOVEMBER 2010: Half a Life by Darin Strauss (Guest Author) 381

DECEMBER 2010: The Girl with the Dragon Tattoo by Stieg Larsson 383

Chapter 15 385

Writing 'Questions for Discussion' for Simon & Schuster and Reading More Great Books (2011)...385

JANUARY 2011: Let the Great World Spin by Colum McCann.......................385

FEBRUARY 2011: Freedom by Jonathan Franzen 387

MARCH 2011: Hotel on the Corner of Bitter and Sweet by Jamie Ford 393

APRIL 2011: Sag Harbor by Colson Whitehead 394

MAY 2011: The Distant Hours by Kate Morton 395

JUNE 2011: The Uncoupling by Meg Wolitzer...396

JULY 2011: Cutting for Stone by Abraham Verghese 397

AUGUST 2011: Unbroken: A WWII Story of Survival, Resilience, and Redemption by Laura Hillenbrand 398

SEPTEMBER 2011: Making Toast: A Family Story by Roger Rosenblatt and Room by Emma Donoghue..399

OCTOBER 2011: Diamond Ruby by Joseph Wallace 402

NOVEMBER 2011: Dreams of Joy by Lisa See...403

NOVEMBER 2011: The Time in Between by Maria Duenas...........................405

DECEMBER 2011: Onward Brave Readers...407

Chapter 16 409

A Year of Highs and Lows: Reading Books, Taking a Walking Tour, Writing 'Questions for Discussion' for Simon & Schuster, Standing Up for Heroes, Reading Throughout Superstorm Sandy, (2012) 409

JANUARY 2012: Another Piece of My Heart by Jane Green 409

FEBRUARY 2012: The Greater Journey: Americans in Paris by David McCullough 410

MARCH 2012: The Paris Wife by Paula McLain 411

APRIL 2012: The Lost Wife by Alyson Richman (Guest Author) 413

MAY 2012: Rules of Civility by Amor Towles...414

JUNE 2012: Istanbul Passage by Joseph Kanon *(Telephone Chat) 415

JULY 2012: Defending Jacob by William Landay..416

AUGUST 2012: The Shoemaker's Wife by Adriana Trigiani 417

SEPTEMBER 2012: Ten Girls to Watch by Charity Shumway.........................418

OCTOBER 2012: The Sandcastle Girls by Chris Bohjalian 419

NOVEMBER 2012: Those We Love Most by Lee Woodruff *(Author Visit)...423

DECEMBER 2012: The President's Club: Inside the World's Most Exclusive Fraternity by Nancy Gibbs and Michael Duffy..425

Chapter 17 427

A New Home for 'The Literary Gallery,' Year-End Recap 2013.....................427

JANUARY 2013: A Wedding in Great Neck by Yona Zeldis McDonough........428

FEBRUARY 2013: The Light Between Oceans by M. L. Stedman 429

MARCH 2013: Gone Girl by Gillian Flynn...430

APRIL 2013: Sutton by J. R. Moehringer...431

MAY 2013: The Secret Keeper by Kate Morton...432

13

JUNE 2013: A Week in Winter by Maeve Binchy............................434

JULY 2013: The Burgess Boys by Elizabeth Strout 435

AUGUST 2013: Fever by Mary Beth Keane.....................................437

SEPTEMBER 2013: Life After Life by Kate Atkinson 439

OCTOBER 2013: And the Mountains Echoed by Khaled Hosseini 440

NOVEMBER 2013: Inferno by Dan Brown 442

DECEMBER 2013: The Girls of Atomic City: The Untold Story of the Women Who Helped Win World War II by Denise Kiernan........................443

Chapter 18 450

Our Year of Reading Women Authors (2014)...............................450

JANUARY 2014: The Supreme Macaroni Company by Adriana Trigiani........450

FEBRUARY 2014: Jacob's Folly by Rebecca Miller 451

MARCH 2014: The Art Forger by B. A. Shapiro.............................452

APRIL 2014: The Manor: Three Centuries at a Slave Plantation on Long Island by Mac Griswold 454

MAY 2014: Beautiful Ruins by Jess Walter...................................456

JUNE 2014: Me Before You by JoJo Moyes 457

JULY 2014: The Husband's Secret by Liane Moriarty 459

AUGUST 2014: Songs of Willow Frost by Jamie Ford 461

SEPTEMBER 2014: The Goldfinch by Donna Tartt..........................463

OCTOBER 2014: Dancing on Broken Glass by Ka Hancock 465

NOVEMBER 2014: Still Life with Breadcrumbs by Anna Quindlen 470

DECEMBER 2014: I Am Malala: The Girl Who Stood Up for Education And Was Shot By The Taliban by Malala Yousafzai and Christina Lamb..............472

2015 AND TO INFINITY AND BEYOND 475

MARK ZUCKERBERG'S YEAR OF BOOKS......................................478

THE HISTORY OF BOOK CLUBS..480

THE ADVENT OF THE eBOOK 484

TIPS ON HOW TO START, LEAD AND ENHANCE YOUR BOOK DISCUSSION ...487

"What We Carry With Us"..494

CALENDAR OF BOOK RECOMMENDATIONS..................................495

INDEX OF QUOTATIONS CITED 503

BIBLIOGRAPHY 504

"THE LITERARY GALLERY" 508

ACKNOWLEDGMENTS 524

15

Useful Definitions:

- **Ultimate (adjective)** – being or happening at the end of a process
  - o Synonyms: final, eventual
- **Hardcore OR Hard-core (noun)** – a small number of very active and enthusiastic members of a group; the most devoted and active members of a group a militant or fiercely loyal faction
  - o Synonyms: Die-hard, staunch, steadfast, absolute and uncompromising
- **High-handed (adjective)** – not having or showing any interest in the rights, opinions, or feelings of other people
  - o Synonym: overbearing
- **Card-carrying (adjective)** - known as an active member of a group or organization strongly identified with a group (as of people with a common interest) registered as a member of a political party or labor union
- **Bibliophilist (noun)** – a lover of books a collector of books
  - o Synonym: bibliophile

PREFACE

It started out quite simply. I mean, I haven't always been "The Ultimate Hard-core, High-handed, Card-carrying Bibliophilist." Just ask my sisters. Diane, my older sister by one year, will tell you that I had a dynamite body, played every sport in high school (but not very good according to her), and that I planned to be a nurse. The fact that I belonged to the Future Nurse's Club of America and was a Candy Striper at Syosset Hospital was a dead giveaway that I had already mapped out my future career. Diane will say that I had many friends and that I always loved to read. She'll probably also tell you that I had a crush on several of the boys in her class, (one Emory Desoffey in particular), but my diary will attest to something else.

Doreen (henceforth, Renee), my younger sister also by one year, will remember me differently. Wedged between two beautiful and very popular sisters who worked very hard at establishing their own identities: Diane in her studies, in theatre and dance (training with the Rockettes) and Renee, taking the opposite route, choosing cheerleading, steno, and dictation, left me at sorts in the middle. Renee was always surrounded by friends and had many boyfriends, one of whom, the boy next door, would later become my brother-in-law. Back then Renee thought of me as being the quiet type, more studious and shy.

SO HOW DID I GET TO BE "THE ULTIMATE HARD-CORE, HIGH-HANDED, CARD-CARRYING BIBLIOPHILIST?"

I enjoyed writing when I was young. I kept a diary and penned short stories at night after I finished my homework. I loved seeing my name at the end of each brilliant entry:

DONNA JEAN ALICIA PERLMAN, author extraordinaire.

But that was then, long before I left high school to study Nursing at Keuka College, an all-girls' institute of higher learning located in the Finger Lakes region of New York State…. long before Mom and Dad's divorce and my decision to bag being a nurse in favor of transferring to Adelphi University on Long Island and studying French.

From bedpans to croissants, I had made the first real decision of my life. I was twenty years old and about to meet the man of my dreams.

"Monday was the diving board poised over the rest of the week. One walked out on the board, reviewed the situation, planned one's strategy, bounced a few times to get the feel of things, and then made a clean dive. Without Monday, one simply bombed into the water, belly first, and hoped for the best."

~Jan Karon, At Home in Mitford (Cross Reference: May 1998)

Chapter 1

The Beginning of My Book Life… With Several Hiccups Along the Way to Becoming the Ultimate Hard-core, High-Handed, Card-carrying Bibliophilist (May – December 1996)

Yes, it started out quite simply. I always loved to read, and Heaven knows I like to talk. When the new mega-bookstore, Barnes & Noble, first opened in East Northport, I decided to pick up the book that was chosen by Dodie Gillman, the librarian who ran the book discussion group I had joined at the Northport Library. The book we were reading was Snow Falling on Cedars, by David Guterson. So, armed with my new book, I approached the check-out counter. "That's a wonderful book," said the salesclerk eyeing my soon-to-be purchase. "I know that you'll enjoy it." "Yes," I replied. "We will be discussing it at our library book club. Do you have a book discussion group here at Barnes and Noble?" "No," she answered. "Would you be interested in starting one?" Momentarily taken off guard, I asked her what I had to do. "Pick a day and time you'd like to meet and choose a book you'd like to discuss," was her immediate reply. My answer came quickly, without any hesitation. "Well, I do love to read, and my husband and children say I talk a lot. That's a pretty good combination in the book world, don't you think?" She said that Mondays were generally quiet days in the store. We decided on the 2nd Monday of each month from 11:00AM – 12:30PM. I would choose *Snow Falling On Cedars*, by David Guterson and she would have our "nouveau" book club announced in their monthly newsletter.

I wanted to start each discussion by giving a brief biographical sketch of the author and providing some background to the story. Our book selections would cover most genres from fiction, (including historical fiction, my personal favorite), to non-fiction, biographies, and memoirs. Crime novels and most mysteries would be excluded since they are not often discussable. Obviously, there are exceptions to this: Gone Girl, by Gillian Flynn, Defending Jacob, by William Landay and The Girl On The Train, by Paula Hawkins, are three examples that quickly come to mind. Likewise, it would not be a discussion of the classics or an analysis of a poem or short story. My expertise did not lie in these areas.

And so it began that first Monday. Four people were in attendance, including me and my dear friend, Hilary. I was the self-designated book facilitator and, as such, it was up to me to select a title and author for our discussion each month.

Qu'est-ce que c'est une, "Ultimate Hard-core, High-handed, Card-carrying Bibliophilist?"

"I miss it if I'm not in it for any length of time; I don't feel comfortable. I want trees and I want frequent rain."

~ *Murray Morgan*

MAY 1996: Snow Falling On Cedars by David Guterson

A bit nervous and anxious to make a good first impression, I started off slowly reading the author's biography. I told the four people seated at the table with me that David Guterson was born on May 4, 1956, in Seattle, Washington, the middle of five children to Murray, a distinguished criminal defense lawyer and Shirley, a stay-at-home mother, Guterson. I stated that he earned a Bachelor of Arts degree in English Literature from the University of Washington, and a Master of Fine Arts degree in Creative Writing, and that he is also a Guggenheim Fellow.

I went on to say that before writing professionally, Guterson worked as a high school English teacher on Bainbridge Island in Puget Sound, was married to Robin (Radwick) and had four children, all of whom had been home-schooled.

"One of the things (Guterson heard from his father) early on was to find something you love to do—before you think about money or anything else. The other thing was to do something that you feel has a positive impact on the world." (1). He believes that there is a moral function of literature. "Fiction writers shouldn't dictate to people what their morality should be. Yet not enough writers are presenting moral questions for reflection, which I think is a very important obligation." (2) (Source: David Guterson from Vintage Books – Reading Group Guide, 1995).

Snow Falling On Cedars is a work of historical fiction.

Set on the fictionalized San Piedro Island, north of Puget Sound in 1954, *Snow Falling On Cedars* tells the story of local fisherman, Carl Heine, who is found suspiciously drowned. Kabuo Miyamoto, a Japanese American, is charged with his murder. Ishmael Chambers, the War Vet, and journalist in love with Hatsue Miyamoto, wife of the accused, is reporting on the trial.

The trial that ensues illustrates the American dream gone awry, collective guilt, and lost love. Part mystery, part love story and hauntingly atmospheric, *Snow Falling On Cedars* chronicles the World War II internment of Japanese Americans in the United States and

shows "how the crucible of war affects those who fight and those who stay at home." (3) and combines "the lucid prose of literary fiction with a compelling courtroom drama." (4)

"Snow Falling On Cedars closely resembles other such courtroom dramas as Anatomy Of A Murder and To Kill A Mockingbird – strong narratives drenched with a small-town atmosphere."(5) It is a book to be savored by all of your senses: SEE the beauty of the Pacific Northwest. SMELL the crisp freshness of the cedar and the salt in the air. TASTE the strawberries. TOUCH the snow falling and HEAR the lapping of the water against the side of the boat and the silent beating of the heart.

We discussed the major characters. We talked about the action of the story and the motive(s) of each of the many figures who peopled this book.

I didn't have a guideline on how to proceed. Aside from Hilary and me knowing one another, we were strangers meeting for the first time.

We agreed that we would meet the following month again and I concluded our discussion with the following quote:

"Ishmael gave himself to the writing of it, and as he did so, he understood this, too: that accident ruled every corner of the universe except the chambers of the human heart."

Quote from Snow Falling on Cedars, by David Guterson

I met Thaddeus, (Ted), in the Snack Bar at Adelphi University in a most inauspicious way. Having recently transferred from Keuka College, I knew I would have to figure out a way to meet people at my new commuter school. No longer a dorm resident, (Allen Hall, Room #105 and Richardson Hall in a suite,) where I was constantly surrounded by my friends, I decided to pledge a sorority as a way to meet both guys and gals. I dated just one boy during my high school years, Bruce Nienstedt, and he was enrolled at Adelphi, so I started off already knowing one person. The only problem was, we broke up during our sophomore year of college, and he was now dating a girl in Delta Delta Delta (Tri Delta), the sorority that was #1 on my Rush Calendar.... oops! I'd need to find a way to work around that little snafu.

College in the 1960s was truly the place to be (1964-1968). I was a Baby Boomer finding my way amidst the music of the Beach Boys, Sonny & Cher, the Mamas and the Papas, Chad and Jeremy, Bob Dylan, the Beatles, and the Rolling Stones.

** Personal note to my son: Sorry, Brett, I was never a Pink Floyd fan.

The Vietnam War was being fought in a faraway land, while protests and riots were taking place right here at home and on campuses across the nation. But here in Garden City, on Adelphi's grassy knoll, we were protected, (at least for a while), and shielded against the battles that raged outside our door. Were we selfish? Yes. Were we callous? No. These were our four years to have fun, to study, to pick our future path in life, and to maybe even find the right person with whom to share it. Years later I would tell our children, Danielle and Brett, as they were about to embark on their own four years of college,

"GRAB A PIECE OF THE WORLD AND MAKE IT YOURS!!!" *Be selfish during this time...look, listen, and learn. You'll never get this precious time back again.*

The world was just starting to open up for young women in the 1960s. At Keuka we were required to wear skirts or dresses to class during the week, **NEVER PANTS** *or* **HEAVEN FORBID!** *"Dungarees" (jeans). They would be reserved exclusively for Saturday classes. And Sundays, of course, were reserved for church. Pantsuits were yet to triumph on the fashion scene.*

In 1964 we were only beginning to branch out to other careers besides nursing, teaching, and secretarial positions. Betty Friedan became a household name with The Feminine Mystique, and Gloria Steinem made us a Ms. Before that time, many women went to college to get their MRS. We were starting to be liberated. New terminology: "women's lib," acts of defiance: "burning bras" and a new Amendment to the Constitution, (the ERA=Equal Rights Amendment), cropped up in conversations, and Erica Jong's Fear Of Flying, gave us permission to act outside of the box. What a glorious, intimidating, fearful, adventurous time it was for me to be a sorority girl, a collegiate pursuing a degree in French, to do what, I still didn't know. Ultimately, I would teach a summer course in French at Adelphi, then go on to work as a bilingual secretary/translator at a French Bank in New York City, (La Banque Verne et Commerciale de Paris), Michelin Tire Corporation and the Berlitz School of Language.

So, I rushed Tri Delta and found that I really liked Jackie Noto, the girl my former high school boyfriend was currently dating. She was petite and pretty, funny and smart, and together we found plenty to gossip about. She became my Tri Delta "Mother" and my entrée into the Greek world of fraternities and sororities.

We didn't have fraternity or sorority houses at Adelphi. We had designated tables in the Snack Bar where we would all congregate before and after class. Chi Sigma (XE) occupied the first table on the right as you entered the Snack Bar. Composed of athletes, scholars, and jocks, the good-looking guys of Chi Sig were just three tables away from us, the often stereotyped "blonde-haired, pearl-necklaced gals of Delta Delta Delta." (Think Hoda Kotb, Farrah Fawcett, Elizabeth Banks, and Katie Couric). I still recall the looks and the flirting that passed between our two tables, the weekend plans and party arrangements being made, the fixups and the blind dates.

And that was when Jackie pointed to two Chi Sigs and asked me if I'd be interested in going to a party with the frat boy on the left.

Dites-le-moi encore une fois, "Qu'est-ce que c'est une "Ultimate Hard-core, High-handed, Card-carrying Bibliophilist?"

* Forty-two years after publication of *Fear of Flying*, Erica Jong followed up with *Fear of Dying* in 2015.

"A man is known by the books he reads."

~ Ralph Waldo Emerson

JUNE 1996: Primary Colors by Anonymous

The next month I selected Primary Colors, by Anonymous, for our group discussion. Six of us sat around the table, wondering who the author could be. (We ultimately learned in July of 1996 that Newsweek columnist, Joe Klein, was the mystery author). After Tom Hanks withdrew his name for the Bill Clinton role in the film version of this political satire, we tossed out names of other prospective actors. Would it be Jeff Bridges, Kevin Kline, John Travolta, Kevin Costner, Richard Gere, Robin Williams or Mel Gibson? John Travolta ultimately garnered that coveted role with Emma Thompson co-starring as Hillary Rodham Clinton. (6)

Although our discussion was lively, it was an odd choice of title for me to have made so early on. I was drawn by the fact that it was "THE" hot book at the time. (Refer to my Tip # 6 re No Politics or Religion).

SURGEON GENERAL'S
WARNING: Smoking by Pregnant Women
May Result In Fetal Injury, Premature Birth and
Low Birth Weight

SURGEON GENERAL'S
WARNING: Smoking Causes Lung Cancer,
Heart Disease, Emphysema, and May
Complicate Pregnancy

JULY 1996: The Runaway Jury by John Grisham

My third month at Barnes & Noble Book Club, eight people assumed a place around the table, sipping coffee and perusing some of the articles I had amassed related to the author and our jury system. I had recently been selected to serve as a prospective juror in a civil case. One of the papers I displayed was a copy of my "Civil Voir Dire Questionnaire," which is designed to assist counsel and the court in selecting fair and impartial jurors.

I had a USA TODAY article dated Friday, May 24, 1996 (Section B, Money, pg.1B) by Melanie Wells, entitled "Court Ruling Gives Tobacco Stocks a Boost" (7). I was a quasi-Library Science student (I received twelve credits towards my MLS (Masters in Library Science) before I temporarily lost my sight and was forced to withdraw from the program). I love to do research on the various subjects mentioned in the books we read; in this case, Jury Selection, tobacco lawsuits (8), and author reviews.

I created my own questionnaire and asked the attendees if they wouldn't mind answering a few questions related to this topic:

1. Do you now smoke cigarettes? Y or N
2. If you answered YES to the above question, how many packs a day do you smoke?
3. And if so, how long have you smoked?
4. If you answered YES to the above, do you want to stop smoking? Y or N
5. Have you ever smoked cigarettes as a habit? Y or N (a stupid question in hindsight)
6. Has any member of your family or someone you know well suffered any disease or illness directly associated with smoking cigarettes? Y or N

7. If you care to elaborate on the above question, you can state the nature of the person's illness and whether or not you feel the person was successfully treated (Optional).
8. Do you believe smoking causes: a) lung cancer (Y or N) b) heart disease (Y or N) c) high blood pressure (Y or N) d) none of the above e) all of the above

I had photos of models ("pucker & blow") training for a 1950s TV ad by practicing the "correct" smoking technique (9) and beautiful women smoking Capri Superslims ("She's Gone to Capri & She's Not Coming Back") and Misty Slim & Sassy.

Clearly, those magazine ads were as outrageous as the questionnaire I asked the group to fill out. While providing a stimulating discussion, it also brought us into the realm of personal experiences. Looking back now almost twenty years later, I can see both the pros and cons of leading your book discussion into this private direction.

I spent hours prepping for our discussion of John Grisham's The Runaway Jury. I had biographical information: John Ray Grisham, Jr. was born on February 8, 1955, in Jonesboro, Arkansas, U.S., the 2nd oldest of five siblings to Wanda (Skidmore) and John Grisham. A graduate of Mississippi State University (1977) with a B.S. in Accounting and the University of Mississippi School of Law (1981), Grisham practiced criminal law for about a decade and served in the House of Representatives in Mississippi from January 1984 – September 1990 before turning his attention to writing. His first novel, A Time to Kill, which he began in 1984, was published in June 1989. A most prolific author, he followed that up with more than a dozen novels, legal thrillers, sportsbooks and books geared to younger readers.

In July 1996, I told the group that, as a boy, Grisham wanted to be a baseball player, and that he has coached three Little League Teams in Albemarle County, VA, where he also helped build six ball fields.

My research was primarily limited to magazine articles and biographical information obtained at the library from Contemporary Authors. We talked about the plot: This 1996 Grisham novel is a complicated courtroom thriller in which tobacco companies set out to steal themselves a jury. "Grisham is fascinated by the bigger issue of tobacco litigation, particularly the theory that a cigarette manufacturer could be successfully sued for product liability." (10)

The book was well received and made for a timely and lively discussion of a habit that was still practiced by many, the harmful effects still not thoroughly known.

*"Every jury has a leader, and that's where
you find your verdict."*

Quote from The Runaway Jury (page 49)

*Mommy always was and still is, beautiful, and we were the
"Father Knows Best" Family. All D's we were....... Diane,
("Smokey,") Donna, ("Muscles,") Doreen, ("Skinny,") Delores,
(Mommy) and Daddy, (Ed). And we had Dog, also a girl.*

*We sang "Sisters" from White Christmas in harmony and were
known as "The Perlman Girls." We went to Mass on Sundays,
spent summers in Bolton Landing, (Lake George), with our
Grandmother, (Grams), and our Perlman cousins from Niagara
Falls, Karyn, our 4th sister, and her 4 brothers, Bobby (Robert),
Chookie (Joseph), Neddy (Edward), and David. How excited we
all were every year as school let out; we'd drive Rte. 9 to our
destination, (no Thruway in the early 1950s), stopping for
Stewart's ice cream sundaes along the way, (chocolate marshmallow
peanut pour moi). We were so eager to see our friends. "Are the
Ciliberti's (Carol and Arlene) up yet?" "Did you see Billy Nolan
(my very first boyfriend?") "Did you see Buddy and Billy Gates?"
(Bill and Dawn Gates gave Karyn and me our very first jobs
waiting the counter at their Diner, now a museum. Karyn loved
Dawn's peach pie; I favored the cherry cheesecake. "Did you see the
Lambs?" "Cobber Pratt?" "Are the caddies, (who came from the
city to work at the Sagamore Hotel Golf Course), up yet?"
"Tommy Larkin?" "Larry Sawyer?" "Barry and Gary Freeman?)"*

*We took our vacations in Florida or on Caribbean cruises when the
export machine- tool business was good.*

*We were each voted "Best Dressed" in High School because we had
a wardrobe for four from which to choose every morning. What fun
our "Back to School" shopping was every August. Poor Daddy, at
the dinner table we used to say, "Who thinks we should all get new
clothes, raise your hand?" and just like that Daddy would be
outvoted 4 to 1.*

*We wore curlers to bed at night so that our hair would hold the
perfect flip, and when the curl was gone, Mom gave us a Toni*

32

Home Perm that you could smell from one end of Drury Lane to the other. We had family jokes, "Daddyisms,": "He talks like a man with a paper fanny," (What?) or "God Bless you and keep you, you little fat slob you," if you sneezed. Better yet, Daddy might jokingly say, "Don't act like a dopey dilldox!!!!" or even, "You look like the 'Wreck of the Hesperus,'" my private tease to Lily, my oldest granddaughter, when she doesn't want to comb her beautiful wavy hair.

We loved going to the movies and sometimes saw the same film two or three times and recited all the lines by heart.

We rooted for the New York Football Giants in the fall and the New York Yankees in the spring, except when Grams lived with us. A die-hard Brooklyn Dodgers' fan, she refused to cheer for those "Damn Yankees."(And Grams would curse Walter O'Malley, owner of the Brooklyn Dodgers, for moving her beloved team out of Brooklyn and cross-country to Los Angeles, California). She would later root for the New York Mets (Metropolitans).

We were the "All American Family" .... until the CRASH OF 1964.

But I'm getting way ahead of myself by going back so far.

Let's return to 1996 when our daughter, Dani, was a Junior at Villanova University and our son, Brett, a freshman playing football at Georgetown University. Can you just imagine the rivalry that existed in our house, especially during basketball season? We were evenly divided between the VILLANOVA WILDCATS and the GEORGETOWN HOYAS.

The encouragement from my children during those first few months was what kept me interested in pursuing this new vocation/avocation. I knew I would have to pace myself and limit my enthusiasm as I dug into my books and research, but it wasn't always easy for me to control those rumblings from within. What did Bruce Banner feel as he morphed into The Incredible Hulk? Could it be anything like what I was beginning to experience?

Qu'est-ce que c'est une "Ultimate Hard-core, High-handed, Card-carrying Bibliophilist?"

"All this happened, and if some of it was hard for me to believe, I had my logbooks and my pound of scraps and papers to prove it to myself – memory in ink. It was only needed that someone should say, 'you ought to write about it, you know. You really ought!'

~ Beryl Markham, *The Illustrated West with The Night*

AUGUST 1996: I Was Amelia Earhart by Jane Mendelsohn

Now, four months into leading a monthly book discussion, I was starting to get into a groove. The same four or five people kept coming back. There was Ellen Davis, Rita Silver, Elvira Lubrano, and Connie Sabatino. They were all very intelligent, avid readers who challenged me and asked stimulating and probing questions.

We all knew of the very famous aviatrix, Amelia Earhart, and her mysterious disappearance off the coast of New Guinea (Howland Island) in the South Pacific in 1937.

Born in Atchison, Kansas in 1898, Amelia studied at Columbia and at Harvard Summer School. A plain, but serious girl, not given to frivolity and often thought to be a tomboy because of the pants and manly shirts she favored, Earhart became known as "Lady Lindy" and preferred "leather and silk but no goggles." She first served as a military nurse in Canada during WWI and then got involved in Social Service work in Boston, MA. Her interest in flying was sparked one day when she was asked to join a crew of men on a transatlantic airplane flight. Apparently, it was thought to be good publicity to take a woman along.

"Amelia Earhart thus made national headlines as the first woman to cross the Atlantic with Wilmer Stutz and Louis Gordon in the Friendship." (11)

A good friend of Eleanor Roosevelt who, like her, believed that women should not stand in the shadow of men, Earhart married publisher George Palmer Putnam in 1931. She was interested in learning about the scientific aspects of flying and became a consulting member of Purdue University's faculty with a specialty in aeronautics. The title of her 1932 autobiography, *The Fun Of It*, referred to Amelia's desire to fly around the world.

She also mentions her predecessor, Harriet Quimby, a pioneer aviator, the first woman to earn a pilot's license.

Amelia Earhart was a woman of many firsts: (The first woman to fly the Atlantic, the first woman to fly non-stop across the U.S., the first woman to receive the Distinguished Flying Cross), too many to list here, yet, she was quick to acknowledge what her predecessor had accomplished.

Amelia Earhart's Lockheed 10 airplane went down somewhere over the Pacific in 1937. Fred Noonan, a first time Pan American navigator, went down with her on that fateful flight.

New evidence came to light in 2012 almost seventy-five years after Earhart's mysterious disappearance. Seeking to chronicle her fate, researchers prepared to look for wreckage of her plane near a remote island where they believe the famed aviatrix may have died as a castaway. Clues indicated that both Earhart and her navigator, Fred Noonan, were marooned on the tiny uninhabited island of Nikumaroro, part of the Pacific archipelago Republic of Kiribati. Organizers of the search had hoped to finally and definitively solve the mystery surrounding Amelia Earhart's death.

About the author and the book according to my notes:

Jane Mendelsohn has fueled the imagination and sparked flights of fantasy in her first novel, our book selection for August 1996, I Was Amelia Earhart. The author, who had created such a lyrical and fictional tale, writes in a totally unique narrative prose, taking the reader at first by surprise and unawares, from the 1st person to the 3rd person, from the past to the present, from fantasy to reality, all the time weaving the life of Amelia Earhart, unhappy wife of publishing scion, George Palmer Putnam, and the world-famous aviatrix into the fictitious life of the independent female heroine she longed to be.

The August 1996 Newsletter from Barnes & Noble featured our discussion group prominently with the following notice:

"Please join our monthly reading group, led by Donna Diamond. Our selection this month is I Was Amelia Earhart, the first novel by current best- selling author Jane Mendelsohn. The author weaves an imaginary tale of what might have happened to famed aviator Amelia Earhart and her navigator, Fred Noonan, after their mysterious disappearance off the coast of New Guinea in 1937.

Come share your thoughts and ideas with us. We look forward to some lively discussions. Please pre-register. Free Starbucks coffee will be served.

Barnes & Noble had advertised our event and provided complimentary coffee. It was now up to me to provide some author background and ask stimulating questions that would spark our conversations.

Because this was the first novel for Jane Mendelsohn, it was difficult to find very much information about her at the library. My research into her background kept leading me to a dead-end, so I decided to call her publisher, Alfred A. Knopf. I spoke with a delightful woman in the Publicity Department, and she was kind enough to send me much of the promotional material that Jane Mendelsohn used on her book tour:

Jane Mendelsohn was born in New York City on July 4, 1965, the daughter of Frederick Mendelsohn, a psychiatrist, and Leatrice, an art historian. She was raised on the Upper West Side of New York and attended the exclusive Horace Mann High School. Mendelsohn attended Yale University where she majored in English and graduated Summa Cum Laude and Phi Beta Kappa in 1987. She returned to New York for a year and interned in the literary section of the Village Voice.

It wasn't until after a one-year stint at Yale Law School, however, that she decided to pursue her childhood dream of becoming a writer. For the next several years she did some free-lance writing for The Voice, The London Review of Books and The Guardian while making yearly moves from one low rent apartment to another. After discovering an article in the paper about someone who had found a wing of Amelia Earhart's plane and it mentioned that she had a navigator, Mendelsohn became enchanted by such a dramatic and romantic idea. She had always thought that Earhart traveled alone. After discovering the Earhart clipping, Mendelsohn slowed her free-lance career to write her first novel. About that same time, she also met her husband, filmmaker Nick Davis, on a blind date.

Mendelsohn was stunned by the rapid success of her novel, and she attributed much of its success to radio talk show host, Don Imus, of WFAN. Deirdre Coleman, Imus's wife, discovered the thin book, I Was Amelia Earhart, on a table at a bookstore in suburban Connecticut. She read it in one sitting, then insisted that her husband do the same. Imus, in turn, read the book and was so taken by it that he raved about the 146-page book on the air for the next several days. The book immediately jumped up on the bestseller list. It was on April 22, 1996, that Imus began talking. Alfred A. Knopf then immediately arranged for interviews with *USA Today*, *People Magazine* and an appearance on the *Today Show* on NBC and the *Charlie Rose Show* on PBS. Book tours were arranged to start in Short Hills, NJ and a Border's Bookstore on Sunday, June 2nd passing through Connecticut, Rhode Island, and Washington D.C. and culminating in a stop in Albany, NY on Saturday, June 29th, 1996. The plan was to let the media appearances build until July 2nd, the date of the 59th anniversary of the disappearance of Amelia Earhart's Lockheed Electra and her birthday July 24th (99 years old).

After I finished reading my notes on Jane Mendelsohn's biography, I continued to discuss with the group some of the details and questions that Mendelsohn had posed regarding Amelia Earhart's fate.

On May 20, 1937, she began her around the world adventure from Miami, FL accompanied by her harmonica-playing navigator, Fred Noonan. The pair was last seen at LAE on July 1st taking off for another leg of flight which was to take them to Howland Island in the Pacific, a distance of over 2500 miles. They never reached Howland Island. One of the largest searches in history was begun when no contact could be made with the fliers. Until this day, there has not been any substantial evidence to prove what had become of the two fliers or their Lockheed Electra. Speculation abounds as to what might have happened to them. For example:

> That Earhart and Noonan had been captured by the Japanese who, four years later, would attack Pearl Harbor.

> That Earhart and Noonan were spies—either for the United States or some other major power and that they were executed, perhaps, by a Japanese firing squad.

> That she died of dysentery in an internment camp, or perhaps, that she survived to become Tokyo Rose, the voice of anti-American wartime propaganda.

> Others have Earhart and Noonan as lovers who wanted to get away from the world and so landed on an idyllic deserted island (maybe called "Heaven").

I created 'Questions for Discussion' in August 1996, long before it became expedient to find questions online or at the back of a book.

My 'Questions for Discussion: I Was Amelia Earhart, by Jane Mendelsohn

"So, what do you think?" I queried the group. Did Jane Mendelsohn take excessive poetic license in writing her novel? What do you think about her style of writing? Of her prose-like narrative? Of her switch from the first to the third person? From fantasy to reality? From the past to the present?

1. Let's talk about Amelia Earhart, herself, as seen through the eyes of Jane Mendelsohn.

   In an article written by Daphne Merkin of the New Yorker she states, "The Amelia Earhart of Mendelsohn's portrait comes across as part Greta Garbo, a glamorous golden-haired creature always wanting to be alone; part Robinson Crusoe intrepidly frying up cocoanut and fashioning furniture out of branches and twine and part Dorothy Parker given to mordant observations about the ways of men and women." He used to smoke after dinner, and I would usually join him, but not until he cajoled me, out of habit, so I could have the pleasure of declining and then giving in." (taken from I Was Amelia Earhart, by Jane Mendelsohn).

It has been written that Mendelsohn's universe is a sensuous and ethereal one. Do you agree? How is the sensuousness expressed? (i.e. "the sky is flesh," page 3.) "The equatorial heatwave which makes Earhart hallucinate and Noonan temporarily go mad?" (page 14) and "nature is bisexual."

2. It has been said that Amelia Earhart's disappearance was attributed largely to her recklessness: She:
    1. didn't know the Morse Code
    2. abandoned the radio's trailing wire
    3. left her life raft behind
    4. chose a drunkard as her navigator
    5. ignored George Putnam's original suggestion of placing a signal on Howland Island. Let's talk about those things.
3. What about George Palmer Putnam and her unhappy marriage? Was she ready or deliberately trying to die?

That was how our book discussion went back in August 1996. I didn't have access to a computer to do my research. I depended on the library's resources to get my information. I used Nexus on the library's computer to gain entry to magazine databases, and I searched Contemporary Authors to glean interesting tidbits about authors. I received invaluable help from the reference librarians, who pointed me in the right direction. Deborah Clark Cunningham, Head

Reference Librarian at Harborfields Library in Greenlawn, in particular, started out as my "go-to" source of information but has since become a close friend and shared book lover. I owe a great deal to her.

Today I googled Jane Mendelsohn and Wikipedia, the free encyclopedia, revealed that she was born in 1965 and is an American author. Her novels are known for their mythic themes, poetic imagery, and allegorical content. Her novel, I Was Amelia Earhart, was a surprise international bestseller in 1996 and a finalist for the Orange Prize.

In August 2015, Paula McLain, author of *The Paris Wife*, (Cross-reference March 2012), produced a second work of historical fiction detailing the life of famed aviatrix, Beryl Markham, *Circling The Sun*. I have read that Amelia Earhart was the first woman to fly over the Atlantic Ocean. Beryl Markham was close on her tailwind.

*So, while I was in the process of composing my life, my parents'
marriage was quietly decomposing behind closed doors. Nothing was
as it seemed.*

*Mommy had moved out of our split-level home in Syosset, taking
our baby brother, Chris (Cubby), just two years old, with her back
to Niagara Falls. Little Chris, born with four mothers, (his own
plus his three big sisters), and one bereft Daddy with a failing
business and a broken heart.*

*Diane was now married and living in Glens Falls, New York.
Doreen (Renee) was working in the city, in advertising, and doing
a little modeling (Taylor wine), and I was commuting to Adelphi
every day in my gold Chevy Impala.*

*Even my "frat boy on the left" didn't turn out to be who I thought
he was. I had mistakenly taken my Thaddeus, (the name given to
him by his best buddies, Frank (François) Canova and Jack
Curphey), to be the frat funnyman, "Gumby," the prankster goof-
off seated on the left, (not that I didn't have Greek spirit).
Thaddeus, the dark-haired Greek with blue, blue, blue eyes, so
beautiful that they would detract from my own, was seated,
oblivious to our scheming, on the right. Looking over her shoulder,
Jackie incorrectly pointed to her left, which was actually my right.
"Are you kidding me?" I uttered an emphatic "NO!" to what would
have been our first blind date.*

*It took another few months, and many missed fraternity parties
before I would go out with Thaddeus. Even then, there were
misunderstandings. I had thought he was a senior to my being a
junior, (I learned that he was a year YOUNGER than me by 359
days, and an Aries like me, to boot), and he was NOT Jewish
(with the name Diamond)? My last name, Perlman, was also
thought to be Jewish, but I was a very religious Catholic, my
German Jewish Grandfather, Nathan Perlman, having converted
when he married my Grandmother, Elizabeth (Lizzie) Kiesel. So*

here I was with a double dose of guilt from both my Catholic and Jewish backgrounds. Thaddeus and I should have been written up in the B'Nai Brith News.

On a dare, Thaddeus ultimately invited me to go to the Chi Sigma (ΧΣ) Surfing Party with him. As the music played, he held me so tight I could barely breathe. (This was long before Mr. Whipple would say, "Please don't squeeze the Charmin.") I asked my Tri Delta sisters, Jackie and Bonnie, if they had ever danced with Thaddeus Diamond, and if so, did he squeeze them as tight as he squeezed me? They laughed knowing that the "squeeze test" was only to find out if my boobs were real or fake.

Was anything as it should be?

Est-ce qu'il y a une "Hard-core, High-handed, Card-carrying Bibliophilist" dans le Snack Bar?

*"Books were my pass to personal freedom. I
learned to read at age three, and soon discovered
there was a whole world to conquer that went
beyond our farm in Mississippi."*

~ *Oprah Winfrey (1954 -)*

SEPTEMBER 1996: The Fourth Estate by Jeffrey Archer and The Deep End of The Ocean by Jacquelyn Mitchard

September 1996 proved to be a perfect storm month for me. Our chosen title was The Fourth Estate, by Jeffrey Archer. I was still relying on Contemporary Authors and the library's magazine database for all of my author research, but a serendipitous trip to Chicago to visit my niece, Allyson Cayce, reinforced my love of books and my desire to continue leading a monthly book discussion at Barnes & Noble.

Ali had secured two tickets for us to go to a taping of the Oprah Winfrey Show on Thursday, September 5,1996. We didn't know who Oprah's guests would be; however, we did go to great lengths to make sure we had the perfect outfit to wear just in case we did manage to show our faces on national TV. Even now I don't recall who the featured guests were on Oprah's show that day, but halfway through the program, Oprah announced that she would be starting an "on-air" book club. Her very first selection would be, *The Deep End Of The Ocean*, by Jacquelyn Mitchard. Copies of the book were distributed to the audience.

With that singular announcement, Oprah Winfrey created a furor in the publishing industry. Heretofore unknown authors rose to superstardom, with a nod of her head. Book clubs were created around the country, libraries attempted to meet patrons' demands, and bookstores clamored for 2nd, 3rd and 4th printings of every book Oprah anointed. Hollywood, too, jumped to attention, spawning movies out of Oprah's Book Club Picks.

From 1996 – 2010 when her final show aired on ABC, Oprah Winfrey captured the attention of book lovers everywhere and made reading really cool. Even avowed non-readers were drawn into the challenge to read books and talk about them with others. I would often hear people discussing Oprah's latest book pick and commenting on a new author. I was proud that our book club at Barnes & Noble was already beginning to gain momentum. Oprah's Book Club could only add to our own literary talks and introduce us to new titles and authors.

The following were Oprah's picks in 1996:

> September – *The Deep End of The Ocean*, by Jacquelyn Mitchard
>
> October – *Song of Solomon*, by Toni Morrison
>
> November – *The Book of Ruth*, by Jane Hamilton
>
> December –*She's Come Undone*, by Wally Lamb

SEPTEMBER 1996: The Fourth Estate by Jeffrey Archer

Blurb from Barnes & Noble EVENTS

16 September, Monday

11:00AM – 12:30PM

Monthly Reading Group

Please join our Monthly Reading Group, led by Donna Diamond. Our September Selection will be The Fourth Estate, by Jeffrey Archer. In his inimitable style reminiscent of his best-seller *Kane And Abel*, the author tells the tale of two press barons who vie for control of the world's media. Come share your thoughts and ideas with us. We look forward to some lively discussions. Free Starbucks Coffee will be served.

The Fourth Estate by Jeffrey Archer

Author Biography -

Jeffrey (Howard) Archer, the British author, and politician, was born on April 15, 1940 in Weston-Super-Mare in England's West Country, Somerset, the only child of William Archer, a career soldier during World War I and the former Lola Cook, a journalist who wrote a column "Over the Teacup" for the Weston Mercury. Lola wrote about the adventures of her son, "Tuppence," that caused Archer to be the victim of bullying while at the Wellington School, a well-known public school for boys, where he was granted a scholarship after his father's death in 1955. Archer was so precocious as a child, as he told Karen De Young in an interview for The Washington Post, (Jan. 5, 1986,) that "when he was three he wanted to be four and when he was four he wanted to be Prime Minister."(12).

Archer subsequently studied at Brasenose College, Oxford University. He was successful in athletics and active as a charity fund-raiser, but there are claims that Archer provided false evidence of his academic qualifications. "He made a name for himself raising money for the then little-known charity OXFAM (Oxford Committee for Hunger Relief) luring both the Conservative Prime Minister, Harold Macmillan, and The Beatles in a charity fundraising drive.

The band accepted his invitation to visit the Senior Common Room of Brasenose College, where they were photographed with Archer and dons of the college, although they didn't play there" (13).

After leaving Oxford, along with his work as a charity fundraiser, Archer began a career in politics and served as a Conservative Councillor on the Greater London Council from 1967-1970. At twenty-nine he was elected Member of Parliament (MP) for the Lincolnshire Constituency of Louth. He subsequently had many public battles with money, fraud, and politics. He was a member of Parliament, (1969-74) and Deputy Chairman of the Conservative Party, (1985-86). He was made a life peer in 1992; however, his political career ended with his conviction and imprisonment (2001-2003) for perjury and perverting the course of justice.

His writing did not suffer. Archer's writing and writing career have been most prolific. He is famous for his Kane And Abel series (Fiction):

➤ *Shall We Tell the President?* (1977)
➤ *Kane And Abel* (1980)
➤ *The Prodigal Daughter* (1982)

as well as his Prison Diaries (Non-fiction):

➤ *Hell* – Belmarsh (2002)
➤ *Purgatory* – Wayland (2003)
➤ *Heaven* – North Sea Camp (2004)

and numerous plays, short stories, and novels that recently include the Clifton Chronicles:

➤ *Only Time Will Tell* (2011)
➤ *The Sins of The Father* (2012)
➤ *Best Kept Secret* (2013)

> *Be Careful What You Wish For* (2014)

But, of course, back in 1996, while I was doing my research on Jeffrey Archer, I was not aware of the fact that he would become Baron Archer, the Right Honourable Lord Archer, and continue his writing and his political career.

In September 1996, as we sipped Starbucks coffee in the café, I was concerned with discussing the storyline of The Fourth Estate with the group. We talked about the struggles and ambitions of immigrants in general, and one, Lubji Hoch in particular, an illiterate Jewish peasant, who would change his name to Richard Armstrong, as he ruthlessly scratched his way up the ladder and seized control of a failing newspaper. And we discussed the moneyed world of the privilege of a second-generation newspaper magnate, one Keith Townsend, who also sought ultimate worldwide media control and recognition. From Berlin to Australia, we would come to know Armstrong and Townsend, two unscrupulous competitors, as their worlds spin out of control and their fortunes hang in the balance.

The Fourth Estate is the timely and compelling story of two men who, though they come from totally different backgrounds, stand face-to-face on the highest precipice, prepared to risk everything to beat each other and control the biggest media empire in the world. (14)

Interesting Fact -

Archer often bases his protagonists on real people. In this instance, the rival newspaper magnates were modeled after the late Robert Maxwell and Rupert Murdoch.

-Taken from *The Fourth Estate*, /Official Website for Jeffrey Archer

"We have our responsibilities as readers and even our importance. The standard we raise and the judgments we pass steal in the air and become part of the atmosphere which writers breathe as they work. An influence is created which tells upon them even if it never finds its way into print."

~ Virginia Woolf

OCTOBER 1996: The Last Don by Mario Puzo

Mario Gianluigi Puzo was born in Manhattan, New York on October 15, 1920, and died at his home in Bay Shore, Long Island (NY) on July 2, 1999, at age seventy-eight, the son of a poor immigrant family from Pietradefusi, Italy. Following military service in World War II, he attended New York's New School for Social Research and Columbia University. An author and screenwriter, Puzo is best known for his crime fiction novels about the Mafia. He co-adapted his masterwork, The Godfather, (1969) into a film by Francis Ford Coppola and subsequently won the Academy Award for Best Adapted Screenplay in both 1972 and 1974.

Puzo's favorite writer was Fyodor Dostoyevsky, and he was deeply influenced by his books as well as by the "Naturalistic writers who focus on the American "cityscape," on the lower orders of the middle class, the streets, the resourcefulness, the upward or downward mobility of emigrants or persons but one generation removed from Europe. Puzo explores the underbelly of social institutions and has a sure sense of the urban social process." (15)

Mario Puzo's early works, The Dark Arena, (1955) and The Fortunate Pilgrim, (1965) had received great reviews yet had not amounted to much. In an interview with Larry King on

August 2, 1996, Puzo revealed that his principal motivation was to make money, to write something that would appeal to the masses. He and his wife, Erika, who died in 1979, had five children and little cash. So, he continued to write (sometimes under the name Mario Cleri) novels, short stories and plays, but it wasn't until the publication of The Godfather in 1969 that he achieved recognition and long-lasting success.

Mario Puzo died of heart failure on Friday, July 2, 1999. He never saw the publication of his book, Omerta, in 2000. OMERTA = The oath of silence or The Family, (2001) completed by his longtime girlfriend, Carol Gino.

Our animated discussion of The Last Don at Barnes & Noble brought us into direct contact with the author, Mario Puzo. Connie Sabatino had taken umbrage over what she thought was the author's derogatory use of the Catholic sacraments, Communion, and Confirmation. In *The Last Don*, Puzo loosely uses the word "Communion" to mean "the body will disappear" and "Confirmation" as a term meaning "the body will be found." Outraged and deeply offended, Connie wrote a letter to the author, who in turn wrote a warm, conciliatory mea culpa reply, thanking her for taking the time to write him and assuring her that these were made up words he used to describe a Mafia shootout.

Connie shared Puzo's letter with the group at our next meeting. It was rewarding for us to know that, as readers, we could make an impact on an author's written word. Sadly, writing a letter in 1996 has become a dying art in 2015 and would ultimately be replaced by email, Twitter, Facebook, IM, and texting.

I suppose I knew that I was going to marry Thaddeus, (Ted), when Adelphi sponsored a weekend ski trip to Jug End, in Massachusetts, the winter of 1967. All of my Tri Delta friends were going and most of the XEs, too (at least the ones we were hoping to end up with).

Sitting by the fire at night after an exhilarating day of skiing or skating or sledding, was the perfect way to get to know someone. Jackie Noto paired off with W.Scott Freeman, Bonnie Vragel with François (Frank) Canova and Thaddeus and I laughed and talked through the night. The boys, of course, teased one another. Thaddeus taunted François and asked him to blow on the fire and make it go "Pff" (that's a line that we still get a chuckle out of more than 49 years later).

I did get to know that "frat boy on the left" a little better that famous Jug End Weekend, especially on the long bus ride home. I remember I wasn't feeling very well and complained about a terrible ache on my right side. By the time we reached Adelphi, I was doubled over with excruciating pain.

I barely said good-bye to Thad, as I rushed to my Dad's welcoming, bear-hug embrace. Forty minutes later, I almost leaped off the examining table when our family doctor pushed down on my abdomen. I was flushed, and my temperature had spiked. The doctor said I needed to get to the hospital immediately and have emergency surgery. "What's wrong?" I asked him. "Not sure," the doctor replied. "Acute appendicitis or infected ovaries. Either way, you need to be operated on tonight." And with that, I was whisked away, not knowing when I woke up sometime later if my appendix or my ovaries had been removed. The doctor feared that my appendix had burst, and peritonitis set in, but I was also concerned that the previous rumblings I had felt were even more insidious than I had originally believed. Could it have anything to do with my being this "Ultimate Hard-core, High-handed, Card-carrying Bibliophilist?"

54

The first question I asked in the Recovery Room was, "What did you take out?"

"Love as powerful as your Mother's for you leaves its own mark...to have been loved so deeply...will give us some protection forever."

~ J. K. Rowling

NOVEMBER 1996: The Deep End of the Ocean by Jacquelyn Mitchard

On September 5, 1996, my niece, Allyson, and I, all dressed up in my new pink outfit from Marshall Field's, waited excitedly outside Oprah Winfrey's HARPO STUDIOS in Chicago. We were instructed beforehand not to wear certain colors, although I can't, for the life of me, remember why.

The show aired on Friday, October 18, 1996.

Author Biography: (As read by me in November 1996).

Journalist and author, Jacquelyn Mitchard, was born in Chicago, IL on December 10, 1956. She graduated from the University of Illinois and Rockford College and became a metro reporter for the *Milwaukee Journal-Sentinel*. Her weekly column, The Rest of Us: Dispatches from the Mother Ship, appeared in the *Journal* and nationwide for more than a decade.

From 1989-1993 Mitchard was the speechwriter for (Secretary of Health and Human Services,) Donna Shalala, while Shalala was Chancellor of the University of Wisconsin. She has written a regular column for TV Guide and is a frequent contributor to *Reader's Digest, Good Housekeeping, Self, Woman's Day* and other publications.

While working free-lance for the *Milwaukee Journal-Sentinel*, Mitchard ventured into fiction with her first novel, The Deep

End of the Ocean. Chosen by TV host, Oprah Winfrey, as the first novel in her book club and "named by USA TODAY as one of the ten most influential books of the past twenty-five years (2nd by a long shot, it is said) to the *Harry Potter* series by J.K. Rowling," (17) Mitchard talked about how she came to write The Deep End of the Ocean in an interview for a Viking Reading Group Guide: "I dreamed the story about three years ago (1993). For a year after that, I didn't do anything with it beyond the notes I made about the dream. I'd never written a novel before, but the dream was clear and astonishing. And I'm not much of a dreamer in the ordinary sense."

The Deep End of the Ocean shot to fame because it was a featured selection by Oprah. The novel sold almost three million copies by May 1998 and was #1 on the *New York Times* Bestseller List for twenty-nine weeks. The film rights were sold to Mandalay Entertainment and later became a feature film starring Michelle Pfeiffer.

Overview of the Story:

While checking into a hotel for her High School Reunion, Beth Cappadora instructs her older son, Vincent, to watch his little three-year-old brother, Ben. In a matter of minutes, Vincent lets go of his brother's hand, and Ben disappears, without a trace. What ensues is every parent's worst nightmare.

Despite a nationwide police search, Ben has vanished, leaving Beth paralyzed and frozen in her agony for nine years and driving a wedge through her marriage to Pat. A kind man who cannot bring his son back, Pat must force his wife to go through the motions of caring for their remaining two children, seven-year-old, Vincent, and infant daughter, Kerry.

The family will be divided in their reactions to the abduction. Vincent will act out and become a delinquent, seeking attention from his parents and trying to break the silence that engulfs his family.

The Deep End of the Ocean delves into the lives of the Cappadora family as we, (the readers) share their loss, their guilt, their anger, and their pain and the many "if onlys" they can but dream about.

Re-reading the notes I had taken on *The Deep End of the Ocean*, on my Villanova notepad, made me think especially of my daughter, Danielle (Dani), herself now the mother of three beautiful daughters, my precious granddaughters Lily, Lauren, and Alice. Dani is currently a member of a book club affiliated with, but independent of, the Port Washington Public Library. If Dani, "The Mother," were to read *The Deep End of the Ocean* today, her reaction would be far different from what it would have been if Dani, my Tri Delta legacy, the collegiate, had read it back in November 1996. It is interesting to imagine how she would have responded to the questions I asked the group.

"THEN vs. NOW"

1. How do you view Beth as a mother? Selfish? Strong? Loving? Intelligent?
2. Who do you think kept the family together through all of their travails? Was it Pat with his strength, patience, and sense of family cohesion? Was it Beth by allowing "Sam" to return to George or was it a combination of both Beth's and Pat's combined wills?
3. Let's review the series of emotions that the family experienced then take each family member as an individual and study his/her reaction to every ironic twist of fate.

58

4. Reese always describes his family, "The Famous Cappadoras," as being dysfunctional. Do you think they were dysfunctional before Ben's disappearance, or did the family just react normally to their tragic circumstances?

5. Candy played a very important role in the families' lives (especially Beth's). She was mother, friend, bodyguard, sometimes played Devil's Advocate to Beth. She was a very interesting character. Let's talk about Candy and the roles she played.

6. What part did "Crazy Loretta's Vision" play in helping to solve the mystery of Ben's disappearance? Beth thought her prediction (vision) meant Ben's demise. Loretta's ESP had them sidetracked, (but then Beth never knew that Ben/Vincent played hide 'n seek in the big cedar chest.)

7. Discuss Tom Kilgor, the psychiatrist, Grandparents Rosie and Angelo and the roles they played in the drama – opera.

The Deep End of the Ocean is the story of one family's journey through hell and back and their ultimate redemption.

"Life is too short not to celebrate nice moments!"

~ Jurgen Klopp

DECEMBER 1996

We concluded our book discussion in December 1996 as we began, with our first selection in May 1996, *Snow Falling on Cedars*, by David Guterson (cross-reference bio May 1996.)

The group had expanded in those eight months. We were now up to fifteen people participating in our monthly book discussions. It was time to celebrate the holidays and our being a book group. We decided to have a luncheon at a local restaurant after our discussion. The next time we would meet it would be a new year, 1997, with so many more books just waiting to be read.

.... It was my appendix, after all.

My Dad and sister, Renee, were waiting for me after I regained consciousness. I was in Plainview Hospital and quite sore but sporting a very sexy "t" scar on the right side of my tummy.

I don't remember much else about what happened that night, except that I told my Dad, "I'm going to marry that man, that Ted Diamond someday."

Chapter 2

CRASH! BOOM! BANG! – Feeling My Way Through Books and Life (1997 and 1998)

Sometimes one book will dominate during the year. It will be on the Bestseller List and be talked about and argued over in book clubs. *Midnight in the Garden of Good and Evil*, by John Berendt, (1994) and *The Horse Whisperer*, by Nicholas Evans, (1995), are two such books. Each rose to the top of the charts and was immediately made into a movie. *Midnight in the Garden of Good and Evil* became a "Destination Book" as tourists clamored to see Johnny Mercer's Savannah firsthand and vie for a glimpse of the notorious Lady Chablis.

Sometimes a book might win a Pulitzer Prize, as Frank McCourt did with *Angela's Ashes*, (1997), his memoir of growing up poverty-stricken in Limerick, Ireland. *The Shipping News*, (1993), E. Annie Proulx's second novel about love and redemption in Newfoundland, won both the Pulitzer Prize for Fiction and the U.S. National Book Award for Fiction.

And sometimes a book might go "under the radar," and yet appeal to book groups because of its subject matter and sheer "discussability." (i.e., A Civil Action, by Jonathan Harr).

There was much to discuss from the books we read in 1997

JANUARY 1997: The Horse Whisperer by Nicholas Evans

British author and first-time novelist, Oxford-educated, Nicholas Evans, received a large advance before his romantic western was completed. It quickly rose to the top of the charts and was immediately made into a movie starring Robert Redford and Kristen Scott Thomas. Nevertheless, despite all of the hype, critic Boyd Tonkin was harsh in his assessment, giving the book a "C" rating and describing the author's language as dissolving into a "sickly purple mush." The story describes thirteen years old, Grace, who is hit by a truck while riding her horse, Pilgrim, and loses her leg. Grace's mother, Annie Graves, a high-powered New York magazine editor, decides to take her daughter to Montana to meet with Tom Booker, a trainer who has mystical powers over injured horses. The book has been described as "spiritual" in nature.

My research in 1997 brought me to the library's magazine database, where I found articles from *Entertainment Weekly* (Oct. 11, 1996) and *People Weekly* (Nov. 6, 1995). My research also brought me to a most interesting piece that appeared in *People Magazine*, dated April 14, 1997, that introduced me to Monty Roberts, a real-life "horse whisperer." While other trainers dismissed Roberts's work as a "flaky version of Doctor Dolittle, his credibility soared in 1989 after Queen Elizabeth read of his exploits in The Blood-Horse, a racing magazine. Intrigued, she summoned him to Windsor Castle for a demonstration of his technique, and immediately enlisted him to train 16 of her cavalry horses and some race-horses for the Queen Mother." With the Queen's endorsement, I quickly ignored any other critical reviews and presented *The Horse Whisperer* for our book discussion in January 1997.

"Cloning represents a very clear, powerful, and immediate example in which we are in danger of turning procreation into manufacture."

~ Leon Kass

FEBRUARY 1997: The Third Twin by Ken Follett

Seven women attended our discussion at Barnes and Noble in February 1997. Little did I know then that these seven bibliophiles would stay with me for more than 12 years. My folder was a real potpourri of information ranging from a Ken Follett biography from Current Biography Yearbook 1990, a pamphlet on *Medical Genetics/Genetic Counseling* from Huntington Hospital, and a Newsday article dated Monday, March 3, 1997, Suffolk, titled "Two Primates Cloned From Embryonic Cells, Now, Monkeys" by Robert Cooke.

The Third Twin in 1997 was a frightening look at cloning, a scientific experiment that would ultimately become "old news."

*"We're all strange inside. We learn how to
disguise our differences as we grow up."*

~ *Annie Proulx, The Shipping News*

MARCH 1997: The Shipping News by E. Annie Proulx

Pulitzer Prize-winning author, (Edna) Annie Proulx, is an American journalist and author, born in Norwich, Connecticut, to parents of English and native American/French-Canadian ancestry. Her novel, The Shipping News, our book selection for March 1997, takes place in the blistery, cold region of Newfoundland. Each chapter, introduced by different sailor's "knots," tells the story of quirky, Quoyle, left to raise his two daughters alone after the accidental death of his wife.

Rescued by a long-forgotten aunt and brought back to their ancestral home in Newfoundland, The Shipping News is a tale of love and commitment, of one man's search for attachment. Barbara Dafoe Whitehead, writing a review in *Commonweal*, December 1, 1995 (v122 n21 p24 (2)), offers her take on the significance of the "knots": "Its central metaphor and motif is the knot, the handmade contrivance that mediates between water and land, tying down all that would otherwise float away. One of the great delights of this book is that it is stuffed with the language and lore of knots, gleaned from a 1944 book on knots that Proux bought for a quarter at a yard sale. We learn about ornamental knots made from hair; knots formed by human handholds; knots created from pieces of rope; knots are woven into braids, leashes, restraints; knots with a hitch or a slip or a snarl. All this would be mere arcana if it did not reinforce the book's larger theme: that commitment both binds us and holds us fast.

For Quoyle, a fumble-fingered man, the triumph comes in learning to fashion sound knots."

The role of Quoyle was played by Kevin Spacey in the movie, with Judi Dench and Julianne Moore also starring.

"Childhood is a short season."

~ Helen Hayes

APRIL 1997: Angela's Ashes by Frank McCourt

Frank McCourt (1930-2009), won a Pulitzer Prize and international acclaim for his memoir of growing up poverty-stricken in Limerick, Ireland. The author's first book, *Angela's Ashes*, (the title derived in part because his mother, Angela, often stared gloomily into the family's cold grate), tells the tale of a childhood often spent hungry and deprived, yet it is a story told without bitterness or anger. "If Angela McCourt were still alive, her son Frank says, he couldn't have published, Angela's Ashes. My mother wouldn't have liked the book. It was too revealing. She was ashamed of our past. Now we're ashamed of being ashamed." (*USA Today*, 4/16/97, by Bob Minzesheimer). Fellow author and memoirist, Pete Hamill said: "The tale has been told before, but the way he tells it is fresh and new. The book is a triumphant work of art." (*People*, 1/20/97, pg.83).

"When I look back on my childhood, I wonder how I survived at all. It was, of course, a miserable childhood: the happy childhood is hardly worth your while. Worse than the ordinary miserable childhood is the miserable Irish childhood, and worse yet is the miserable Irish Catholic childhood." (from *Angela's Ashes*, by Frank McCourt).

Give this book a read for the innocence and laughter to be found amidst the squalor and pain. Give this book a read because the author, who was an avid reader but never finished high school, connived his way into college at New York University and became a "Teacher Man" for thirty years. And then, after having read the book, check out the movie, *Angela's Ashes*, which starred Emily Watson as Angela.

"Rule number one: Always stick around for one more drink. That's when things happen. That's when you find out everything you want to know."

~ John Berendt, Midnight in the Garden
of Good and Evil

MAY 1997: Midnight in the Garden of Good and Evil by John Berendt

I've been a collector for most of my life. It wasn't surprising that, when I first began to lead book discussions at Barnes & Noble in May 1996, I began researching and "collecting" information pertaining to the book we would be reading each month. I saved newspaper and magazine articles, New York Times Bestseller Lists, and anything else that would highlight the book's appeal.

My sign-in sheet lists the names of seven women, some of them still active members of our book club today. We gathered together to discuss this murder story, the screen version of this non-fiction work ultimately directed by Clint Eastwood and starring John Cusack as a " reporter who travels to Savannah, Georgia to cover an elite party given by Kevin Spacey, who ends up on trial for murder." (USA Today, Friday, Nov. 21, 1997 pg. 9D, Movie Reviews/by Mike Clark, "' Midnight Movie Drags On'").

Although the movie may not have garnered great reviews, *Midnight in the Garden of Good and Evil*, the book, was filled with fascinating characters, like the Lady Chablis, Jim Williams, the nefarious antique dealer, Johnny Mercer and the city of Savannah, itself. The book jacket, with its low hanging trees and the (forsaken) statue of the young girl seemingly balancing the scales of justice, immediately draws

70

the reader in, but it is necessary to read through to page 247 to fully comprehend the title, *Midnight in the Garden of Good and Evil.*

"Okay. Now, you know how deadtime works. Deadtime lasts for one hour – from ½ an hour before midnight to ½ an hour after midnight. The ½ hour before midnight is for doin' good. The ½ hour after midnight is for doin' evil."

*"You never know what worse luck your bad luck
has saved you from."*

~ *Cormac McCarthy*

JUNE 1997: All the Pretty Horses by Cormac McCarthy

We met in a Chinese Restaurant, Tian Tian in Commack, to discuss Cormac McCarthy's, All the Pretty Horses. One of our very dear friends, an original member of 'The Literary Gallery,' as was Elvira Lubrano, who chose this restaurant for our discussion, would be moving to Florida to be closer to family. We knew we would miss Ellen Davis, but we promised to keep her apprised of any future books we would be reading.

Sixteen years old, John Grady Cole, is the protagonist in this western cum coming-of-age story that takes place in modern times. The year is 1949. Death and divorce conspire to leave former rancher, Cole, without skills or money to navigate his way in modern society. He and a friend, Lacey Rawlins, will work their way to Mexico, "where a horse is still a thing of value, and breaking one is considered a worthy feat." (Guide to All the Pretty Horses, by Cormac McCarthy).

Cormac McCarthy was born in Rhode Island in 1933 and spent most of his childhood in Knoxville, Tennessee. He served in the U.S. Air Force and studied at the University of Tennessee. His novels are set in Tennessee, the Southwest and Mexico and include *The Orchard Keeper* (1965), for which he won the Faulkner Award for a first novel, *Outer Dark* (1968), *Child of God* (1973), *Suttree* (1979), *Blood Meridian* (1985), *All the Pretty Horses* (1992), and *The Crossing* (1994). The last two books are part of McCarthy's Border trilogy.

72

All the Pretty Horses won the National Book Award for Fiction and the National Book Critics Circle Award for Fiction.

*"The air was so thick with testosterone that the
wallpaper was getting soggy."*

~ Nelson DeMille, Plum Island

JULY 1997: Plum Island by Nelson DeMille

Nelson DeMille's Plum Island met all of the criteria for
consideration by the Long Island Reads Committee:

1. The author must BE FROM Long Island, or his/her
   book must BE ABOUT Long Island.
2. The book must appeal to Men, Women, and Young
   Adults.
3. The book must be available in all formats (Hardcover,
   Paperback, Audio, Large Print).

But, Alas! There was no Long Island Reads Committee in
1997. Our Book Selection Committee would not come into
play until 2002 with our choice of *The Great Gatsby*, by F.
Scott Fitzgerald.

In 1997, when DeMille wrote his novel, Plum Island was the
Animal Disease Center, part of the U.S. Department of
Homeland Security. Full environmental studies were being
conducted on the soil and water for contamination from
animal disease testing. The timing was ripe for the author to
introduce his cocky new character, John Corey, whose wit
and tongue-in-cheek retorts keep the novel flowing:

"I was wearing Mr. Ralph Lauren's blazer, Mr. Tommy
Hilfiger's oxford shirt, Mr. Eddie Bauer's pants, Mr. Perry
Ellis's boxer shorts, Mr. Karl Lagerfeld's aftershave, and
Messieurs Smith and Wesson's revolver."

~ Plum Island, p.218

Plum Island is a fast-paced mystery that will keep you guessing (and laughing) until the last page. I highly recommend it.

*"No man is an Island, entire of itself; every man
is a piece of the Continent, a part of the main."*

~ John Donne

SEPTEMBER 1997: Songs in Ordinary Time by Mary McGarry Morris

Oprah chose *Songs in Ordinary Time*, a voluminous novel, part coming-of-age, part thriller, part family drama, as her Summer Selection 1997. This unforgettable story takes place in the fictional town of Atkinson, VT during the summer of 1960, and opens on the day that Omar Duvall sauntered in. Peopled with a chorus of characters, from young Benjy Fermoyle, his sister, Alice, and his over-burdened mother, Maria, to Sonny Stoner, the local cop and his dying wife, to insurance salesman, Bob Haddad, and the youthful priest, Father Gannon, *Kirkus Reviews* wrote: " A good sweep of a novel: Morris, like a contemporary Dickens, creates a world teeming with incident and characters, often foolish, even nasty, but always alive."

The title of the book suggests the songs or stories of ordinary people living their lives. But it also implies Ordinary Time in Christian Liturgy, that period in which there are no holy days; the summer being the only complete season in Ordinary Time.

I thoroughly enjoyed reading and discussing this book with the ten people who gathered together at Borders on Sept. 8, 1997. Make this your next summer book! I'm sure you'll enjoy it, too.

'When you make a mistake, there are only three things you should ever do about it: admit it, learn from it, and don't repeat it."

~ Paul Bear Bryant

OCTOBER 1997: The Reef by Edith Wharton

In 1997 I was "feeling my way," still experimenting with format and book titles. I found that I was most comfortable discussing current bestsellers, both fiction and non-fiction, and my favorite genre, historical fiction. Our attempt at a classic, The Reef, by Edith Wharton, ended with some people reading the Olde English Version and others reading the American English Edition. Our discussion became almost impossible to follow. We ultimately realized that we were talking about two very differently interpreted books.

Oops! My faux pas, hopefully never to be repeated again.

"Siddons has never written a sentence that did not have music in it."

~ Pat Conroy

NOVEMBER 1997: Up Island by Anne Rivers Siddons

My mother-in-law, Dorothy Diamond, linguist and perennial book lover like me, was the first to introduce me to this very versatile author. Sybil Anne Rivers was born in 1936 in Fairburn, GA, just outside Atlanta, where her family has lived for six generations. The only child of wealthy parents, a true Southern Belle, she became a cheerleader, Homecoming Queen and ultimately a member (comme moi) of Tri Delta (Delta, Delta, Delta) sorority at Auburn University. Siddons became a senior editor for Atlanta Magazine. This author of many novels divides her time between her homes in Atlanta and Brooklin, ME.

Up Island's central character is Molly Bell Redwine. Also, a Tri Delta, a middle-aged woman whose life is completely upended when her Mother dies and her husband announces that he's leaving her for a much younger woman. On a whim, Molly decides to join her friend, Liv, at her home on Martha's Vineyard for the summer. It is there that she will continue her journey towards self-reliance and happiness.

"Whether in truth or fiction, I have never read a more compelling chronicle of litigation."

~ *John Grisham*

DECEMBER 1997: A Civil Action by Jonathan Harr

When I addressed those who had gathered for our discussion of Jonathan Harr's a Civil Action, I got a chuckle out of my notes, which spoke of the literary gift exchange we used to look forward to at our annual year-end meeting. I can still recall the 'Secret Santa' type presents we would buy, mugs, posters, signs, or books themselves with a literary bent, in the price range of $15-$20. It was a tradition we would continue for another year or two, or until our book club became too big.

The true story of a lawsuit initiated by a young mother living in Woburn, MA, who accused two of the nation's largest corporations, (W.R.Grace and Beatrice Foods), of causing the death of children because of dumping a cancer-causing industrial solvent into the water table, A Civil Action pits personal-injury lawyer, Jan Schlichtmann, (portrayed by John Travolta in the movie), who risks losing everything, against two corporate Goliaths, represented by William Cheeseman and Jerome Facher. But the truly maniacal villain of the story is Federal District Judge Walter J. Skinner, (John Lithgow in the film). I won't tell you why. I won't tell you how. You'll have to pick up this very true, sadly, very current, tale of environmental pollution. Sometimes truth really is stranger than fiction.

He played the drums and had me at "CRASH! BOOM!, BANG!"

Frog Hollow Frolics was the big event at Carle Place High School, where Ted was to play and afterward introduce me to his family for the first time. But before I was to walk into the lion's den, we had become a couple.

Three days after my appendix operation, we were dancing to the music of Johnny Mathis singing,' Chances Are' at a Tri Delta party. We double-dated with my cousin and confidante, Karyn, and Ted's playboy buddy, Jack Curphey, and went to see a Dean Martin MATT HELM movie. I vividly recall the outfit I wore that night. I actually laughed so hard in one scene that I split the zipper of my skirt, (a Keuka-inspired blue tweed A-line with coordinating sweater).

It was still the 1960s and, although our pocketbooks and shoes no longer had to match, we were still wearing skirts on Saturday night dates. Mini-skirts were all the rage (de rigueur,) thanks to London designer, Mary Quant, who is credited with the creation of the leg-baring mini-skirt and hot pants. Tights and pantyhose had been introduced, HALLELUJAH!! Freeing us from girdles, roll-ons and garter belts.

The 1960s was a decade filled with great social and cultural upheaval. Fashion was dictated by the styles of the leather-wearing rockers, and the preppy art and music inspired Mod Movement, epitomized by Twiggy, with her pixie haircut and dark, heavy eye makeup.

SHALIMAR became my signature scent.

U.S. First Lady, Jackie Kennedy, impeccably wore Oleg Cassini coats and pillbox hats. And Audrey Hepburn's wide-brimmed chapeau and oversized sunglasses had us all wanting to take BREAKFAST AT TIFFANY'S, (a wonderful 1961 film, based on the book by Truman Capote, and also starred George Peppard).

Tie-die shirts, à la Woodstock (August 15-18, 1969), were worn by both men and women. There was a style for everyone in the '60s. I found my own "Donna style" in 1963 after seeing Shirley MacLaine in IRMA LA DOUCE. Like Irma in her black satin sleep mask, and Holly Golightly, (Audrey Hepburn in BREAKFAST AT TIFFANY'S), in her turquoise sleep mask, I started to wear (eye) blinders to sleep during my Junior Year of High School.

There was many a morning that I woke up yelling, "I'm blind! I can't see!" forgetting that I was still wearing my sleep shades.

Little did I think that one day I truly would be blind.

JANUARY - DECEMBER 1998

By 1998 our book discussion group was living up to its name. We were in the process of moving to another of the mega-bookstores, Border's Books and Music, and the group was expanding. Mothers brought their daughters, friends brought other friends, and two brave men, fellow bibliophiles, John McGuinness, and Nick Siciliano, entered our circle on their own. Suddenly, we were a group of almost twenty people. I thought of my son, Brett, who had slipped me a note back in May 1996. "Don't worry, Mom. Today there were four people. Next month there'll be five or six and then maybe fourteen. I'm so proud of you."

Looking around at the thoughtful faces of so many intelligent, well-read men and women, I knew that I had chosen the proper moniker for us, "THE LITERARY GALLERY."

"You spend your whole life stuck in the labyrinth, thinking about how you'll escape one day, and how awesome it will be, and imagining that future keeps you going, but you never do it. You just use the future to escape the present."

~ John Green, Looking for Alaska

JANUARY 1998: Larry's Party by Carol Shields

In January 1998, we discussed a second book by one of Canada's foremost authors, Carol Shields, (The Stone Diaries), this time about garden mazes and horticulture, *Larry's Party*.

Dan Cryer, a Staff Writer for *Newsday* in 1997, wrote, "Larry's Party chronicles 20 years in the life of an ordinary Joe, a Canadian baby boomer, Larry Weller, born in 1950." The reader views Larry through the eyes of an omniscient narrator, as he takes stock of his life so far at age 40. He has 1 parent, 1 sibling, 2 wives, 1 child, several diplomas, and has lived in 2 cities/countries, Winnipeg and Chicago. At his party (August 17th,) he thinks about what it means to be a man today (in 1997) and the roles of discomfort and confusion between men and women. The Chapters, as with Larry's life, are defined by floral mazes and vivid descriptions of the hedges of England, particularly the Hedge Maze at Hampton Court, England.

Shields has said she likes to write about survivors, about reality and the texture of ordinary life and the way people appear and relate. Her works are rich in domestic detail and intelligent compassion for her characters. Often her writing is funny, like her hilarious description of Larry's penis on pages 123-124.

In *Larry's Party*, her 9th novel, Shields addresses the rhythm of life itself.

"….and somewhere else, just out of earshot, he senses that his life is quietly clearing its throat, getting ready, at last, to speak."

Quote from Larry's Party by, Carol Shields

> *"…that we here highly resolve that these dead shall not have died in vain; that this nation, under God, shall have a new birth of freedom; and that this government of the people, by the people, for the people, shall not perish from the earth."*

> ~ *(President) Abraham Lincoln*

FEBRUARY 1998: Cold Mountain by Charles Frazier

We read both Fiction and Non-fiction in 1998 and were introduced to many new authors.

Cold Mountain is a historical novel by Charles Frazier, which won the U.S. National Book Award for Fiction in 1997. A first novel, Cold Mountain became an immediate success, selling roughly 3,000,000 copies worldwide. The reader follows the solitary trek of W.P. Inman, a wounded deserter from the Confederate Army near the end of the American Civil War. Persistent and determined to return to Ada Monroe, the love of his life, Inman walks alone for months across the Blue Ridge Mountains. The story was adapted into an Academy Award-winning film in 2003. Frazier has said that the real W. P. Inman, portrayed by Jude Law in the movie, was actually his great-granduncle, who lived near the real Cold Mountain, (Pisgah National Forest, Haywood

County, North Carolina). Nicole Kidman and Renee Zellweger also starred in the movie.

It has been said that the story shares several similarities to Homer's *Odyssey*.

> *"God is the color of water. Water doesn't have a color."*

> ~ *James McBride, The Color of Water: A Black Man's Tribute to His White Mother*

MARCH 1998: The Color of Water: A Black Man's Tribute to His White Mother by James McBride

The Color of Water, a National Book Award winner, was published in 1995. It is James McBride's autobiography, as well as a memoir and a tribute to his mother, Ruth, who was White and Jewish. James called her Mommy (just as my sisters and I still call our Mother, "Mommy." My brother calls her "Ma"). This memoir sold more than 2.1 million copies worldwide and has been translated into more than sixteen languages. Considered an American classic, The Color of Water was a New York Times bestseller for two years. It is required reading in many high schools and colleges across America.

This beautifully written story speaks of Ruth, born in Poland and raised in Suffolk, VA, the daughter of a wayfaring rabbi and a loving Mother, who spoke no English and was, herself, disabled. "At 17, Ruth fled the South, landed in Harlem, married a black man in 1941, founded a church, was twice widowed, and raised 12 children in New York City. Despite hardship, poverty, and suffering, Ruth sent all 12 of her children to college." ..... "James was working as a tenor sax sideman with jazz legend Jimmy Scott when he penned this book, which was written in hotel rooms, vans, airports, libraries and on buses." .... "He set about interviewing Ruth McBride Jordan and searching out her mysterious past, a process that took 14 years and resulted in a book that is regarded as a landmark work. Says McBride of *The Color of Water*," If I had known so many people were going to read that book, I would've written a better book." (From James McBride, Author, and Musician).

McBride's book was overwhelmingly given a 'Thumbs Up' rating by 'The Literary Gallery' in March of 1998. Our Long Island Reads Committee would choose this title in 2007, but in 1998, our reading choices put us at the vanguard of the literary world.

"At his best, man is the noblest of all animals;
separated from law and justice, he is the worst."

~ *Aristotle*

APRIL 1998: A Certain Justice by P.D. James

Legendary author of fourteen bestselling crime novels, P. D.
James, (Phyllis Dorothy), "reigning queen of the British
detective novel" (*USA Today*, Tuesday, July 20, 2010, *LIFE*,
Section D), Baroness James of Holland Park in London,
introduced us for the first time to Scotland Yard
Commander, Adam Dalgliesh. Known for her intense
research and courtroom settings, James "interviewed
barristers, attending trials at the old Bailey, reading from her
volumes of "Notable British Trials." (Newsday," Talking with
P.D. James, Tea With the Baroness, Currents, and Books,"
pg. B11).

Active in politics, a public figure, magistrate, on the board of
the British Council and a governor of the BBC, in addition to
being a writer, James has said that she understands the male
psyche, and has never felt threatened by men. "This witty,
complex and intelligent character – grandmother,
homemaker, cat-lover, devilish describer of blood and
mayhem, lay expert on murder and architecture – pauses.
And as P. D. James pauses, one can imagine, watching her
furtive but friendly face, a host of future fictional deaths
making their gleeful way across her mind." (Newsday,
"Talking With P.D.James, Tea With the Baroness, Currents &
Books, Pg. B11).

We all thoroughly enjoyed reading this author.

"Mitford would simply like to be the pause that refreshes."

~ Jan Karon, *At Home in Mitford*

MAY 1998: At Home in Mitford (The Mitford Series) by Jan Karon

Like "chicken soup for the soul," Mitford represents a safe haven, a joyful escape, an idyllic setting in which to kick back and enjoy life. Peopled with very human characters who represent the good in all of us, we meet Father Tim, Cynthia Coppersmith, and their faithful dog, Barnabas. The author's newsletter, 'More From Mitford', is Christian and spiritual in nature. Her missives begin with 'Gentle Reader' and close with 'Yours faithfully.

My niece and Goddaughter, Kirsten would bring this book to my attention in May of 1998.

Start your very pleasant reading with this Book I of the Mitford Series.

"At the temple, there is a poem called "Loss"
carved into the stone. It has three words, but the
poet has scratched them out. You cannot read loss,
only feel it."

~ *Arthur Golden, Memoirs of a*
Geisha

JUNE 1998: Memoirs of a Geisha by Arthur Golden

Wow! What a book! What guts! What chutzpah! Somehow a 41-year-old father of two from Brookline, MA has managed to cross both gender and racial barriers to write his book, Memoirs of a Geisha. A member of the Ochs/Sulzberger family which owns and publishes *The New York Times*, Arthur Golden grew up in Chattanooga, TN, was educated at Harvard College, where he received a degree in Art History, specializing in Japanese Art. In 1980 he earned an M.A. in Japanese History from Columbia University. After college, Golden spent fourteen months living in Japan. He speaks both Japanese and Mandarin Chinese.

It took the author nine years to research and write his novel. First published by Alfred A. Knopf in the fall of 1997, *Memoirs of a Geisha* had more than 150,000 copies in print after ten press runs. And sales were further fueled by the Winter Olympics in Nagano, Japan.

Golden has rendered to perfection the voice of a young Japanese girl (Chuyo at age nine), as she recounts her transformation from a simple child to a sought-after Kyoto geisha named Sayuri. The voice came after Golden had rewritten the book twice with a third-person narrator. Only on the third try did he gain the confidence to write in Sayuri's voice.

My research folder of this incredible novel overflowed with information: a New York Times article dated Sunday, August 29, 1999, "Putting a Face on a Culture by, Luchina Fisher; People, 5/21/01, "Conflicting Memories", by Christina Cheakalos, Nobuko Matsushita in Kyoto, Danielle Anderson in New York City and Ron Arias in Los Angeles, pg. 103-104,; Spielberg Loves a 'Geisha' (USA TODAY, Thursday, April 30, 1998 by, Andy Seiler; a Reading Group Guide to 'Memoirs of a Geisha' provided by Alfred A. Knopf dated 5/28/99; further New York Times, Newsday and USA TODAY articles; an NPR Cassette tape of an interview with the author, Arthur Golden.

It was very exciting for me to read this book because it was easy to bring the pages to life through Golden's descriptions and first-hand experience. My husband had been traveling extensively to the Far East, especially China and Japan for the past twenty-five years, and I myself had the opportunity to witness this exotic land when I accompanied him for one month almost five years ago. I brought in some of the Chinese dolls, opera masks, tea sets, and other memorabilia I had collected. They enhanced our pleasure as we discussed this beautifully written novel of life in the inner world of geisha society.

For Christmas the next year my Father-in-law, (TaTa) painted two oils of the heroine, Pumpkin (Hatsumiyo), that hang prominently in my living room today.

"May a man live well-enough and long-enough, to leave many joyful widows behind him."

JULY 1998: A Widow For One Year by John Irving

In July, John Irving told the story of *A Widow for One Year* (Ruth Cole), a sometimes raunchy love story about the passage of time and the lesions left by grief. A dark comedy, Irving's style post *The Cider House Rules*; a dysfunctional family of writers. Two decades have passed since this New Hampshire native wrote, *The World According to Garp*.

There were eleven of us gathered around the table that day, including Elvira Lubrano, Ellen Davis, Ann Monaco, Rita Silver, Gina Henry, Liane Buix, and her mother, Muriel Walker. The book was listed at #2 on Newsday's Bestseller List, Sunday, June 28, 1998. Yankee great, Derek Jeter, was "seeing" singer Mariah Carey (very stressful), Leonardo Di Caprio was mulling over his future roles after the colossal success of the movie, 'Titanic', and, according to USA Today,(Thursday, May 21, 1998), "Sinatra's legacy fills the shelves….."Like an undertaker keeping an eye on a nursing home (or a newspaper preparing an obituary in advance), book publishers awaited the death of Frank Sinatra. It's a big event in commercial publishing, up there with the death of Princess Diana or the cinematic sinking of the Titanic."

Such was the state of the world in July 1998 as we were reading *A Widow For One Year*.

We chose a dual selection for August 1998, both short narratives, Wait Till Next Year, by Doris Kearns Goodwin and Colony, by Anne Rivers Siddons (Cross-reference November 1997).

"The past is not simply the past, but a prism through which the subject filters his own changing self-image."

~ *Doris Kearns Goodwin*

AUGUST 1998: Wait Till Next Year by Doris Kearns Goodwin

Pulitzer Prize-winning author, Doris Kearns Goodwin, has created in *Wait Till Next Year*, a memoir of growing up in Rockville Centre, Long Island (NY) during the 1950s. We meet Doris's beloved family, father Michael, with whom she shared a love of baseball, her frail and sickly mother, Helen and her two older sisters, Charlotte and Jeanne. We meet her best friend, Eileen as they share stories sipping soda at the corner drugstore. It is the postwar era when neighborhoods were equally divided between Dodgers, Giants and Yankee fans. We follow Doris's love of her Brooklyn Dodgers, Jackie Robinson, Pee Wee Reese, and Gil Hodges. It was a fun romp through a simpler, more innocent time.

Choose this book for your next discussion but add some peanuts and Cracker Jacks. (Refer to my Tip #21 re Food/Beverage Themed Books and Tip # 24 re Dual Titles).

93

"It was lovely wine, soft and full of flowers."

~ Anne Rivers Siddons, Colony

AUGUST 1998: Colony by Anne Rivers Siddons

Prolific author, Siddons, who generally pens her novels in the "low country" of Georgia, takes the reader up north to Maine, to a Colony simply called "Retreat." We meet Southern Belle, Maude Gascoigne, fresh from her Charleston plantation, as her husband, Peter Chambliss, from a Boston Brahmin banking family, drops his wife into the chaos of life with his opinionated and hostile mother, Maude's "beloved enemy". You will revel in the drama of Colony and perhaps choose this title as a light summer or comfort read. (Refer to my Tip # 27 at the back of the book).

"The major fortunes in America have been made in land."

~ John D. Rockefeller

SEPTEMBER 1998: Philistines at the Hedgerow: Passion and Property in the Hamptons by Stephen Gaines

In September we went North of 25A for prime real estate, *Philistines at the Hedgerow: Passion and Property in the Hamptons*, by Stephen Gaines. Gaines gives us an insider peeks at the lifestyles of some of the rich and famous and provides a few chuckles and anecdotes as the reader acts as a voyeur. We encounter "...the rich and dishy cultural history of the Hamptons from the time when Georgika's Pond, one of the most expensive pieces of real estate in the world, was the fishing ground of a lone Indian named Jeorgkee. He traces unending Hamptons litigation and squabbling from Goody Garlick in 1658 up to Martha Stewart (Goody Garlick was tried for witchcraft, and Martha has an ongoing feud with her neighbor, real-estate mogul Harry Macklowe). (*Kirkus Review*).

I guarantee you'll get a kick out of this tale of clashing egos and name dropping.

"Accept what people offer. Drink their milkshakes. Take their love."

~ Wally Lamb, She's Come Undone

OCTOBER 1998: She's Come Undone by Wally Lamb

We chose Oprah's pick, *She's Come Undone*, by Wally Lamb in October of 1998. Lamb's break-out hit introduced us to a troubled, overweight, Dolores Price, as she grapples her way out of depression and self-loathing and searches for acceptance and self-confidence.

On Thursday, January 30, 1997, USA Today captured the story of "How an Oprah book star is born" by Jacqueline Blais:

Q: What's more remarkable than the way the Oprah Book Club sells books?

A: How selections are kept secret.

Here is how 750,000 copies of *She's Come Undone*, by Wally Lamb, were printed and distributed in time for Oprah Winfrey to announce on Jan. 22 that novel for her club.

Jan. 10: Winfrey calls Lamb at home in Mansfield, Conn., and swears him to secrecy. He does tell his wife and three children. Winfrey says Lamb should alert his publisher, Pocket Books.

Jan. 12: Liz Hartman and Kara Welsh of Pocket Books meet him at home.

Jan. 13: Oprah's film crew goes to the Lamb house and Norwich Free Academy in Norwich, Conn., where Lamb teaches writing. They film a class of high school juniors.

Jan. 13 – 17: Pocket Books prints 750,000 paperbacks at presses in five states, and the books are shipped to a warehouse in Bristol, Pa. Booksellers offered the mysterious (but effective) *Untitled Oprah's Book Club #4*, buy three-quarters of a million copies sight unseen.

Jan. 17 – 22: Lamb's book is shipped "wherever books are sold," Welsh says.

And that's how *She's Come Undone*, by Wally Lamb became a # 1 bestseller.

"There can be no failure to a man who has not lost his courage, his character, his self- respect, or his self-confidence. He is still a King."

~ *Orison Swett Marden*

DECEMBER 1998: For Kings and Planets by Ethan Canin

'The Literary Gallery' now consisted of fifteen eager bookworms as we ended the year 1998. Our last selection was *For Kings and Planets*, by Ethan Kanin, an author described as being "a worthy successor to Philip Roth." The novel introduces us to two students at Columbia University and the woman they both love. Life, for them, ends up being a test of their friendship and morality.

Ethan Andrew Canin is an American author, educator, and physician and a member of the faculty of the Iowa Writer's Workshop.

We followed our discussion with our 3rd Annual Luncheon at Taormina Restaurant in Commack.

Chapter 3

Turning the Page on the Book and the 20th Century (1999) Author Friends and Invited Guests

THE YEAR 1999

The Year 1999 marked the end of the decade and the end of the 20th Century. Many Western nations viewed this time, (the '90s), as a period of peace and prosperity between the end of the Cold War and the start of the War on Terror.

As the New Millennium approached, a theme of death and foreboding surfaced. Nostradamus's predictions were being cited; the End of the World was near. Dr. Jack Kevorkian, (aka Dr. Death), the man who brought the taboo topic of assisted suicide to the forefront, was convicted.

Hugo Chavez was elected President of Venezuela, two students murdered thirteen people and then took their own lives in the Columbine High School massacre in Colorado, Napster sparked a revolution in music distribution with its digital file-sharing application, Nelson Mandela stepped down as President of South Africa and world-wide panic spread as many feared the Y2K bug.

Yet nothing happened at midnight on New Year's Eve 1999. We continued to watch *The Sopranos, SpongeBob SquarePants, Who Wants to Be a Millionaire*, and *The West Wing* on television. We went to the movies to see *Toy Story 2, American Beauty, The Sixth Sense, Austin Powers: The Spy Who Shagged Me, Star Wars Episode I: The Phantom Menace.*

In sports that year (1999), David Cone pitched a perfect game for the New York Yankees who would ultimately beat the Atlanta Braves in the World Series, Tiger Woods* won the PGA Championship, (*his infidelity scandal in 2009 ultimately led to the loss of many sponsors and endorsements. He and wife, Elin Nordegren, divorced in 2010. Tiger Woods returned to competition at the 2010 Masters Tournament) and the Denver Broncos defeated the Atlanta Falcons to become the NFL Champions once again in Super Bowl XXXIII.

And in the book world in 1999, "all nine editors of the New York Times Book Review began to worry that fewer outstanding books seemed to be coming their way." (The NY Times on the web, Dec. 5, 1999- Editors' Choice: The Best Books of 1999).

They chose eleven Best Books of the Year including, An Affair of State: The Investigation, Impeachment, and Trial of President Clinton, by Richard A. Posner in the non-fiction category and Disgrace, by J.M. Coetzee for fiction. Today you can google "Listopia," which didn't exist in 1999, to find other book titles that are as popular today as they were back in 1999:

1. *Harry Potter and the Prisoner of Azkaban*, (Harry Potter # 3), by J.K. Rowling *
2. *Girl with A Pearl Earring*, by Tracy Chevalier *
3. *The Perks of Being a Wallflower*, by Stephen Chbosky *
4. *Chocolat* (Chocolat # 1), by Joanne Harris *
5. *White Oleander*, by Janet Fitch (Note: This became an OPRAH Book Selection in May 1999).
6. *Waiting*, by Ha Jin
7. *'Tis*, by Frank McCourt (Note: This last line of his Pulitzer Prize winning, Angela's Ashes, became the title of his sequel to it).
8. *It's Not About the Bike: My Journey Back to Life*, by Lance Armstrong. (In October 2012 Lance Edward Armstrong, former road racing cyclist, was stripped of his seven Tour de France titles (1999-2005) and

100

stepped down as head of his Livestrong Foundation. He was found guilty of doping and cover-up. An exclusive Oprah Winfrey interview wouldn't come until fourteen years later on January 17th and 18th, 2013 on Oprah's OWN network (Oprah Winfrey Network).

9. *A Walk to Remember*, by Nicholas Sparks *
10. *The Girl's Guide to Hunting and Fishing*, by Melissa Bank
11. *Interpreter of Maladies*, by Jhumpa Lahiri

Designates a movie made from the book.

In January of 1999, 'The Literary Gallery' read, *A Man in Full*, by Tom Wolfe. Following the successful run of his first novel, *The Bonfire of the Vanities*, A Man in Full, would take eleven years for Wolfe to complete.

In February 1999 we read *The Loop*, by Nicolas Evans, author of the widely received *The Horse Whisperer*.

Our introduction to Barbara Kingsolver came, (even before Oprah selected her book in June 2000), when we discussed her epic family drama set in post-colonial Africa. *The Poisonwood Bible* tells the tale of an evangelical Baptist named Nathan Price, his wife, and four daughters, who embark on a mission to the Belgian Congo in 1959. Narrated in the alternating voices of the five women of the family: Orleanna, Nathan's long-suffering wife, Rachel, their self-centered eldest daughter, Leah, the most outspoken and the tomboyish twin to silent sister, mathematically inclined Adah, and Ruth, the youngest of the Price girls, inquisitive and perceptive, The Poisonwood Bible explores the beliefs and challenges that one family will face in their tumultuous new environment and displays Kingsolver's thorough knowledge of biology, ecology and the political climate of the Congo in 1959. (April 1999).

We read British novelist, Ian McEwan's, *Amsterdam*, (May 1999), a morality tale for which he received the Booker Prize in 1998. The novel begins at the funeral of Molly Lane, where two friends, Molly's former lovers, newspaper editor, Vernon Halliday, and lauded composer, Clive Linley, make a strange euthanasia pact. Their relationship will dissolve and culminate in disaster in Amsterdam, but not before each man exacts his revenge.

The Reader, by Bernhard Schlink, is a love story, set in post-Nazi Germany, and deals with themes of guilt and atonement. We had a very animated discussion of that book in June 1999. Kate Winslet would ultimately win an Academy Award in 2009 for 'Best Performance by an Actress in a Leading Role' for that movie. (June 1999).

Anita Shreve's, *The Pilot's Wife*, (September 1999), asks the question: "How well do we know our own spouse" and "To what lengths will we go to try to rectify a wrong, (perceived or real) done to us?" Readitforward.com pursued this question on April 30, 2013, in an interview with Nichole Bernier, author of The Unfinished Work of Elizabeth D, who shared a list of books that remind us, "you never really know the hearts and minds of others." "Books that reveal that things are not what they seem have always fascinated me. Here are some of my favorites that show the hidden pains and motivations rolling beneath the surface of us all." (21) :

1. *Crossing to Safety*, by Wallace Stegner
2. *Devotion: A Memoir*, by Dani Shapiro
3. *Gone Girl: A Novel*, by Gillian Flynn
4. *Bartleby the Scrivener*, by Herman Melville
5. *The Light Between Oceans: A Novel*, by M.L. Stedman
6. *The Silent Land*, by Graham Joyce
7. *A Gift from the Sea*, by Anne Morrow Lindbergh

8. *The Language of Flowers: A Novel*, by Vanessa Diffenbaugh
9. *Extremely Loud and Incredibly Close*, by Jonathan Safran Foer
10. *The Pilot's Wife*, by Anita Shreve

We read English author, Alex Garland's, *The Beach*, (October 1999), a novel about backpackers in Thailand in search of a legendary pristine beach, far from the hustle and bustle of the outside world. *The Beach*, reminiscent of such classics as Thomas Hardy's, *The Heart of Darkness*, and William Golding's, *Lord of the Flies*, in its noir descriptions, was adapted into a film in 2000, directed by Danny Boyle and starred Leonardo Di Caprio.

Many of my titles for 1999 were reflected in the books that Oprah had selected that year. *The Reader*, by Bernhard Schlink, *The Pilot's Wife*, by Anita Shreve and *Midwives*, by Chris Bohjalian, made instant stars of those authors.

Chris Bohjalian became my first "author friend" after I sent him a letter telling him how much my book discussion group and I enjoyed reading his very gripping birthing drama, Midwives. For several years after he would send me a postcard of his current book jacket cover saying simply, "I hope you and your book club enjoy my latest work." (November 1999)

"Choose an author as you choose a friend."

~ Sir Christopher Wren

Midwives by Chris Bohjalian

Author Biography: (as I would read in 1999 in Contemporary Authors, Vol.139, p.54-5, (1992.)

Personal: Born August 12, 1960, in White Plains, N.Y.; son of Aram (an advertising executive) and Annalee (a homemaker; maiden name, Nelson) Bohjalian; married Victoria Blewer (a photographer and artist,) Oct. 13, 1984.

Education: Amherst College, B.A. (Summa Cum Laude,) 1982.

Career: Burlington Free Press, Burlington, VT, book critic and columnist, 1987-; Vermont Life Magazine, Montpelier, VT, book critic, 1991-; free-lance journalist and novelist. New England Young Writers Conference at Breadloaf, faculty member, 1991-92.

Writings:

- ➤ A Killing in the Real World, (a mystery,) 1988

- ➤ Hangman, (a ghost story,) 1991
- ➤ Past the Bleachers, (a quiet novel about fathers and sons and Little League baseball,) 1992
- ➤ Contributor to numerous magazines including Reader's Digest, Cosmopolitan, and Boston Globe Magazine.

Work in Progress: a novel about dowsing ("water witching") with divining rods and a ski resort in the midst of the worst drought in Vermont history, to be completed in early 1993.

Bohjalian told CA (Contemporary Authors) in 1992: "I view myself fundamentally as a novelist. Although I am also a weekly newspaper columnist and free-lance journalist, it is my novels that matter to me most. I have no particular agenda for my writing – especially my fiction – no particular goal. I write because it gives me enormous pleasure, and I can't imagine I'd be happy doing anything else."

Chris Bohjalian's work has been translated into over twenty-five languages and three times become movies, (SECRETS OF EDEN starring John Stamos, MIDWIVES starring Cissy Spacek as Sibyl Danforth, and PAST THE BLEACHERS).

Note: Chris Bohjalian is the author of seventeen books including the NY Times Bestseller, *The Sandcastle Girls*, (2012) which tells the story of the Armenian genocide, "The Slaughter You Know Next To Nothing About," a timely novel today considering the present massacre in Aleppo, Syria. Bohjalian has called *The Sandcastle Girls*, the "most important book he will ever write."

I attended the launch of Chris Bohjalian's 16th book, *The Light in the Ruins*, with Carolyn Deegan, a very special friend, and bibliophile, a member of my 'Page Turners' Book Discussion Group at Northport Library, in July 2013. Carolyn exemplifies to perfection my Tip # 28 regarding favorite quotes from the book we had just read. The luncheon, book signing, and video presentation were held at the Armenian American Society in New York City and were presided over by the author, who spoke eloquently about his characters, his research, and his story.

Bohjalian hit the book tour circuit again in July 2014 with the publication of Close your Eyes, Hold Hands, the story of his two beloveds "Emilys," Emily Shephard and Emily Dickinson.

To this day, Chris Bohjalian remains one of my favorite author friends. He has participated in numerous telephone, and SKYPE chats with my three book discussion groups, (Barnes & Noble, East Northport, NY---/Elwood Library, Elwood, NY,) Harborfields Library (Greenlawn, NY) and Northport Library (Northport, NY), to everyone's delight.

In 1999, author Joel Glenn Brenner became my first invited guest to speak about her book, a work of Non-Fiction called, *The Emperors of Chocolate: Inside The Secret World of Hershey & Mars.* A former Washington Post business reporter, Ms. Brenner wrote an award-winning feature on Mars, Inc. in 1992. It was published in The Washington Post Magazine. She expanded her research into the candy industry and the personal style of each candy patriarch, Milton Hershey and Forrest Mars, Sr. As one who has been "addicted" to M & M peanuts for most of my adult life, I enjoyed reading about "how the famous American chocolate given away by Allied soldiers during WWI and WWII differed from the chocolate we eat today." (The Emperors of Chocolate, by Joel Glenn Brenner, Non-Fiction review – Yahoo! Voice.) I vicariously savored every bite of European milk chocolate and compared it to Hershey's. I learned of the rivalry between these two corporate "Emperors" and how these competitors organize their companies. And, because of Joel Glenn Brenner's meticulous decade-long investigation, in which unprecedented access was granted by both companies, I discovered why E.T. followed a trail of Reese's Pieces instead of some other tasty delight. *

Ms. Brenner came to our book discussion at Border's Books, and Music prepared to serve us chocolates of many varieties, dark, milk chocolate, and white chocolate. She had us close our eyes as we sampled Godiva, Hershey, Cadbury, Lindt, Nestle, Ghirardelli, and Suchard chocolate. What fun we had! Years later, and many M&Ms pounds heavier, I would still recall that luscious taste of chocolate on my lips, un gout délicieux et inoubliable.

Note: Elliot used Reese's Pieces to lure E.T. into the house. Director Steven Spielberg wanted to use M&Ms candies but the makers of M&Ms, the Mars Co., did not want to be associated with the alien character and did not want to bankroll the publicity of the film, which was a Spielberg requirement. OOPS! Hershey's did. Reese's Pieces sales exploded with an increase of 65% for a total of $35 million in sales in 1983. (Source: "Buy the Way..." Insights on Integrated Marketing Communication).

We got so good at hosting our author that we did it again the following month. Barbara Rogan, the author of eight novels, joined us for a very lively discussion of her novel, Suspicion. I telephoned Ms. Rogan in August of 1999 to personally invite her to talk to us about her life, (born in New York, lived and worked in Israel, worked extensively in publishing, starting as an editor then as director of the Barbara Rogan Literary Agency, (Israel) teaching fiction writing at Hofstra University and SUNY). She currently teaches for Writer's Digest University and is a frequent lecturer on both the business and craft of writing. Her books have been translated into a dozen languages, featured by the major book clubs, optioned for movie and television and issued as audiobooks and ebooks.
(www.writersonlineworkshops.com/our instructors/barbara-rogan/ Barbara Rogan Writer's Digest University.) Her works include:

➢ Hindsight
➢ Rowing to Eden
➢ Saving Grace
➢ Suspicion

➢ A Heartbeat Away

And in December, in that last month of the last year of the 20th century, we discussed Doris Kearns Goodwin's Pulitzer Prize Winner, No Ordinary Time: Franklin and Eleanor on the Home Front. A great historian and biographer, all of Goodwin's books give us an informative, insider's look at a world gone by. Franklin and Eleanor, and their united front at home during the Second World War came to life and eased our fears. We would read another book by this brilliant author in April 2008, Wait Till Next Year. And, our Long Island Reads Committee unanimously made Doris Kearns Goodwin, and her childhood story of growing up on Long Island in the 1950s and loving the Brooklyn Dodgers, our Island-wide selection in 2009, (*Wait Till Next Year*).

 It was another great year of reading for us in 1999 from start to finish. Our book group, 'The Literary Gallery,' moved its monthly meetings over to the competition, the other mega-bookstore, Border's Books & Music. In addition, I became a book discussion facilitator at Harborfields Library in Greenlawn, New York. Moderating this new group gave me the opportunity to meet many other intelligent book lovers, who would share my love of reading, and challenge me to present other authors with different styles of writing and different points of view. Unlike the books I would choose at Border's, the titles selected at the library would have to be at least six months old, and available in all formats, (hardcover, paperback, large print, audio and occasionally "Talking Books"). In order to accommodate this larger group, books had to be borrowed from other libraries on Long Island through Inter-Library Loan, (ILL). This introduced a greater variety of books into the library pool. In Suffolk County, the Suffolk County Library System (SCLS) operated as a separate entity from the Nassau County Library System (NCLS). The two systems would come together, however, to form other committees, one of which, the Long Island Reads Committee, (the concept of 'One Island-One Book') established in 2002*** I would join in 2003 as a book discussion group leader. I was, and still am, the sole non-working librarian book discussion facilitator on the Committee. Each April, I would discuss, in both book clubs, the title and author chosen by our Long Island Reads Committee that year. My twelve credits towards my MLS (Masters in Library Science) had helped to prepare me for my future career in "books."

*** *The L.I. Reads Committee is an Island-wide initiative sponsored by the Nassau Library System and the Public Libraries of Suffolk County. Its purpose is to promote the reading and discussion of the same book, bringing communities together through literature.*

LONG ISLAND READS SELECTIONS

- 2015 – *The Museum of Extraordinary Things*, by Alice Hoffman
- 2014 – *The Manor: Three Centuries at a Slave Plantation on Long Island*, by Mac Griswold
- 2013 – *Sutton,* by J.R.Moehringer
- 2012 – *The Lost Wife*, by Alyson Richman
- 2011 – *Sag Harbor*, by Colson Whitehead
- 2010 – *The River of Doubt: Theodore Roosevelt's Darkest Journey*, by Candice   Millard
- 2009 – *Wait Till Next Year*, by Doris Kearns Goodwin
- 2008 – *Aloft*, by Chang-Rae Lee
- 2007 – *The Color of Water: A Black Man's Tribute To His White Mother*, by James   McBride
- 2006 – *Amagansett*, by Mark Mills

- 2005 – *Travels With Charley: In Search of America*, by John Steinbeck
- 2004 – *Snow In August*, by Pete Hamill
- 2003 – *How the Garcia Girls Lost Their Accents*, by Julia Alvarez
- 2002 – *The Great Gatsby*, by F. Scott Fitzgerald

Ted had a really great pick up line in those days. Forget the corny, "What's your major?" query. He hit the jackpot, went straight for the heart, (or maybe the pocketbook,) when he casually asked, "Wanna see my yacht?" "No kidding around, he really did ask me that." My mother always said it was "just as easy to marry a rich man as (marry) a poor man" but could it really be this easy? He already had me with a drum roll and a CRASH! BOOM!, BANG!, but a yacht, too?

The "Mister D," a 42' Chris Craft, was the name of his mistress, his seafaring love, the pride and joy of Ted's family. I met his Mother and Father, Dorothy and Dimon Diamond, his older sister, Diane, who they affectionately called DeDe, and younger brother, Billy. Dorothy (Dot) and Dimon Diamond, (they called him "Double D") were two brilliant, old school Greeks, mired in their history yet surprisingly ahead of their time. Socrates would be quoted by Ted's father in Greek while Edith Piaf records would be played and sung by his mother, a fellow Francophile like me. Grade school sweethearts, they were both multi-lingual, articulate, well-read, and educated and politically astute. On weekends Dimon's brother, George, a successful New York City architect and his wife, Beverly, a lovely and savvy real estate broker, two of Ted's, and ultimately my, favorite people, would come to the house in Carle Place or meet on their own boat, the "Bye George" and have a raucous time discussing a particular senator or the Cold War or the President's policy on education. (That topic always struck a nerve and led to endless hours of raised voices, laughter, and opinionated conversation). I loved listening to, and joining in on, these weekly diatribes, always stimulating and thought-provoking. And for me, quant à moi, it was especially enjoyable to have someone with whom I could practice speaking French and honing my linguistic skills. Ted's mother was a French teacher and later an English (AP) teacher par excellence. Both of his parents were heavily entrenched in the Carle Place community and school district. Dimon served as Treasurer of the Board of Education for many years, and Dorothy

111

led a group of students and parents on trips into New York City to see Broadway Shows.

Years later, my daughter, Dani, and I would join the "Culture Vultures" on those bus trips to the Great White Way. And in 2012, Ted and I would continue the Broadway tradition by taking each one of our grandchildren to the theatre to celebrate their kindergarten graduation. From The Lion King and Mary Poppins to Cinderella and Aladdin, musical theatre had become a very special and important part of our lives.

C'était le bonheur de vivre, une certaine je ne sais quoi joie de vivre.

Chapter 4

When One Door Closes Another Door Opens (2000)

With school behind me, I was now able to read whatever I wanted, whenever I wanted. Love Story, by Erich Segal, had captured the hearts of many young girls, including starry-eyed moi, the hopeless romantic. My sister, Diane, asked me to join her in New York City while she took the test to, hopefully, qualify as a contestant on JEOPARDY! Our plan was to answer the questions then try to catch a matinee showing of "Love Story," the movie starring Ryan O'Neal and Ali McGraw. What a perfect afternoon! Diane passed the test with flying colors and would ultimately appear on JEOPARDY! with Art Fleming a few months later. (She did well but was unable to take that coveted first place after Final Jeopardy! Blame it on the Audio Roar of the Metro Goldwyn Mayer Lion). That left us free to stuff our mouths with popcorn and sob along with Ali McGraw, whose Jenny Cavalieri told her heart-broken, Oliver, (Ryan O'Neal) "Love Means Never Having to Say You're Sorry."

I read QBVII, by Leon Uris, The Exorcist, by William Peter Blatty and The World According to Garp, by John Irving. I fell in love reading Colleen McCullough's The Thornbirds and immersed myself in Alex Hailey's Roots: The Saga of an American Family. My taste in books was eclectic. I loved reading Rich Man, Poor Man, by Irwin Shaw and The Gang That Couldn't Shoot Straight, by Jimmy Breslin. I read The Winds of War, by Herman Wouk well into the night, until my eyes finally closed at dawn.

Books have always been an important part of my life. When I was at Keuka, I became acutely aware of the care and study of books because my roommate's older sister had received her MLS (Masters in Library Science) and was a practicing Reference Librarian in a public library on Long Island. I admired the details, and the search for knowledge that was required, and I marveled at the respect that was given to those sacred leather-bound pages. I adhered to the rules and would NEVER (pas du tout, jamais!) even think of writing or taking notes in a book that didn't belong to me. I was starting to become very possessive of my own books, however, my college reference books, and my private collection of leisure reads, best-sellers and coffee table books.

My books became my diary, my thoughts recorded with dates written in the margins. Like Thomas Jefferson and the Billy Collins poem, "Marginalia," I "talked back" to the books I read. (The New York Times, Sunday, February 2, 2014, page 9. Opinion by Andrew D. Scrimgeour, Dean of Libraries at Drew University). I became quick to slap a "Property of Donna Perlman" bookplate on the first page of every book I owned, rather than the more demure, "From the Library Of ----, " label. I wrote the date and my physical location when reading each book. I loved the touch and smell of a hard-cover (paperbacks didn't appeal to me). I would make lists of the books I had read and the movies I had seen, but somehow, they got lost in the shuffle. Quel dommage!

Could this have been the seed that would eventually ripen into the creation of the dreaded "Ultimate Hard-core, High-handed, Card-carrying Bibliophilist?" If I were to have closely looked in the mirror, would I have seen an evil face? Would my long, baby fine, blonde hair, (compliments of Clairol Flaxen Blonde,) have resembled the wiry gray locks of Oscar Wilde's Picture of Dorian Gray?

I would come to regret that I didn't have that list of books I'd read through the years, ("so many books, so little time," to quote Frank Zappa), but I was busy living my life.

"I worked in a number of high schools in New York, and I wound up at Stuyvesant High School, which is known nationally for producing brilliant scientists and mathematicians, but I had writing classes. I thought I was teaching. They thought I was teaching, but I was learning."

~ *Frank McCourt*

JANUARY 2000: 'Tis by Frank McCourt

The year 2000 for 'The Literary Gallery' at Border's Books & Music began with *'Tis*, the sequel to Pulitzer Prize Winner, Frank McCourt's, Angela's Ashes. Deirdre Donahue, reviewing for *USA Today* on Thursday, September 16, 1999, wrote: *"'Tis: A Memoir* by, Frank McCourt. "How's 'Ashes'? 'Tis brilliant! The Sequel? 'Tisn't." Hugh Kenner critiquing *'Tis* in the *Wall Street Journal* on Friday, September 17, 1999, caught our attention with the headline, "Alas, Tain't," but those harsh assessments of McCourt's writing only added to our already animated discussion.

'Tis opens when McCourt first arrives in New York at age 19 and continues when he gets his first job emptying ashtrays at the Biltmore Hotel. The book speaks of how the young Frank is taken under the wing of a Roman Catholic priest with a drinking problem, how he finds work on Manhattan's loading docks, his service in the Army and ultimately how he becomes a High School English teacher, a career that spanned more than 30 years.

'Tis takes the reader on McCourt's journey from adolescence to middle age, "focusing on his intellectual growth and on his social odyssey as an immigrant." (22) (New York, Sept.27, 1999).

I had the pleasure of meeting the charismatic Frank McCourt, with the twinkling eyes and the mischievous grin of a leprechaun, at the Book Revue in Huntington (L.I.), NY when he did a book signing for Angela's Ashes. Many years later, in July 2009, the brilliant Colum McCann did a reading and book signing also at the Book Revue for the launch of his fascinating social novel, *Let the Great World Spin*, a series of stories linked together by the tightrope walk/ dance of the unnamed Philippe Petit between the World Trade Towers on August 7, 1974. That evening McCann told his audience that his dear friend, Frank McCourt, had died. I will never forget how Colum McCann, himself with a grin and a sparkling smile, spoke of McCourt and how the night before, "we sang him into the dark." And I wondered, what better tribute could one possibly receive?

Colum McCann's work, *Transatlantic*, was released in June 2013. Once again, the Book Revue in Huntington, NY hosted McCann, as he discussed his decade-spanning, multi-generational novel that, like Let the Great World Spin's high wire act, takes the reader on a compelling flight across the Atlantic from Ireland to New York.

"I wonder this: If you take a woman and push her to the edge, how will she behave?"

~ Anita Shreve, The Weight of Water

FEBRUARY 2000: The Weight of Water by Anita Shreve

We were exposed to the writing of Anita Shreve for the second time after *The Pilot's Wife*, when we read *The Weight of Water* in February 2000. A story within a story, alternating between the past and the present, *The Weight of Water* simultaneously recounts two parallel random acts of passion and the tragic consequences that result. In the telling of each story, the author brings the reader to the precipice and then retreats, leaving him breathless and eager for more.

Story # 1 begins on March 5, 1873, when two Norwegian immigrants, Anethe and Karen Christensen, were murdered on the Isles of Shoals off the coast of New Hampshire. A third woman, Maren Hontvedt, survived, hiding in a sea cave ("Maren's Rock").

In Story # 2, told primarily by Jean, a magazine photographer, we meet four adults and one child living on a boat ---- Rich, who owns the sailboat, Adaline, Rich's girlfriend, Thomas, a poet, Rich's older brother married to Jean, and Billie, the five-year-old daughter of Jean and Thomas.

The author leaves clues and foreshadowings of what is to come. There is poetry, suspicion, obsession, and betrayal in The Weight of Water and, during our discussion of the novel, three of the questions posed to the group were:

1. If you take a woman and push her to the edge, how will she behave?
2. What are the consequences of a single random act?

AND

3. How well do we know our own spouse and to what lengths will we go to try to rectify a wrong done us?

The Weight of Water is a compelling, thought-provoking, novel of passion, and secrets that will lead to very animated discussions in your book group.

"I remember these moments not solely for themselves, but for the knowledge that beyond these memories lies an instant in time that cannot be erased. Each image a steppingstone taken in innocence or, if not in innocence, then in a kind of thoughtless oblivion."

Quote - from The Weight of Water, by, Anita Shreve

"It is 'where we are' that should make all the difference, whether we believe we belong there or not." ...

~ *Chang-Rae Lee*

MARCH 2000: A Gesture Life by Chang-Rae Lee

My first introduction to the writing of Chang-Rae Lee came in the new millennium. Born in Seoul, South Korea, his parents emigrated to the United States when Chang-Rae Lee was just three years old. "I went from one language, lost it, and picked up another. I have to think that has a lot to do with my being a writer. That's when I became almost obsessive about language." (23)

A Gesture Life, Lee's sophomore novel, tells the story of Franklin "Doc" Hata, who remembers treating young Korean girls who served as comfort women for Japanese soldiers during WWII. A model citizen, the man behind the Chamber of Commerce smile, Franklin Hata freely admits to wishing to "pass through with something more than a life of gesture."

Lee explores the prominent themes of language, assimilation, and the immigrant experience in his works. His fictional novel, Aloft, was chosen by our Long Island Reads Committee in 2008 and read by librarians and book clubs throughout Nassau and Suffolk Counties in New York. Lee subsequently wrote other novels including, *The Surrendered*, and his novel of a dystopian future which was released in 2013, *On Such A Full Sea.*

"You cannot find peace by avoiding life." ...

~ Michael Cunningham

APRIL 2000: The Hours by Michael Cunningham

We read a very different kind of story, (actually, three short parallel stories coming together as one), when I selected Michael Cunningham's, The *Hours* for our April 2000 discussion. Winner of the Pulitzer Prize and made into a hit movie starring Meryl Streep, Julianne Moor, and Nicole Kidman, *The Hours* is loosely based on the life and work of Virginia Woolf's 1925 novel, Mrs. Dalloway. The action takes place during one pivotal day in the life of three characters, each struggling with her own feelings of doubt, sexuality, loss, detachment, longing, life, and death.

The Hours is the perfect choice for your book club to discuss and follow up with viewing the movie.

"Men are afraid that women will laugh at them.
Women are afraid that men will kill them."

~ *Margaret Atwood*

MAY 2000: Alias Grace by Margaret Atwood

Historical fiction at its best, a mystery, a murder, jealousy, servitude, insanity, Alias Grace has it all. Written by acclaimed Canadian author, Margaret Atwood, the novel won the Giller Prize, the Premio Mondello and was short-listed for the Booker Prize.

The story describes the notorious 1843 murders of the wealthy Thomas Kinnear and his housekeeper and mistress, Nancy Montgomery, by two servants in the household, 16-year-old Irish immigrant, Grace Marks, and James McDermott. Convicted of the crime, McDermott was hanged, and Marks was sentenced to life imprisonment.

Atwood's 9th novel, Alias Grace, details the grisly murders and the events leading up to them but allows the reader to determine whether the protagonist is guilty or innocent, evil or insane.

Book groups will haggle over what actually transpired. Was Grace Marks an innocent or a villain, and what did the author hope to reveal in telling her (in) famous tale? Dig in and enjoy this very satisfying novel.

Christmas has always been a very special time for me. Growing up Diane, Renee, and I would watch 'A CHRISTMAS CAROL' with Alastair Sim as Scrooge on 'The Million Dollar Movie', over and over and over again, until we had memorized every line, from Ebenezer's "Can you forgive a pigheaded old fool for having no eyes to see with, no ears to hear with, after all these years?" to Tiny Tim's gentle supplication, "God Bless Us, Everyone!" We would sneak into each other's beds on Christmas Eve and try to guess what gifts were waiting for us under the tree. We would have written our letters to Santa and placed the cookies and milk in a spot he couldn't miss as he came down the chimney. Actually, we didn't really have a fireplace in our home on Drury Lane. We had to improvise a bit but, nevertheless, the magic was there as we whispered and giggled beneath the covers while sugarplums truly danced in our heads.

Renee and I were very playful and imaginative, Diane the more clear-headed realist. Funny that I was the one who wanted to be a nurse, despite the fact that I hated science, and it is fitting that Diane would become the nurse and future Director of Nursing at major health care facilities. Even back then, my sisters called me a 'Pollyanna.' There was no hint of the "Ultimate Hard-core, High-handed, Card-carrying Bibliophilist" I was destined to become.

Ted and I got engaged on Christmas Eve 1970. Although he was far from what you might call old fashioned like me, he still adhered to age-old traditions by calling my Father and requesting my hand in marriage. He was more a rebel than a rule follower, my beloved Ted, (Theodore, Thaddeus, my Theo), someone who answered to his own set of demands, the drummer who played to his own beat.

My pear-shaped, marquis-set diamond ring was nestled under the tree in the tiniest of several different size boxes in the style of the Russian matryoshka dolls----it was, truly, a Christmas to remember!

*I had graduated from Adelphi University in August of 1968 and
been granted a graduate assistantship to continue my studies in
French at Ohio State University. Mon reve était d'étudier à la
Sorbonne à Paris and, perhaps, get a job as a translator at the
United Nations in New York City. Instead, 'What I Did for
Love' was to remain on Long Island and wait for Ted to make up
that one year difference in our ages, get his degree and then find a
job. I was twenty-four years old when we got engaged, old by
"Perlman" standards at least. Both Diane and Renee were now
married, and each had a baby. I became the favorite aunt, the
cosmopolitan working girl to Diane's Kirsten, (my Goddaughter)
and Renee's Lance.*

*I commuted to the city with Dad every morning, frequently stopping
at Ted's home on the way, to enjoy a cup of my future father-in-
law's Turkish coffee. Dimon Diamond's coffee was so strong that
a spoon inserted inside the cup could easily stand up straight all by
itself. He would tease that my coffee was so weak it could pass for
tea. And when the rich, dark coffee had been consumed, Dorothy,
my belle-mère- to- be, would read our fortunes from the grinds
remaining in the cup.*

*Occasionally Dad and I would take the Long Island Railroad to
work and leave our car in the parking area at Wyandanch Station.
One evening in early 1971, Dad and I exited the train and
walked to our car, which was parked on a side street just off
Straight Path Road. I had the key in my hand as I approached the
driver's side (of the car). Dad walked across to the passenger side.
I saw the man rise up behind my Dad at the same time I felt the
blunt object digging into the small of my back. "DON'T TURN
AROUND, DON'T SAY A WORD," "DON'T TURN
AROUND, DON'T SAY A WORD," he repeatedly chanted in my
ear. I was afraid for my Father, afraid for myself, fearful that
Big Ed Perlman, the boxer in college, the entertaining pugilist in
the Army, would try to fight the thugs who took our money. It was*

123

no time for risky bravado. I silently prayed that the men would be satisfied with just taking our wallets and flee, that they wanted no more than some fast cash to buy drugs. I thought quickly and somehow managed to turn my engagement ring around so that the stone was facing the inside of my palm. I carried a purse and a small satchel which contained my book, (The French Lieutenant's Woman, by John Fowles), a lipstick and a box of Tampax. I remember that it was a Friday because Dad had just cashed his check and was carrying a few hundred dollars on him.

*What felt like an eternity was over in less than a few minutes."
DON'T TURN AROUND, DON'T SAY A WORD," "DON'T TURN AROUND, DON'T SAY A WORD." They fled in the darkness taking my Father's money, my book, and my Tampax. I was shaking; Dad was in control. I tried, unsuccessfully, to put the key in the door but my hand was trembling, and my knees started to buckle. There was no way I could drive to the Police Station to file a report. Dad had to physically take my hand and put me in the car. He drove. I shook. He talked. I stammered. "DON'T TURN AROUND, DON'T SAY A WORD," "DON'T TURN AROUND, DON'T SAY A WORD." The petty thieves fled, and we were left physically unscathed, but I was not so lucky in trying to escape the nightmares that haunted me for more than a year afterward, the similar, but yet utterly different, nightmares that would dog my dreams of my son, Brett, after September 11th.*

"All endings are also beginnings. We just don't know it at the time."

~ Mitch Albom

JUNE 2000: Tuesdays With Morrie: An old man, a young man, and life's greatest lesson by Mitch Albom

When Mitch Albom, syndicated Detroit Free Press sports columnist, radio host and ESPN, The Sport's Reporter's Panelist, at the time, set about writing *Tuesdays With Morrie* in 1995, he hoped only that sales would defray the medical expenses of his beloved Brandeis Sociology professor, Morrie Schwartz, who was dying of amyotrophic lateral sclerosis (ALS), also known as Lou Gehrig's disease. Instead, it became 1998s top-selling non-fiction book.

Albom re-encountered his former professor sixteen years after having studied under him. Their Tuesday afternoons spent together became the basis of the novel. Mitch's visits lasted three months, each final "class" teaching lessons about the power of love, acceptance, compassion, and courage. In dying, Morrie taught Mitch how to live a life fully.

Tuesdays With Morrie is the most successful memoir ever published. It spent more than four years on the New York Times Bestseller List and was made into a TV movie which aired on December 17, 1999, and starred Jack Lemmon and Hank Azaria. Tuesdays With Morrie is assigned reading at scores of colleges.

Below are some of Morrie's lessons ("Aphorisms"):

1. "Accept what you are able to do and what you are not able to do."

2. "Accept the past as past, without denying it or discarding it."
3. "Learn to forgive yourself and to forgive others."
4. "Don't assume that it's too late to get involved."
5. Love each other or perish" (Poet Auden) – "Without love we are birds with broken wings" (Morrie.)

6. "Be prepared to die. Once you learn how to die, you learn how to live."

Morrie's lessons remain timeless.

"Horse sense is the thing a horse has, which keeps it from betting on people."

~ W. C. Fields

JULY 2000: Horse Heaven by Jane Smiley

American novelist and Pulitzer Prize Winner for Fiction (A Thousand Acres), Jane Smiley has hit the racing trifecta with Horse Heaven. According to *Publisher's Weekly*, in its book review, "The Chinese calendar aside, 2000 may be the Year of the Horse. Almost neck and neck with Alyson Hagy's Keeneland, this novel about horses and their breeders, owners, trainers, grooms, jockeys, traders, bettors, and other turf-obsessed humans is another winner."

As I read about the world of horse racing, I thought of my seventy-five-year-old Mother, the unabashed gambler, who loved to go to the track, be it Yonkers, Aqueduct, or Belmont. Every summer, her vacation would take her to Saratoga, 'The August Place To Be,' to cheer for her horses with funny names because it reminded her of me, or my sisters, Diane and Renee, my brother, Chris, or one named for one of her eleven grandchildren. I still have her SARATOGA RACE COURSE POST PARADE MAGAZINE 2000 Official Past Performance Program. My Mom usually favored the gray horses, but on this particular day in July of the year 2000, she placed a $4.00 bet on the Daily Double with her favorite number combination 3 & 5, 5 & 3. Neither the #3 nor the #5 horse was gray; however, the #3 horse, Glitter n Glimmer, ridden by jockey Diana Gillam and the #5 horse, Iron County Xmas, with jockey Chip Miller, paid off with a big win for her that day!

*"My origins do not haunt me. Attitudes about
my origins do."*

~ Michelle Paulse

AUGUST 2000: Half a Heart by Rosellen Brown

Author Rosellen Brown (Before and After, Civil Wars),
tackles themes of motherhood and racial bias in her latest
novel, Half a Heart.

As a young woman and civil rights activist in Mississippi in
the 1960s, Miriam Vener becomes involved with her Black
professor, Eljay Reece, and bears his biracial child, a daughter
named Veronica (Ronnee). Miriam was White and Jewish,
Eljay, Black. Eljay said they were "Klan Bait," the Blacks and
the Jews, the least understood and the most passionate and
imaginative. For seventeen years, Ronnee was kept from her
birth mother. Our discussion brought us into the realm of
nurture vs. nature and the bond of love between parent and
child.

"How many grilled cheese sandwiches did it take to be a
good parent?" Miriam wondered. The title of the book poses
its own dilemma: "She had lived these seventeen years with
half a heart, but comfort had provided the other half, had
kept her alive."

Pick up this book and decide for yourself.

"There on the beaches of Normandy, I began to reflect on the wonders of these ordinary people whose lives were laced with the markings of greatness."

~ Tom Brokaw, The Greatest Generation

SEPTEMBER 2000: Flags of Our Fathers by James Bradley

A letter from DONNA J. DIAMOND to:

James Bradley, Flags of Our Fathers,

c/o Bantam Books, 1540 Broadway, New York, N.Y. 10036

July 10, 2000

Dear Mr. Bradley;

It was with deep joy and bittersweet sadness that I turned the last page of your beautiful book, Flags of Our Fathers. I can only try to tell you the impact that it has had on my life.

Like you, I, too, am the child of a World War II veteran "of common virtue." Born in 1946 the middle of three daughters, (my older sister, Diane was born in 1945 and my younger sister, Doreen, in 1947 – a brother, Christopher, came 18 years later in 1964), fathered by a devout Roman Catholic, 2nd Lieutenant INF., Company +++, 378th Infantry Regiment, Edward Charles Francis Perlman.

129

My Father served in the U.S. Infantry stationed in Europe during WWII. He won the Purple Heart for valor and bravery when he led his men to the beaches of Normandy during the second wave of action there, and he was awarded two Bronze Stars, (one received on April 7, 1945, in the vicinity of Rhynern, Germany, where he continued to lead his platoon against the enemy, despite being hit by a rifle shot and having shrapnel in three places). Like your Dad, John, "Doc" Bradley, my Dad, "Big Ed" Perlman, never spoke about his war years to his family. With a smile always on his face, (his lifelong motto was, "a smile and a few kind words can go a long way"), he might reluctantly show us the spot where he had been hit by shrapnel in the legs and shoulder. But he never spoke about the battles he had fought or the medals he had won. We knew nothing about the time he spent in France and Germany or the pain behind the smile. He saw close friends die and he carried that grief with him just as "Doc" Bradley bore "Iggy's" memory with him. How they must have suffered, these brave young fathers of ours! And how terribly sad I am that I couldn't have been there to listen if he had wanted to talk.

My Dad, my beloved friend, (I was always such a "Daddy's girl"), died in August 1988 of a fatal heart attack. He was accorded a military funeral and is buried at Calverton National Cemetery on Long Island, New York.

Eddie Perlman had a wonderful life after the war. He returned to his family and raised his girls and took pleasure in seeing his grandchildren come into the world. (He was overseas for the births of my sisters and me, so he was overjoyed to be present whenever one of his grandchildren was born). He traveled extensively, as he worked in the International Machine Tool arena, taking his family with him on domestic vacations whenever possible. He was so proud of the commemorative statue of "The Photograph" at Iwo Jima in Washington, D. C. I can still remember our first family trip to our nation's capital and Dad's joy and pride in showing us what our men in the service had accomplished. And our Father, "Big Ed" Perlman, always had his faith and love of God.

I am an avid reader, and I lead two monthly book discussion groups, (one at Border's Books and Music in Commack, L. I., which I do on a strictly voluntary basis, and one at our local library). I would like to make your book, Flags of Our Fathers, our selection for September 2000 and, although I am not an employee of Border's, I would like to extend an invitation to you to join us and speak about your research and about your father and the other boys of Easy Company.

Our group of approximately 22 men and women generally meets on the 2nd Monday of each month (with an exception in September – the date being September 18th this year) from 11:00 – 12:30PM. If you would prefer to meet at night, I know that Border's would be thrilled to welcome you at any time that is convenient for you.

As I said at the beginning of this letter, Mr. Bradley, it was with a bittersweet feeling that I read the final pages of your book. I searched whatever "archives" my family has of my Dad's service in the army, but I could not come up with much of a story to fill in the gaps between the medals and the shrapnel – "the silent years."

If you would consider speaking to my book discussion group, it could be my way of paying tribute to my Father and saying, "Thank You," as you did, for being a part of "The Greatest Generation."

Thank you again for bringing my Father alive through the pages of your book.

Sincerely,

Donna

J. Diamond

Note: My original letter to James Bradley is still intact in the folder I had created for Flags of Our Fathers, by James Bradley, September 18, 2000. It was never sent. I became quite ill and had to cancel our book discussion.

"And the wicked thing is, that when we're really upset, we always take it out on the people who are closest and whom we love the most."

~ Rosamunde Pilcher, *Winter Solstice*

OCTOBER 2000: Winter Solstice by Rosamunde Pilcher

In the Northern Hemisphere, the winter solstice is the shortest day of the year; the sun is at its most distant, and all seems dark and dreary. That was not the case with this book by an author that I always adored, (*The Shell Seekers*, September, Coming Home). One of the things I always tell my book clubs is TIMING IS EVERYTHING! Especially when it comes to reading – Quite often "when" we read a book may be important – not the time of day or the month or year, but rather "what period" in our lives we may decide to start turning the pages. After a particularly bad or sad experience, we may have a negative view of a book. If we were to re-read that very same book, months or even years, later, at a happier time, our opinion would, undoubtedly, be different. (Refer to my 'Tips On How to Start, Lead and Enhance Your Book Discussion' at the back of the book).

This warm and fuzzy read was perfect for me as I underwent IV infusions at Huntington Hospital; yet, it was sad at the same time, because I knew this was Rosamunde Pilcher's final work. Rosamunde Pilcher had always been my "go-to" author, especially when I was feeling sick, troubled, or out-of-sorts. What author would I find to replace her? Who would fill that empty place in my soul and on my bookshelf? I would have to wait six more years before I would meet Adriana Trigiani, a very talented, larger-than-life, writer par excellence, who would come to fill that void. Although each

133

would have a very different writing style, and their subjects and characters hail from opposite ends of the pond, their storytelling would project a similar kindness and generosity of spirit.

"Love is a temporary madness; it erupts like volcanoes and then subsides. And when it subsides, you have to make a decision. You have to work out whether your roots have so entwined together that it is inconceivable that you should ever part. Because this is what love is."

~ Louis de Bernieres, Corelli's Mandolin

NOVEMBER 2000: Corelli's Mandolin by Louis de Bernieres

Corelli's Mandolin, also released as *Captain Corelli's Mandolin*, by Louis de Bernières, an Englishman with a French name, was originally published as a best-selling book for children, but in 1994 it became a very popular book club choice. We, in "The Literary Gallery," enjoyed reading this colorful historical novel in November 2000.

Set on the breathtakingly beautiful island of Cephalonia, (Kefalonia,) surrounded by rugged mountains and sparkling blue waters in the Ionian Sea, de Bernières' extraordinary novel is based on a historic episode: c'est à dire, the Nazis' occupation and slaughter of thousands of Italian troops from Mussolini's army after Greece's defeat by the Axis.

One of the Italian officers billeted with the elderly Dr. Iannis and his lovely seventeen-year-old daughter, Pelagia, is the young, high-spirited, Antonio Corelli, a captain in the 33rd artillery regiment of the Aqui Division, who "plays the mandolin like an angel and inspires impromptu opera performances among his troops." (24)

The book's hero is a composite figure based loosely on the real Amos Pampaloni and de Bernières' own mastery of the mandolin.

The author has written a (love) story, played out among the harsh reality and cruelty of war, set on an idyllic island. Corelli's Mandolin has been simultaneously praised and criticized for being overly sentimental. It is up to you, the reader, to make that judgment.

This book was of particular interest to me because the story takes place on the Greek Island of Cephalonia, (Kefalonia,) not far from where my father-in-law was born. Like Corelli, he too would periodically play the mandolin, as his nimble fingers moved up and down the scale rhythmically humming "Never On Sunday" .... Yasou!

In 2001, *Corelli's Mandolin* was made into a movie starring Nicolas Cage and Penelope Cruz.

"Beauty exists where you least expect to find it."

*~ Gail Tsukiyama, The Samurai's
Garden*

DECEMBER 2000: The Samurai's Garden by Gail Tsukiyama

Gail Tsukiyama's, *The Samurai's Garden,* was our final read in December 2000. This very talented and prolific author, who writes sensitive stories about the suffering and courage of Chinese and Japanese people, was soon to become another favorite of mine for many reasons. During the late '70s, '80s, and 1990s, Thaddeus was taking frequent, extensive business trips to Asia, to China and the Far East. When she was a mere two years old, my little daughter, Danielle, would tell family and friends that her, "Daddy was in KO RE' A."

I became fascinated by the long history and traditions of the Chinese people and wanted to learn to speak at least a few simple phrases when I joined Thad on two such trips. This led me to study Mandarin so that I could smile and say, "ni hao" or "ni hao ma?" "xie xie," and "zai jian," (which means hello, how are you, thank you and good-bye), pleasing phrases that will take you almost anywhere.

Our book clubs would later go on to read Tsukiyama's, *Women of the Silk,* and *The Language of Threads.*

It started with a slight tingling and numbness, facial neuralgia, and weakness on the right side. "Nerves," one doctor said. "Pre-wedding anxiety" was a second diagnosis. "It's either a brain tumor or spinal meningitis," yet another specialist flatly declared.

Then "IT" attacked my eyes. For days I felt as if I had a hair or piece of dust in my left eye. I kept rubbing it, trying to remove whatever had lodged itself inside. I continued to go to work in the city, enjoying my Wall Street job as a Bilingual Administrative Secretary/Translator to the President of a French bank. It was November 1971, three months before our wedding. Seated at my typewriter, (with a French keyboard — computers like Hal in '2001 A Space Odyssey' were still just imagined creations of some quirky lab-sequestered scientist). My hands were raised, fingers poised to strike the keys, when they froze, locked in place like the useless paws of a declawed kitten. Suspended in the air in a painful clenched position, I was powerless to move. Minutes passed before I was able to react and ask my co-worker to call my father and tell him I would meet him outside the office. She asked if I would be alright, or if I needed assistance, but all I could think of was that I had to get out of there. I had to get to safety, had to go home. I stumbled out of the building, disoriented and untethered, my eyes blurry, and blended with the crowd.

And then I blacked out.

I don't remember what happened next or how I got to a place with bright lights and people hovering over me. I heard someone ask if I was drunk or on drugs, and then I heard my father's angry voice yelling, "NO! my daughter is neither intoxicated nor taking any drugs." I was dizzy, lightheaded, and my left eye was throbbing.

Dad put me in the car, and we drove to Long Island Jewish Hospital (LIJ) in Lake Success. My friend, Libby Canova, was working in a Dialysis Unit there and I knew she would get me in to see an (eye) doctor as quickly as possible.

I was instructed to cover my left eye and try to read the chart in front of me. So far, so good. I was then told to cover my right eye and read that same chart. "What chart?" I asked. I could see nothing with my left eye. There was a stunned silence when no one spoke. "How long have you been blind in your left eye?", the examiner asked. "I can't be blind," I distinctly remember saying. "I'm getting married in three months!"

Who is to say if this account is what actually happened? I have thought about this sequence of events and pondered over what still stands out so vividly in my memory. Is it possible? Yes. Is it true? Yes, again. If a memoir is based on one's own recollection of what transpired, then this is, indeed, a memoir. I would never want to be accused of fabricating the truth as James Frey did when he wrote 'A Million Little Pieces. '

"…half of memory is imagination anyway."

~ as Bart said in Kevin Powers', The Yellow Birds (page 186).

Chapter 5

The End of Camelot (2001)

2001

January 2001 – The start of a bright, new year in the 21st century. After all the hoopla and prognosticating, after all the fears and anticipation surrounding the Y2K bug, we seemed ready to move forward and settle into this new period.

In the United States, in 2001, the average cost of a new car was $25,850.00 and a gallon of gas was $1.46. You could mail a letter with a .34 cent postage stamp and buy a dozen eggs for .90 cents.

In Italy, the Leaning Tower of Pisa reopened after eleven years of repairs to stop it from falling over, and on June 8th, Tony Blair and the British Labour Party were elected for a second term in Great Britain.

In 2001, *Publisher's Weekly* named, A Painted House, by John Grisham, #3 on the Hardcover Fiction List and, John Adams, by David McCullough, #4 in Non-Fiction. Amazon Customer's Favorites of 2001 had John Adams at #1, A Painted House at #7, The Corrections, by Jonathan Franzen, at #9 and, The Red Tent, by Anita Diamant, and several books in the Harry Potter series by J.K. Rowling, at #10.

Amazon's Best of 2001 Editor's Picks found Leif Enger's, *Peace Like a River*, at #1, *The Corrections* at #2, Laura Hillenbrand's, *Seabiscuit: An American Legend*, at #6 and *John Adams* at #7.

In 2001, in Fiction, *Desecration*, by Tim LaHaye and Jerry B. Jenkins' 9th volume in the 'Left Behind' series, sold for

$24.99 and the Non-Fiction list offered, *The No Spin Zone*, by Bill O'Reilly for $24.95.

"As a kid, I was pretty obsessed with dinosaurs and the day that my parents took me to Dinosaur National Park, I didn't think life could get any better."

~ Chelsea Clinton

JANUARY 2001: Tyrannosaurus Sue: The Extraordinary Saga of the Largest, Most Sought Over T. Rex Ever Found by Steve Fiffer

In our reading world, in 'The Literary Gallery,' we veered off the traditional path with our first two book selections in January and February, *Tyrannosaurus Sue: The Extraordinary Saga of the Largest, Most Sought Over T. Rex Ever Found*, by Steve Fiffer and Morgan's Run, by Colleen McCullough. With Tyrannosaurus Sue, our book discussion was scientific, contemporary, and theoretical. One of our gentlemen members at Border's, Nick Siciliano, a retired history teacher, posed the question that was the premise of the book: "Is a fossil personal property?"

We discussed the legal battle between big government and the absent-minded professor, (i.e., the scientific community,) and we learned, in-depth, of that famous dispute when Tyrannosaurus Sue was sold to Chicago's Field Museum in 1997 for $8.4 million.

"Don't worry about the world coming to an end today. It is already tomorrow in Australia."

~ *Charles M. Schulz*

FEBRUARY 2001: Morgan's Run by Colleen McCullough

Morgan's Run, by Colleen McCullough, is a voluminous tome that speaks of the birth of Australia, which was founded and populated mainly by British convicts, sent in the late 1700s, to settle the land then called New South Wales. Although we unanimously agreed that Morgan's Run could not hold a candle to McCullough's previous triumph, *The Thornbirds*, it was, nonetheless informative, when it did not get too bogged down with seemingly useless trivia (i.e., 18th-century fire engine construction and rum distilling methods). Then again, if you are a JEOPARDY! fan, like me, no information or learning can ever be considered trivial.

*"You have to believe in yourself despite the
evidence."*

~ Kent Haruf

MARCH 2001: Plainsong by Kent Haruf

Our March selection 2001 was *Plainsong*, written by Kent
Haruf. Verlyn Klinkenborg, writing for the New York
Times, described *Plainsong* as "a novel so foursquare, so
delicate and lovely, that it has the power to exalt the reader."
The action takes place over a short period of time in the
small town of Holt. We meet Tom Guthrie, a high school
teacher, struggling to raise his two young sons, when their
depressed mother closes herself off in a bedroom, then
moves away to her sister's house. During the reader's slow
drive through the town, we meet a cast of characters who
come together, bound by their community and landscape.
Plainsong is a story of shared grief and abandonment, of
kindness and hope. Michiko Kakutani, writing for the New
York Times on October 8, 1999, (pB45(N) pE47(L) col 3 (18
cols in,) said re *Plainsong*, "Everyone's a neighbor in a small
prairie town." Lisa Michaels, *The Wall Street Journal*, October
8, 1999, (sOpW10(W)pw10 (E col3 (15 col in,) called
Plainsong "a West Side Story" and Dinitia Smith, The New
York Times, December 1, 1999, (pB4(N) pE1(L) col 3 (35 col
in,) wrote in her review of Kent Haruf's, *Plainsong*, "Eyes
covered but seeing, a novelist looks inward; embracing the
smallness of a town, and the big hearts of its people."

In the summer of 2014, Haruf finished his last novel, *Our
Souls at Night*, which was published posthumously in 2015.

"Their lungs full of fluid, they drowned in their bed, first my mother, then my father. I was helpless to hold them back."

~ *Christina Schwarz, Drowning Ruth,*

APRIL 2001: Drowning Ruth by Christina Schwarz

Oprah had selected Christina Schwarz's suspenseful debut novel, *Drowning Ruth*, for her Book Club in September 2000, less than a year before we, in 'The Literary Gallery,' read it in April 2001.

The setting is bleak: Winter 1919, Nagawaukee Lake, Wisconsin.

A story of sisters, the ties that bind and the forces that tear them apart, *Drowning Ruth*, embraces early 1900s mores, social restraints, and tensions. The author presents the reader with a strong sense of foreboding and of place and questions the nature of love and guilt. Drowning Ruth is a good book club choice and will lead to thought-provoking discussions of family loyalty and love and of taking responsibility for people and things.

"He saw things in a way that others did not so that a city I had lived in all my life seemed a different place so that a woman became beautiful with the light on her face."

~ Tracy Chevalier, Girl With a Pearl Earring

MAY 2001: Girl with A Pearl Earring by Tracy Chevalier

In April 2013, the Rijksmuseum, the Dutch National Museum of Art & History (Amsterdam), where masterpieces by Rembrandt van Rijn and Johannes Vermeer mingle with Delft blue pottery, re-opened its doors to the public after ten years of comprehensive renovations. Thaddeus and I spent a most enjoyable afternoon at the Rijksmuseum in July 2013. I was most anxious to see the painting that had launched thousands of copies of its namesake book, *Girl with a Pearl Earring*, by Tracy Chevalier, but, alas, it wasn't meant to be. I was disappointed to learn that the precious painting had been returned to her rightful home in Delft and, although we made the trip to this incredibly quaint, step- back- in- time, blue and white village, it was a cold and rainy Sunday and the museum was closed. We did manage to stop for some famously delectable, thin, powdered sugar, Dutch pancakes, which didn't disappoint.

Tracy Chevalier vividly brought to life 17th century Holland and the work of the famous Dutch painter, Johannes Vermeer, (1632-1675) in her historical novel, *Girl with A Pearl Earring*. Chevalier's second novel, *Girl with A Pearl Earring* won the Barnes & Noble Discover Award, has sold more than 3,500,000 copies worldwide and was made into a film starring Colin Firth and Scarlet Johansson. Her inspiration for the book was a poster of Johannes Vermeer's painting, *Girl with a Pearl Earring*. She bought the poster as a nineteen-year-old, and it hung wherever she lived for sixteen years. Supposedly, the "ambiguous look" on the girl's face left a lasting impression on her. Chevalier describes the girl's expression, "to be a mass of contradictions: innocent yet experienced, joyous yet tearful, full of longing and yet full of loss." She began to think that the girl had directed all these emotions at the painter and began to think of the "story behind" that look." (25)

Girl with A Pearl Earring is a work of historical fiction, which centers around Griet, a quietly perceptive sixteen-year-old Dutch girl, who becomes a servant in Vermeer's household in the 1660s after her father becomes blind while working as a tile painter. Although Griet makes enemies in the household, Vermeer takes a liking to her, and employs her as his assistant, and ultimately has Griet sit for him as a model. Chevalier vividly evokes the tensions created, in large part, by Vermeer's perpetually pregnant Catholic (Papist) wife, Catherine, and her stern, unflinching mother, Maria Thins, Vermeer's mother-in-law and the owner of the home they share. Griet is also opposed by Cornelia, Vermeer's sly, arrogant daughter, who knowingly and intentionally pits Griet against her mother, (and thus her father and grandmother). Nevertheless, Griet takes pleasure in her mundane tasks, particularly when cleaning her master's studio, (from which his clumsy wife is forbidden), grinding the paints and arranging the background objects.

> "I came to love grinding the things he brought from the apothecary—bones, white lead, madder, massicot – to see how bright and pure I could get the colors. I learned that the finer the materials were ground, the deeper the color. From rough, dull grains madder

became a fine bright red powder and, mixed with linseed oil, a sparkling paint. Making it and the other colors was magical."

~From Girl with A Pearl Earring, by Tracy Chevalier

Griet will ultimately become Vermeer's muse when one of his wealthy patrons' requests that Griet be the subject of his next painting.

Indeed, *Girl with A Pearl Earring* is "a jewel of a novel." ~ The Miami Herald

Girl with A Pearl Earring quickly became a Book Club favorite. Celebrations and parties using a menu of gouda cheese and Dutch beer (Amstel) took place, with copies of Vermeer's artwork displayed on the walls and lovely blue and white Delft figures adorning coffee tables.

> *"The truth is life is full of joy and full of great sorrow, but you can't have one without the other."*
>
> *~ Andre Dubus III, House of Sand and Fog*

JUNE 2001: House of Sand and Fog by Andre Dubus III

House of Sand and Fog is one of those books that has stayed with me, searing my memory more than thirteen years after I turned the final page, saddened and spent. Shortly after I started my book club at Barnes & Noble in May of 1996, my mother-in-law, Dotty Diamond, created her own book club at the Tarpon Springs, (Florida), Library. Although Dotty emphasized the author's writing and creative style at her monthly meetings and engaged more in the study of the Classics than I, we often shared one another's notes and held private two-way discussions after we had read a book, similar to the way Will Schwalbe and his mother, Mary Anne, held their discussions. (*The End of Your Life Book Club*, by Will Schwalbe). Thankfully, our rendezvous was neither inspired by a terminal illness nor held in a hospital venue.

Andre Dubus III found his calling as a writer and teacher after having worked for a time as a bounty hunter, private investigator, and actor. He published his first book in 1989 and his first novel, Bluesman, in 1993. "He taught and did odd jobs as a carpenter while working on House of Sand and Fog. Much of the book was written in his car, which he often parked at a local cemetery in search of quiet and solitude. His characters were inspired by two people whose predicaments had stuck in his mind for years: a woman he read about in the newspaper who was wrongly evicted from her home and forced to live in her car, and a college friend's father, (in the book, Colonel Massoud Amir Behrani), who had been a colonel in the Iranian Air Force and could only find menial jobs after fleeing to the United States." (Taken from *Vintage Books Reading Group Guide: House of Sand and Fog*, by Andre Dubus III.)

As we have encountered with other authors who have written about the immigrant experience and assimilating into American society, (*The Namesake*, by Jhumpa Lahiri, *A Gesture Life*, by Chang-Rae Lee,) Dubus presents his Iranian national, Colonel Massoud Amir Behrani, as a proud man attempting to get a foot in the door of the American dream. For him, the house on Bisgrove Street represented all of that. But, for Kathy Nicolo, the house on Bisgrove Street was a reminder of a kinder, gentler past. Can a house be your whole identity? Do we all want to capture the American dream?

Those were just a few of the many questions we discussed as we read House of Sand and Fog. We talked about how everyone in the book was obsessed with ownership of the bungalow and with the opinions of others. We talked of misplaced materialism and foolish pride. We talked about parent-child relationships and about marital bliss and its difficulties. And finally, we spoke of the strong emotions that this book evoked in each of us---anger, fear, frustration, sympathy, and sorrow. Like a Greek tragedy, House of Sand and Fog is a "perfect storm" of emotions colliding inevitably and irreversibly.

Dubus's novel was an Oprah Book Club Pick in November 2000 and a finalist for the National Book Award.

In 2003, House of Sand and Fog was adapted into a film of the same title starring Ben Kingsley and Jennifer Connelly. The movie's ending differs from that of the book.

I would highly recommend this novel for any group, large or small, men and women. Because of the in-depth conversations that are generated, I chose this title again for our discussion at the Northport Library in September 2013.

I wish to leave you with the poem from "The Balcony" by Octavio Paz that is referenced in the book.

> "Beyond myself
>
> Somewhere
>
> I wait for my arrival."

"You have a 5% chance of having Multiple Sclerosis," Dr. Balkin, the eye specialist at LIJ, sadly informed me. "If you have no episodes or further symptoms in the next five years, then you will be "out of the woods." "Am I going to die?" was my feeble,

frightened question to him. "No," he replied, with a serious but unreadable expression on his face.

And because I was getting married in a few short months and wanted to be able to see at my wedding, the doctor gave me a steroid injection directly into my left eyeball.

⁂

(An Aside: I have a very touching picture to remind me of how my three-year-old Goddaughter, Kirsten, who was the flower girl at our nuptials, reaches up to give me a kiss on our wedding day. I was having trouble putting on my makeup because I had double vision and couldn't see clearly out of my left eye. Diane and Renee, my co-Matrons of Honor and Karyn, one of several bridesmaids, were getting dressed with me. More than a little frustrated because I didn't want to have black smudges on my eye make-up, I blurted out loud, "Who will help me?" And then I heard a quiet voice reply, "I will, Bride." That was my Kirsten, my little pal as a child, now my friend, a grown woman.

⁂

Libby and Bonnie were waiting for me when I left the doctor's office. I was sobbing as I told the girls about my possible diagnosis of Multiple Sclerosis. "How can I tell Ted?" I cried. "How can I tell him about the future that possibly awaits me/us?" He would certainly have every reason to flee, to break our engagement and cancel the wedding. And why shouldn't he when so much was at stake? I didn't know if I would be blind or in a wheelchair, would walk with a limp or be incontinent. Would I be able to talk? To remember? The doctor said I wasn't going to die, but how would I be living?

Once again, things weren't as they should be. I felt disconnected and fearful. Things were happening so fast. It was all surreal. So, I decided to pray, "Please Dear God........"

"We'll deal with each day, with each symptom, IF and it's still a big IF "IT" ever comes," my practical realist consoled me. "I know that you're frightened, but I also know you're going to be OK." "Let's not worry about what might be, what may happen." "Let's continue with our wedding plans and get you feeling better right now."

My Ted, my Theo, loving, calming, protective, strong. My Thaddeus, my frat boy on the left, my drummer, who had me with a CRASH! BOOM! BANG! My Thaddeus, with his family's yacht, the Knotty Knee bartender, the High School wrestler with the muscular physique. My blue-eyed Greek would stand by me and fight for me.

And because of that, I loved him even more.

*"I try to make my characters kind of ordinary,
somebody that anybody could be. Because we've all
had loves, perhaps love and loss, people can relate
to my characters."*

~ *Maeve Binchy*

JULY 2001: Scarlet Feather by Maeve Binchy

In July 2001 "The Literary Gallery" gleefully plunged into
Maeve Binchy's, *Scarlet Feather*. This popular author of short
stories and novels such as *Circle of Friends, Tara Road* and *Light
a Penny Candle*, was born in Dalkey, a small village outside of
Dublin, Ireland on May 28, 1940. She left a grieving nation
and fan-base when she died on July 30, 2012, at age 72 after a
short illness.

Binchy's novels take place in her beloved Ireland and most
focus on women and their day to day lives. She has recurring
characters in her books, (like Brenda Brennan,) and Quentin's
Restaurant/Pub is a frequent hang-out and hot spot for her
colorful people to meet. Her books predominantly appeal to
female audiences and address themes of alcoholism and
divorce, homelessness and child neglect. In *Scarlet Feather*, the
author has given us a contemporary backdrop from which to
view the new Ireland "where children take care of their unfit
parents and where the social worker has replaced the priest as
the country's conscience." (26) (*Newsday*, Thursday, March
29, 2001, "In a New Ireland, the Same Old Business," by
Anna Mundow.

Without preaching, Binchy tells her story with a keen eye for
domestic detail and social commentary. "Nowadays women
realize that they are dealt a hand of cards and must play it,"
Binchy told The Chicago Tribune in a 1999 interview.

152

"There are no makeovers in my books. The ugly duckling does not become a beautiful swan. She becomes a confident duck able to take charge of her own life and problems."

Maeve Binchy's books make for a delightful vacation read and discussion of Ireland and all of our day-to-day experiences. Perhaps, you might wish to serve a cup of tea, or a hearty stein of dark Guinness ale and a slice of Irish soda bread when reading a book by this delightful Irish treasure.

Sadly, we would read what we thought was her final novel, A Week in Winter, in June 2013; however, in the *New York Times Book Review* dated Sunday, April 27, 2014, (pg. 2,) there appeared a lovely illustration of a book jacket with the title, Chestnut Street, by Maeve Binchy. There is a quote by *Publisher's Weekly*: "One finds here insightful observations about human nature—all with Binchy's thoughtful and loving touch that will be sorely missed" and, on the side of the Times Review, adjacent to the photo of the multi-colored doors of Dublin, the words: "The late, great Maeve Binchy imagined a street in Dublin with many characters coming and going, and every once in a while over the years she would write a story about one of these people. She would then put it in a drawer, "for the future," she would say. The future is now.

"Because it is my name!..."

~ Arthur Miller, The Crucible

AUGUST 2001: Salem Falls by Jodi Picoult

Jodi Picoult's gripping 7th novel about witchcraft and the practice of Wikkan, about rape and accusation, was an ideal selection for generating a heated discussion of a Y2K re-telling of Arthur Miller's, *The Crucible*.

Chosen as a featured selection of the Literary Guild and a Book Sense 76 Pick, *Salem Falls* takes the reader on a roller coaster ride of twists and turns, surprises and unexpected revelations.

Jodi Picoult, née Jodi Lynn Picoult, was born on May 19, 1966, in Nesconset, (L.I.,) NY. She studied writing at Princeton, graduated in 1987 and followed with a Master's Degree in Education from Harvard University. She currently resides with her husband, Tim Van Leer, and three children, Sammy, Kyle and Jake in Hanover, New Hampshire.

A prolific writer, (more than twenty-one books,) Picoult's novels are thoroughly researched and frequently deal with timely and ethical issues, (teenage suicide, eugenics, organ transplants and donations, anti-semitism, autism, and bullying). Her stories are told from several perspectives, with each chapter written in a different character's voice. She presents multiple sides to every argument and opinion, withholding her own bias to allow the reader to reach his or her personal conclusion. The author's final courtroom scenes commonly bring the action taking place to a crescendo and render unexpected "gotcha!" moments.

I have had the pleasure of meeting Jodi Picoult several times at the Book Revue in Huntington, NY. She is a natural, a glib speaker, comfortable and knowledgeable discussing her craft or her latest novel. We, in the 'Literary Gallery,' in our 'From Cover to Cover' Book Discussion Group at Harborfields Library, and in our 'Page Turners' Group at Northport Library, would subsequently read some of this author's other books:

- ➤ *Plain Truth* - 2002
- ➤ *My Sister's Keeper* - 2004
- ➤ *Vanishing Act* - 2005
- ➤ *Nineteen Minutes* - 2007
- ➤ *House Rules* - 2010

Ms. Picoult will frequently make use of recurring characters in her novels. For example, Jordan McAfee, his son, Thomas, and wife, Selena, are featured in *The Pact, Salem Falls* and *Nineteen Minutes*. The charming Patrick Ducharme appears in *Perfect Match* and again in *Nineteen Minutes*.

> "It's always great fun to bring a character back because you get to catch up on his/her life, and you don't have to reinvent the wheel – you already know how   he speaks, acts, thinks." (27)

Many of Jodi Picoult's books have been made into film and TV adaptations:

- ➤ The Pact – 2002
- ➤ Plain Truth – 2004
- ➤ The Tenth Circle - 2006
- ➤ My Sister's Keeper - 2009
- ➤ Salem Falls - 2011

I remember once hearing Ms. Picoult chuckling over a question she was asked about whether her childhood was dysfunctional enough to supply fodder for her novels. Her smile and the slight shrug of her shoulders was sufficient to answer as she fondly looked out at her beaming family in the audience.

Picoult's last seven novels, including *The Storyteller*, have debuted at #1 on the *New York Times* Bestseller List. *Leaving Time* and her ebook novella, *Larger Than Life*, came out in the fall of 2014.

"Sam Houston: You will remember this battle!
Each minute! Each second! Until the day that you
die! But that is for tomorrow, gentlemen. For
today, Remember The Alamo!"

~ Author Unknown

SEPTEMBER 2001: The Gates of the Alamo by Stephen Harrigan

Our regularly scheduled meeting of "The Literary Gallery" took place on Monday, September 10, 2001, just one day before our nation and the comfortable world that we knew, would be forever changed. I had chosen, The Gates of the Alamo, by Stephen Harrigan, for three reasons: The first was that I was curious to read something by this heretofore unknown, (to me) author. The second was because I had recently seen an old movie, (Fess Parker? John Wayne?) about the Alamo. And the third, and possibly the most outrageous reason, was because in May I had giddily celebrated Cinco de Mayo con la bandera Mexicana, verde, blanca y roja. I was curious as to the origins of that guacamole-eating, taco-stuffing, feast of margaritas and wanted to know if it was, indeed, the same war that was fought over the Alamo.

Note: Cinco de Mayo has ultimately become one of our favorite holidays. My daughter-in-law, Rebecca, is of Mexican-American heritage. She and my son, Brett hold their annual green, white and red fiesta on the first Saturday in May, complete with a burro, enchiladas, and a piñata, to the delight of all the adults and children.

Simple reasons, innocent musings................

Brett called Ted and me from work early Tuesday morning, September 11, 2001. We each picked up an extension. It was a little after 9:00AM. "TURN ON THE TV!" our son commanded with a catch in his voice. "I'm looking out the window from my office, and I just saw a plane crash into the World Trade Center. Do you think......? OH, MY GOD, NOW ANOTHER PLANE JUST FLEW INTO THE TOWERS!" My heart stopped, my jaw agape, as I gawked at the screen. Ted screamed to Brett, "GET OUT OF THERE RIGHT NOW, USE THE STAIRS, DON'T TAKE THE ELEVATOR, JUST RUN, NOW!"

Brett had already thrown down the phone. The connection was lost.

You know the rest. We all have our "Where were you when?" stories, our horror tales and "There but by the grace of God go I" anthems.

This is mine:

Brett was on the 31st floor of his office at 60 Broad Street with a direct view of the World Trade Center. After he dropped the phone, he ran for the nearest exit to the stairs. Brett played football at Georgetown. He was a wide receiver accustomed to running sprints. So I fervently prayed, "Dear God, please protect my boy. He's fast. Please keep him safe."

The same images were repeatedly projected on the TV screen......the plane crashing into the North Tower and the horrendous, Hiroshima-like mushroom of smoke inching behind the fleeing mob. In my new nightmare, Brett was one of those people trying to outrun destiny. September 11, 2001, a giant mushroom cloud, my boy running........." DON'T SAY A WORD, DON'T TURN AROUND," "DON'T SAY A WORD, DON'T TURN AROUND!"

Dani was in New Jersey on September 11, 2001, working with a focus group for Lowe Advertising. Far from a radio or TV and at a distance from the city, she was totally unaware of what had taken place just moments before. Our phone call signaled that moment for her when life and living in New York City would change irrevocably.

Dani's fiancé, Greg, was working uptown for Arthur Anderson when the Towers were struck. My sister Renee's daughter, Jaime, was also in midtown, just four blocks up from Greg. The kids had their cell phones, but how long would they hold a charge? They knew they would have to get out of the city and find their way to our home in East Northport, but how would they get here? The bridges and tunnels were closed. The trains were running sporadically. People were walking, NO! RUNNING across the Brooklyn Bridge.

Ted and I would serve as middlemen, relaying messages between Dani and Brett, Greg and Jaime, our nephew, Doug, and Brett's three friends, who had apartments in the city, that were being evacuated. They came from New Mexico, Connecticut, and Delaware and had no place to go.

Dani and Greg, (and Brett temporarily,) were sharing an apartment in the Murray Hill section. That would become the meeting place, the spot where they would all reunite IF they could find one another. IF they were all safe.

It was chaos. A pall hung over the city. The smell of smoke was pervasive for miles and miles.

We waited for the phone to ring. We prepared beds, my husband and I, and we started dinner. We busied ourselves doing anything that would keep our minds clear and our fingers moving. We got calls from Ted's folks, YaYa and TaTa, and from my Mom, sister-in-law, DeDe, and my two sisters, Diane and Renee.

The hours passed. We held hands. And we prayed.

160

Then they all came together, Dani and Brett, Greg and Jaime, Doug, and Brett's three Georgetown friends. We held each other and cried and then we talked until the early morning hours. It was almost impossible to sleep. We watched the news and the photographs, the same horrific images over and over.

That's what we did for the next four or five days. Like most of America, we were numb. We were frightened, but above all else, we were thankful. We were lucky to have survived. We were blessed to be sitting together, sharing this joint nightmare, which could have had a very different ending. Brett had been recruited by Cantor Fitzgerald, right out of college. Following his graduation from Georgetown in 1999, he would have been working on the 104th floor of the World Trade Center Building on September 11th, had his Father not convinced him that he was too much of a "people person" to be chained to a desk, too gregarious and out-going, a "born salesman." So, he took an alternate route. Sadly, Brett lost a few football buddies who did take the path to Cantor Fitzgerald.

There's no need for me to go into any more detail about that day. For some, there was psychological counseling at the workplace. For others, there was church. Some retreated into their own ways of forgetting, while others had to fight their way through the recurring nightmares.

Dani and Greg were to be married on October 20, 2001, a mere one month away. Would they be able to move forward with their plans? We were expecting to host close to 300 people. Would they be willing to celebrate so soon after this terrorist attack? Would people be traveling freely across the country again or would they choose to stay safely at home, far from the uncertainty of New York City, even though the wedding was to take place on Long Island?

We would all be tested in those days leading up to Danielle and Greg's "I Do's."

161

SEPTEMBER 11, 2001

There is a highly researched and cataloged list of September 11th, 2001 attacks books. The bibliography of said books includes out-of-print titles and famous and notable books in both fiction and non-fiction. The list below consists of books that were discussed in either one or several of my book groups, (not necessarily in 2001), or more likely were just obsessively read by me:

1. *The Emperor's Children*, by Claire Messud (Harborfields Library discussion)
2. *Leadership*, by Rudy Giuliani and Ken Kurson (read by me, privately, not discussed) – (See Tip #6- Religion & Politics at the back of the book)
3. *The 9/11 Commission Report* (Ditto above)
4. *Chicken Soup for the Soul America*, by, Jack Canfield (Ditto above)
5. *Bush at War*, by Bob Woodward (See Tip #6 - Religion & Politics)
6. *Extremely Loud and Incredibly Close*, by Jonathan Safran Foer

9/11: A NEW CHAPTER IN OUR READING HABITS
(Source: Taken from *USA Today*, Tues., Dec. 18, 2001, Page 9D)

"Just as Sept. 11 redefined normality in America, so too did the terrorist attacks bring major changes to the *USA Today* Best-Selling Books List."

"I felt the kind of desperation, I think, that cancels the possibility of empathy…that makes you unkind."

~ Sue Miller, While I Was Gone

OCTOBER 2001: While I Was Gone by Sue Miller

We, in "The Literary Gallery," read *While I Was Gone*, by Sue Miller in October 2001. This suspenseful novel illustrates how a marriage can crumble in the blink of an eye and shows us the ways in which we can invent a new life for ourselves. The characters that make up this story are intelligent, likable professionals who somehow lose their direction. I loved Jo Becker's life, her job as a veterinarian, her loving husband, and three grown daughters until it slipped away from her.

The author of The Good Mother, Miller's tale will hook you from the first page and make you want to shake some sense into this very human but flawed woman.

"Life was always a matter of waiting for the right moment to act."

~ *Paul Coehlo*

NOVEMBER 2001: Waiting by Ha Jin

As per Wikipedia, "*Waiting* is a 1999 novel by Chinese-American author Ha Jin which won the National Book Award that year. It is based on a true story that Jin heard from his wife when they were visiting her family at an army hospital in China." Lin Kong is a dedicated doctor caught between his love for two very different women. As he tries, again and again, to get a divorce from the woman his family has chosen for him, the reader, like Lin Kong, is forced to wait and wait and wait. It isn't hard to imagine why the title of this book is so appropriate.

"Old minds are like old horses; you must exercise them if you wish to keep them in working order."

~ John Adams

DECEMBER 2001: John Adams by David McCullough

We concluded the year at Border's Books & Music with a biography of a Founding Father, our second President, John Adams. Written by David McCullough, one of our greatest historians, the book won the 2002 Pulitzer Prize for Biography or Autobiography. It was made into a TV miniseries by HBO and starred Paul Giamatti as John Adams, and Laura Linney as his faithful wife, Abigail.

Our discussion was lively and educational, informational, and apolitical.

So, while Danielle and Greg were basking in the honeymoon sunshine of St. John, Ted and I were traipsing along the cobblestone streets of Nantucket. Their wedding at Flowerfields, in Nesconset, on that 80-degree October day was "almost" Cinderella perfect. (The qualifying "almost" because many family and friends were still reeling from the September 11th attacks and feared flying).

Their union was joyous and bittersweet, as we celebrated and thanked our dear ones who had come so far to share our special day----Mom and Luke, YaYa and TaTa, Diane and Chris, (a high school friend, Chi Sig fraternity brother and soon-to-be Diane's husband,) Renee and Jim, DeDe, Aunt Beverly, Karyn and Jim, and the Perlman cousins, François and Libby Canova, (and their sons, Chris and Frank), Jack Curphey, Bonnie and Walter Naef, Jackie and Scott Freeman, our Aruba friends and so many more.

The hors d'oeuvres and the cocktails were served in abundance, the photo-taking clicked away, the band rocked the house, the food pleased every palate and the Viennese Table, and the Cigar Bar was open until the wee hours. We had buses that shuttled people to and from their hotel. And, because Dani and Greg, Brett, Jack, Thad and I didn't want the party to end, we missed the last shuttle bus leaving the reception and were forced to all squeeze into somebody's compact car, (I don't remember whose). I only remember that Dani's and my "poof" gowns, crinolines and netting, took up the entire back seat. All six of us happy celebrants piled into the Volkswagen-Beetle-sized car, the way fifteen clowns or slapstick Keystone cops disembark from a telephone booth at the circus.

We all stayed at the same hotel and continued the party the next morning, with a complimentary brunch, to which everyone was invited.

Danielle and Gregory (the new Mr. & Mrs. Westfall's) wedding was truly a celebration of life!!

167

Nobody whistles anymore.

Dad, (Big Ed), was a whistler. He would always round up his girls with a special call that I have since come to almost duplicate on my iPhone, (my recent concession to 21st-century technology).

Lauren Bacall famously taunted Humphrey Bogart, (Steve), (her future husband, "Bogie") in the film, 'To Have and Have Not:' "You know how to whistle, don't ya, Steve? You just put your lips together and blow."

Chevy Chase was a whistler, too, in the movie, 'Seems Like Old Times.' He played the Nick Gardenia character opposite Goldie Hawn's, Glenda Parks. In the final scene, Nick is portrayed proudly walking away, whistling, "The High and the Mighty."

And who can possibly forget Earle Hagen whistling 'The Fishin' Hole,' the theme from 'The Andy Griffith Show'?

Big Ed's whistling on our wedding day helped me navigate that very long and narrow red carpet walk down the aisle of Our Lady of Mercy, R.C. Church in Hicksville, (L.I.) on that cold and snowy Saturday, February 26, 1972.

Diane, Renee, and I had it all worked out from the time we were teens with slam books playing around with our imagined future lives. ("Who do you want to marry? Name five people. Where do you want to live? Name five places. How many children do you want to have?") We naively assumed that Diane would marry first since she was the oldest. She did, as a matter of fact, marry first and I was her maid- of- honor. Renee was to be my maid- of- honor, and Diane would be Renee's. But, the best-laid plans can, and often do, run astray. Renee married the best looking guy in her high school class, the quarterback who lived next door, a few

*years later and Diane was nine months pregnant with Kirsten, so I
served as maid-of-honor in her stead. That meant that I was
maid-of-honor to both my sisters. How and who would I choose to
play this special role in my wedding? The answer was: I couldn't,
and I didn't choose. I asked my two beloved siblings to be my joint
matrons-of-honor.*

*My Mom and Dad had both remarried in 1969, Dad to Sharon
and Mom to Luke. I was living with Dad and Sharon and my
Grandmother, (Grams) on Long Island. Mom, Luke and my baby
brother, Cubby, now eight years old and set to be our ring bearer,
were up in Niagara Falls and Diane and Renee were neighbors
living in Glens Falls, NY.*

*Planning became a bit complicated. How would we word our
invitations? Where would my Mother and Luke sit? Would there
be any tension between the families and guests? We settled on a
simple invitation with italic font and the following wording:*

Mr. & Mrs. Edward Perlman

Request the honour of your presence

At the marriage of his daughter

Donna Jean

to

Mr. Theodore Arthur Diamond

Son of

Mr. & Mrs. Dimon Diamond

On Saturday, the twenty-sixth of February

Nineteen hundred and seventy-two

At twelve o'clock in the afternoon

169

Our Lady of Mercy R.C. Church

Hicksville, New York

I decided that my bridal party would wear a beautiful mix of colors---- navy, lavender, and hot pink, to brighten up the dull February sky. Diane wore a lavender empire waist gown which highlighted her "smokey" brown eyes and frosted hair. Blue-eyed, blonde-haired, Renee, my look-alike, mirrored Diane but in a deep shade of hot pink. And my four bridesmaids donned the identical gown in a dark shade of navy blue. Three-year-old flower girl, Kirsten, wore a long purple velvet dress with a coordinating cap.

Rather than a traditional headpiece, I chose a multi-colored fabric in hues of hot pink, navy, and lavender, which Grams made into flowing scarves to be worn in the girls' hair. Their floral bouquets, fashioned in matching hues, completed their red carpet look, (or so I thought). Blonde-haired blue-eyed, dark-haired blue-eyed, blondes with deep chocolate brown eyes and dark-haired, brown-eyed beauties, made up our wedding party.

*Is this too much unnecessary detail for you, dear reader? My sisters said that this is totally annoying sartorial chatter. I, however, love reading about all of the fine talks regarding the color of curtains, the thickness of hair, and exotic names of nail polishes, ("life's a bowl of cherries RED"). Perhaps, this deep appreciation for minutiae carried over to my 'Ultimate Hard-core, High-handed, Card-carrying Bibliophilist' behavior with regard to the treatment and return of MY BOOKS!

Thad's brother, Billy, was his Best Man. His brother-in-law, "What's his name?", François Canova and two other Chi Sig fraternity brothers rounded out the groom's posse. (Jack Curphey sent a congratulatory telegram from California, which was delivered to us during our reception).

170

Billy was on crutches from a football injury he had sustained in high school, but that didn't hold him back from making the funniest, most memorable toast at the Four Seasons Country Club, where our reception was held. He was seven and ½ years younger than Ted, and had always been around on those days and nights that I spent with the family, either on their boat, the 'Mister D,' or at their home on Aspinwall Street--- those delicious nights when I would awaken to the aroma of Ted's Dad, (he called him, Pop,) making French Toast using a secret family recipe. He would only divulge the ingredients after you'd sworn eternal allegiance to the cooking of Greek food, your love of dolmades, souvlaki, feta cheese, and moussaka and signed your name in the drippings of saganaki. OPA!

Billy was smart and talented. He played a very royal King Arthur in 'Camelot,' Carle Place High School's Senior Class Musical. Billy could do the greatest impersonations, constantly fooling and confounding my children, Dani and Brett, in later years, as my husband's future business travels with my Dad, Big Ed took him to Egypt, Jordan, and Japan. But, for our wedding toast, Billy stuck to the basic younger brother raunchy jibes.

Our families were dressed elegantly. Typically, a Saturday evening reception on Long Island (and New York City) suggested formal attire. My Mother looked stunning, her hair swept up, in a rose-colored velvet gown with a matching coat. My Father's wife wore a striking navy-blue chiffon with white beaded details on the collar and cuffs and Dorothy, who I would soon call, "Mom," (belle-mère) was fabulous in a floral swirl of oranges, blues, and pinks. The men, naturally, were in tuxedos.

And now let's talk about the bride, c'est-à-dire, MOI, and what I wore as Big Ed marched me down the aisle. Oh, and did I mention that my Dad looked exactly like the late actor, Phil Silvers? When we were in high school, our friends used to call him "Sergeant Bilko," (Master Sergeant Ernest G. Bilko,) for the role Silvers

171

played in the television sitcom called, "The Phil Silvers Show," which aired on CBS from 1954-1959. Like Sergeant Bilko, Dad was a jokester, filled with a "joie de vivre" like no one else I have ever met. He would often say, "A smile and a few kind words go a long, long way." I tried to make that my mantra in dealing with people. I knew the lesson was learned when my daughter brought me home a plaque she'd found at a craft fair on the North Fork (of L.I.) which reads:

A SMILE IS SOMETHING THAT IS STILL FREE!

My wedding gown was a long-sleeved, high collared, silk jersey knit fabric with beaded V-neck, cuffs and bodice, which fell gracefully into a soft train. My matching jeweled headpiece, which framed my face, was, for me, the show stopper, the pièce de résistance. I felt like Elizabeth Taylor must have felt playing Cleopatra as she was borne into her palace. (Well, at least my head felt regal).

I wore a made-to-order brocade cape to and from the church and reception and wanted to carry a white fur muff like Sonja Henie used to warm her hands in one of her ice skating movies.

But I didn't.

Like most brides, I was jittery, teary, and nervous on our big day. I didn't want any mascara tears running down my face to shock Thaddeus, as my veil was lifted at the altar. So, I chuckled instead when Dad squeezed my hand and whispered, "Don't worry, Muscles, no one is looking at you. Everyone came here today to see me."

***

"Do you take this man to be your lawfully wedded husband?" And when no one stood up to make any objections, our vows were exchanged, and Billy presented our rings to Father Christensen. Being very much into my "I love everything French," phase, and

172

working for the French Company, Michelin Tire, I wanted the inscription on our rings to express my love. On my husband's gold wedding band, I had engraved:

"Je t'aime, plus qu'hier, moins que demain. A nous deux pour toujours.»

(I love you, more than yesterday, less than tomorrow. To us, always)

I wish I had the storytelling skills and sense of humor of the very gifted author, Adriana Trigiani. If I did, I would describe our wedding reception the way she wrote the laugh-out-loud Roncalli Family Wedding scene at Leonard's, (of Great Neck,) in the first book of her Valentine Trilogy, Very Valentine. I would have painted a portrait of Thad's dour Greek matriarch, Aunt Sophie, the way the curmudgeonly Aunt Feen was depicted in Brava Valentine and The Supreme Macaroni Company. After all, I did have the right ingredients to create my own "Big Fat Greek Wedding."

My father-in-law danced the "men only" sailor dance with Uncle George, Nick Stavrides, Ari Amandapoulos, Stephan Volanopoulos, Gregory Callas, and a few of the others. We, the new Mr. & Mrs. Theodore Diamond, danced to our wedding song, "If Ever I Would Leave You," from Lerner & Lowe's CAMELOT.

The catering hall asked if there was going to be any plate throwing, (which there wasn't, but it certainly would have been great fun).

« A nous deux pour toujours »   To our « Big Fat Greek Wedding! »

Our life together as Mr. & Mrs. Theodore Diamond began on Saturday, February 26, 1972, after a courtship of more than five years. My new "Mom and Dad" held a brunch in our honor the *next morning, before we embarked on a fourteen-day Caribbean cruise aboard the 'SS Amerikanis' (Greek Registry).*

Upon our return, we set up house at 99 Foxhollow Road, Woodbury, the Fairhaven Garden Apartments, which would be our home for the next three years. We bought a bedroom set and cushy shag carpeting in pale blue and paired it with a chocolate brown colored couch. We had a TV in the living room where we watched 'Happy Days' and the 'Evening News with Huntley and Brinkley.'

I was commuting to Lake Success and saying "Bonjour" to my boss, "le chef du département technique" à Michelin Tire Corporation. Ted was working in the Accounting Dept. of Harvey Radio. On weekends we'd play cards, charades or work up a sweat playing ATARI with Libby and Frank and our other friends or drive out East to look at houses. We were "water people" and needed to get our daily dose of what living on Long Island so beautifully provides......saltwater beaches in every direction. We'd take excursions to the North Fork and look at homes in the Northport/Centerport area.

And every year for three years, on our anniversary, Ted would take a picture of me in my wedding gown (I needed to make sure it still fit).

The first year, (1973), the Polaroid picture was of a smiling "moi" holding a beautiful bouquet of flowers.

The following year, I shared the lens with Sham ("La Chamade"), our pure white German Shepherd puppy. Everyone thought Sham was brilliant, since I taught him all of his commands in French, and he readily responded to:

PARLEZ! – Speak!

ASSEYEZ-VOUS – Sit!

Since he was a German Shepherd, I probably should have taught him to respond to SPRECHEN UND SITZEN, but my French romance language was far more pleasant to hear.

and

On February 26, 1975, I was tightly squeezed into (and bursting the zipper) on my bridal gown. I was beaming as I cradled our one-month-old baby girl, our Aquarius, Danielle. Sham and my floral arrangement were relegated to a distant second place, lying on the floor by my side.

NOTE: (Sadly, I would put my wedding gown in the drop-down attic of our apartment and forget to retrieve it when we moved into our home at 23 Carrol Place, Greenlawn. I did call the management at Fairhaven Gardens many years later asking if they would check the kitchen attic at 99 Foxhollow. They politely informed me that the apartment attic had been permanently sealed off, no longer used for storage. Alas, it was "Bonjour Tristesse" pour moi!

Life was good, and we were happy.

Ted joined my Dad in the export machine tool business in 1975, and so began the traveling that would become a mainstay of our marriage. Their overseas' trips together would take them to Iran, Jordan, Egypt and throughout the Middle East.

How different the world, and flying in general, was back in the 1970s. Pan Am, TWA, Braniff, Northwest, Continental, United, Eastern, Delta, National, and Southwest vied for pre-merger ticket sales. It was at this time when the OPEC (Organization of Petroleum Exporting Countries) oil embargo that began in October 1973 and lasted until March of 1974, would impact the lives of every American. Long lines at the gas stations and increased pricing forced us all to allot extra time at the pumps and forego our lunch hour breaks.

I have a postcard of the SHAHYAD Monument, Tehran, dated January 24, 1976, which reads:

"Hi,

Long trip to get here – but worth it so far – Beautiful scenery – Quite a large city

Love, Dad "

And another from the Royal Tehran Hilton, ("Chez Maurice," le restaurant le plus sélect de Téhran, fondé en 1975, le plus Parisien des Restaurants Français de la Ville), touting the restaurant as being the most Parisian of Tehran's French restaurants.

I have a postcard from Iraq stating how interesting the land of Ali Baba (No, not THAT Alibaba, the Chinese retail search engine) was, but the weather was lousy. Still another carte postale from Dad shows a color view of the Sphinx and the Pyramid of Giza with a man riding a camel. It reminded him of me my senior year of high school when I traveled with Big Ed to Cairo and Athens. (Perhaps, in that case, Diane and Renee were justified in saying that "I got everything").

Traveling in the 1970s was an exciting experience, an adventure that warranted dressing up for the occasion. In-flight food was edible, and airport restaurants offered fine dining. Movies were shown on long-distance flights, and I always made sure to pack plenty of books for Ted to take with him. While I was reading, Once Is Not Enough, by Jacqueline Susann and Looking for Mr.

176

Goodbar, by Judith Rossner, he would peruse business journals or books like, The Billion Dollar Sure Thing, by Paul E. Erdman or The Seven-Per-Cent Solution, by Nicholas Meyer.

My sister-in-law, DeDe, and I got pregnant at the very same time. We chose to share our exciting news with her parents one night over dinner. The four of us, (DeDe and "what's-his-name?" and Ted and I) had only recently shared a bottle of home-made wine, the grapes lovingly trampled by Mrs. Soupa next door. Could our pregnancies have been the joyful after-effects of Mrs. Soupa's potion? What a chuckle we had over that.

During the summer of 1974, we rented a house on the bay in Southampton. Ted and I and Sham, (before his broken leg,) joined DeDe, "what's—his-name?" and their young son, Gregory, for a few weeks. We swam all day and watched the news at night. And our reading material was always within arm's reach. I re-read Le Petit Prince, par Antoine de Saint-Exupéry, and L'Etranger par Albert Camus. J'ai lu des poèmes de Baudelaire, Verlaine, Rimbaud et Valéry. (OK, so it wasn't exactly light summer reading!)

We saw a dejected and defeated President Nixon give a sad, parting wave of resignation to all Americans (and the world,) as he reluctantly boarded Air Force One for the last time. We were glued to the TV, waiting for news on the abduction of Patty Hearst, (Tania) by the Symbionese Liberation Army (SLA). Was she a victim, or did she willingly join her captors in their demands? "Stockholm Syndrome" became the new catchphrase.

***

I had a beautiful pregnancy with Danielle, and her 6 lb. 10 oz. bodyweight made for a relatively easy delivery. (My Theo being in the Labor Room as my La Maze coach, however, was far from ideal. I distinctly remember screaming at him, "TAKE BACK YOUR

SPERM!!!!" every few minutes I was told to "BREATHE!"). I'm grateful he didn't pay me much heed.

Sheer delight she was our babbling daughter, Danielle Lizabeth Diamond. I chose her middle name for my Grandmother, Grams, who was Elizabeth, but I didn't want my little girl to have the dreadful initials, DED (superstitious, I suppose,) so I changed it to Lizabeth instead (DLD). (In 2005 I would fall in love with another Lisbeth (with no A and an S in the name Stieg Larsson gave to the heroine of his Millennium series, Lisbeth Salander,) aka The Girl with the Dragon Tattoo.

She was funny and loquacious, my Dani, with big blue eyes and dark hair and, much to my inexperienced maternal horror, Dani started to walk at nine months old, leading her older cousins, Kirsten and Ali, to give her the nickname, "Dancing Dani Doodle."

She was wishing the family a "Merry Missmas" at eleven months old while her cousin, Doug, (DeDe & "what's-his-name's?" youngest son), just three days her junior, laughed alongside her and tore open his gifts. And at age two, Dani was singing "Feelings" ("Whoa, whoa, whoa feelings") with great gusto.

***

A little more than two years later, our Dukie Boy was born. Like his Dad, he was bonny and blithe and good and gay, born on the Sabbath day. (Danielle and I were Friday's children, loving and giving). The nurses at Syosset Hospital loved his dimpled smile and hairy pate. According to the old wives' tales, if a child is born with a lot of hair, the mother was asked if she had heartburn or acid reflux. I had neither, blessed again with an easy nine-month gestation period and quick finish- up- our- Saturday- evening-game- of- Hearts, to head back to Syosset for my 5:12PM delivery on April 3rd, 1977.

178

My Brett weighed in at a hefty 6 lbs. 11 oz., just one ounce more than his sister. When I was pregnant with Danielle, I was smoking a little less than a pack of cigarettes a day, (LARK charcoal filters, if you please, L&Ms for Ted). Once we became aware of the dangers to the fetus of inhaling tobacco, I quickly gave up the habit. Another thing I gave up when Brett was born was to have his father in the delivery room shouting vicious commands like "PUSH!" and "EASY BREATHS!". He almost passed out the first time. I wasn't taking any chances with our second born.

With Brett, we now had a household of three Aries, (Ted on April 6th and me on April 12th) and one Aquarius, Dani, on January 31st).

Dani loved her little brother and before long had him taking tea and collecting Cabbage Patch Kids, (Cedric), with all the other little girls on the block, (any boys living on Carroll Place at that time were at least six years older than Brett). This female-dominated situation would be recaptured thirty-four years later with my lone grandson, also a Brett, ("Puma") being surrounded by his twin sister, Brielle, and three Westfall cousins, Lily, Lauren, and Alice. Both Bretts would become the charming prince or the swashbuckling pirate in their fantasy games; however, out of self-defense or sheer "boyness," my little Brett exhibited his sports acumen early on. He could always charm us with his engaging smile and physical coordination. He had no problem keeping up with the big boys on the ball field. And, as Dani gathered "Hello Kitty," "Strawberry Shortcake" and "Smurf" stickers and figures, our Dukie boy ("Puke," "Cool Rider Shakespeare" to his cousins,) collected baseball cards, Star Wars, and WWF Action Figures.

It was about this time that I first started to write short poems and children's stories. As I recall, my titles were, "Wishing Well," "When I Grow Up," and "Sticks and Stones." I personified a dandelion and gave him the name "Dandy." In my mind's eye, Dandy resembled the curly-haired lad from Asteroid B612, "Le

179

Petit Prince" of Antoine de Saint-Exupéry. Dandy would often wear a top hat and carry the ubiquitous dandy's walking stick. My college pal, Bonnie Naef, now herself the mother of two girls, would do the thumbprint drawings and illustrations for our book.

Our collaboration continued for just a short time. We received rejection letters from five or six publishers, and so our short-lived careers as author/illustrator disappeared, as our lives moved on to raising our kids and immersing ourselves in their daily activities.

I would continue to read books by Leon Uris, (Trinity), Peter Benchley, (The Deep), Sidney Sheldon, (A Stranger in the Mirror), and my most favorite, which I read on the beach of Avalon, New Jersey, War, and Remembrance, by Herman Wouk.

Chapter 6

"Il n'y a pas de roses sans épines." ~ Every Rose Has Its Thorns, But Chocolate Cream Pie In The Face Can Make It Better (2002)

I had collapsed in the shower shortly after Brett was born. I was dizzy and disoriented with pins and needles and tingling on the right side of my face and leg, and my eyes were blurry double vision.

The spinal tap taken late at night at Glen Cove Hospital showed definitively that I had Multiple Sclerosis (MS). It was 1977, long before the advent of MRIs, (Magnetic Resonance Imaging) could detect the lesions on my brain and spinal cord.

Ted, my parents, and my sisters were devastated when they heard the news. Renee offered a little levity when she sobbed, "I'm so sorry that you have Muscular Dystrophy." I laughed through my tears and said, "Please get my illness straight." I have Multiple Sclerosis (MS) NOT Muscular Dystrophy (MD). I guess that wasn't much of a consolation. I was now thirty-one years old. MS "the crippler of young adults" had hit me in my prime.

The Doctor, (now I had a fancy doctor, a "neurologist,") said I probably should NOT have any more children because of the stress and trauma to the body. I was so blessed to have two beautiful, healthy children, my beloved Danielle (then age two) and my newborn son, Brett. I had always dreamed that I would have four children, like both my sisters, so naturally, I resented being told that having any more children was no longer an option. Diane tried to cheer me up by saying, "You have two adorable, healthy kids, a daughter, and a son, and you have just two hands for them to hold. You're very lucky." Yes, "Lucky Me." When my sisters used to say that I get everything, I don't think even they expected me to get this. Of the three of us sisters, all born just one year apart, what

181

germ or virus found its way into my system and not into theirs? I wasn't feeling sorry for myself, (well, maybe just a little). I just wanted to know WHY?

Back in the '70s, so many theories circulated regarding the cause of MS:

1. *Was I a twin? – YES. My twin brother died when my mother fell down the stairs and had a miscarriage early on in her pregnancy. The Doctors did a D&C procedure, but still, my mother's stomach grew bigger. They thought she had a tumor. Nine months later, I was born. My mother never knew she was carrying twins. To this day, I often kid her when I say, "I'm not a tumor!" as Arnold Schwartzenegger proclaimed in one of his movies – Kindergarten Cop? (IT'S NOT A TUMOR!!) Note: The aforementioned must be said imitating Schwartzenegger's Austrian accent for effect.*

   > *My Mother's Father had been a twin, himself. He was dark-haired while his twin brother had light-colored hair. They were called "Blackie" and "Whitey."*

   > *So, I definitely fell into the first category, (being a twin), with regard to my diagnosis of Multiple Sclerosis.*

2. *The next theory was based on having a rabid dog at some point in our family. The answer to that question was, once again, a resounding YES! We had many dogs growing up, two German Shepherds, one named Major and the other Brandy, a French Poodle named Jacques Henri, a black Collie named Chad Hannah and a Fox Terrier that we called Linky, (the formal name that was registered to*

182

establish his pedigree was "The Missing Link"). It was Linky who sadly contracted rabies at the kennel. We ultimately had to have him put to sleep; thus, I was a viable candidate for the second theory as well.

3. *Studies showed that more women than men got Multiple Sclerosis. (I carry two X chromosomes). The predominance of the disease was found to be in people living in the Northeastern section of the U.S. (Long Island and New York are considered to be in the Northeast) and affected people with a higher educational level.*

None of these studies made me feel any better. Doctors said that MS was "familial," but our family history showed no record of it affecting anyone prior to my diagnosis. My main concern was for our children. Would they inherit this insidious disease? Was there anything I could do to protect them? How long would I be sick? How would it impact my marriage and my childrearing?

I was terrified.

> *"Lucky from the outside was an illusion."*
>
> *~Anna Quindlen, Still Life with Breadcrumbs, pg. 89*

"The man who has experienced shipwreck
shudders even at a calm sea."

~ *Ovid, Poet*

JANUARY 2002: In the Heart of the Sea: The Tragedy of the Whaleship Essex by Nathaniel Philbrick

I selected our January 2002 title, In the *Heart of the Sea*, by Nathaniel Philbrick, after reading a fascinating review of this National Book Award Winner. The story of the Essex, if it was remembered, was thought to be the story that inspired the climax of *Moby Dick*.

I knew that the author was a leading authority on the history of Nantucket and that he lived on the island from which the Essex whalemen set sail. I sent him an email inviting him to join our two book discussion groups, (at Border's Books & Music and at Harborfields Library). He sent his regrets in a return email dated Thursday, January 10, 2002. He wrote, "I'm currently chained to my desk working on my next book, so will be unable to venture off the island"; however, he did attach a brief biography which I read to the group:

> "Nathaniel Philbrick, 45, is Director of the Egan Institute of Maritime Studies on Nantucket Island and is a Research Fellow in History at the Nantucket Historical Association. He has degrees from Brown and Duke Universities and is the author of *Away Off Shore: Nantucket Island and Its People* (1994) and Abram's Eyes: The Native American Legacy of Nantucket Island (1998). In the Heart of the Sea: The Tragedy of the Whaleship Essex, won the National Book Award for non-fiction in 2000. In

184

addition to being named one of the year's best books by *Time*, *Entertainment Weekly* and *The Boston Globe*, as well as a notable book by the *New York Times*, In the *Heart of the Sea* received the Alex Award from the Young Adult Library Services Association, the Ambassador Book Award from the English-speaking Union of the United States, the Premio Mazzotti Award, and was a finalist for the *Los Angeles Times* Book Award and the Massachusetts Book Award. A *New York Times* bestseller for five months in hardcover and five months and counting in paperback, In the *Heart of the Sea*, has been translated into fifteen languages and was a number one bestseller in England and Ireland. The book was optioned by Intermedia/Baltimore Spring Creek, producers of *The Perfect Storm* and in September 2001 a two-hour documentary titled 'Revenge of the Whale, narrated by Liam Neeson and featuring Philbrick's commentary appeared on NBC.

The bio goes on to discuss the author's credentials as a former inter-collegiate All-American sailor and North American Sunfish Champion, some of his writings and other awards.

I was so excited when I first read, *In the Heart of the Sea*, that immediately following our daughter's wedding on October 20, 2001, I asked Ted to take me to Nantucket so that I could experience, (if not firsthand, then at least as close as possible,) what the crew of the Essex felt almost two hundred years ago. As we took the high-speed ferry from Hyannis to Nantucket, I felt as if we were brought back in time to another era, to another place where Captain George Pollard, Owen Chase, and Thomas Nickerson once walked. We went to the whaling museum, where an entire room is devoted to

185

the Essex. I took pictures of the route that the Essex took in 1819-20, the names of crew members and "the attack," most of which are included in the book. We took a walking tour and saw Captain Pollard's and Thomas Nickerson's homes.

I think I enjoyed the book as much as I did because it was rich in history. Not only did the author bring the characters to life for me, but I learned a great deal about the influence of the Quakers on the whaling industry, about sperm whales and the science of starvation and the nutritional value of cannibalism. I know now why Herman Melville was inspired to write, *Moby Dick*, based on the hardships endured by the crew of the Essex.

> ➤ Note: The feature film, based on Nathaniel Philbrick's 2000 National Book Award-winning, *In the Heart of the Sea: The Tragedy of the Whaleship Essex* and directed by Ron Howard, premiered in March 2015.

"To learn to read is to light a fire; every syllable that is spelled out is a spark."

~ *Victor Hugo*

FEBRUARY 2002: The Bee Season by Myla Goldberg

We read *The Bee Season*, by Myla Goldberg in February 2002. This debut novel describes what happens to an ordinary American family when their eleven-year-old, (Eliza,) surprises and defies everyone's expectations by becoming a champion speller. The book appealed to me because of my fascination with words and languages and their correct spelling.

The Scripps Howard National Spelling Bee, that lovely tradition that takes place annually, has managed to keep pace with an ever-changing vocabulary of new words. In 2002, for example, students aged eight to fifteen years were asked to spell such words as "Anschluss," (the annexation of Austria by Germany in 1938), "escabeche" (a Spanish dish consisting of fried fish that is marinated and served cold), and "pickelhaube" (from the German, a spiked helmet worn by military, firefighters, and police in the 19th and 20th centuries, "headgear." Only 90 of the 175 students who took the written test following the first round got 16 of the 25 words correct. They were asked to check the appropriate box indicating whether the word was spelled correctly or incorrectly, for example: (28)

	Correct	Incorrect
1. sample		
2. Ebenezer		
3. dyskinesia		

4. Decoupage

My husband of forty-three years, never the speller, still
grapples with the word "cabinet." In his (spelling) Bee
Season the letters would be arranged like this, "c – a – b – i –
n – a – t – e" and pronounced "cabin ate."

It's too bad I wasn't eligible to enter the Scripps National
Spelling Bee Championship in 2014. There might have been
a three-way tie between me, the French major, who would
have known and used the word "feuilleton," ("a part of a
European newspaper or magazine devoted to material
designed to entertain the general reader"), Ansun Sujoe and
Sriram Hathwar.

"Either write something worth reading or do something worth writing."

~ *Benjamin Franklin*

MARCH 2002: The Amazing Adventures of Kavalier and Clay by Michael Chabon

What a fun romp through the world of comic books and superheroes we experienced, when we read this 2001 Pulitzer Prize winner by Michael Chabon. Epic in length and scope, Chabon takes the reader from New York City in 1939 to Europe, as Hitler is poised to strike. We meet cousins, Joe Kavalier, and Sammy Clay, who hope to create heroes and villains and stories for the new comic book craze.

The book was well received by the men and women of 'The Literary Gallery;' however, my visiting relatives, Diane and Kirsten, found fault with the "convoluted story" and "plethora of characters," (their words, not mine!) Book Groups reading today, (March 2015), would do well to give this book another look based on the box-office domination of comic book films, (Thor, Hulk, Captain America, and The Avengers). And, OH, the appeal of Comic-Con on a grand scale!

*"It is one of the blessings of old friends that you
can afford to be stupid with them."*

~ Ralph Waldo Emerson

APRIL 2002: Hateship, Friendship, Loveship, Courtship, Marriage by Alice Munro

When I read an article in the British newspaper, *The Guardian*, in which Canadian short story writer, Alice Munro, announced that there wasn't going to be another book following the release of her 2001 collection, *Hateship, Friendship, Loveship, Courtship, Marriage*, I suggested that we switch genres for a change and try our hand at reading short stories. (29)

Although my April 2002 title bombed, I am happy to note that the author continued to write. In 2013, Alice Munro won the Nobel Prize for her story collection, *Dear Life*.

"Kindness is a language which the deaf can hear,
and the blind can see."

~ *Mark Twain*

MAY 2002: The Heart is a Lonely Hunter by Carson McCullers

I should think I would have learned my lesson (as cited in my Tip #3) about choosing and staying in a particular genre after the debacle of my previous choice of title in April, 2002, *Hateship, Friendship, Loveship, Courtship, Marriage* by, Alice Munro, but apparently, for what I considered to be very good reasons, I selected a "modern classic" in May, *The Heart is a Lonely Hunter*, by Carson McCullers. There was a resurgence of interest in the author with the opening, (albeit short-lived), of a new off-Broadway play, "Carson McCullers— Historically Inaccurate," playing at the Women's Project Theatre on West 55th Street.

McCullers was twenty-three when her first novel was published in 1940. A Southern writer, Georgia born, critics were immediately taken by her tale of five lonely, isolated people searching for expression and spirituality. The main character, John Singer, is a deaf-mute.

There was much to discuss about this book and, despite the switch in the genre, in this case, *The Heart is a Lonely Hunter*, was a tremendous hit with the group. I was able to secure a copy of the movie, (a real tear-jerker), starring Alan Arkin as John Singer, the deaf-mute protagonist. We, obviously, weren't able to view the movie at Border's Books and Music, but I invited everyone to join us at Harborfields Library the following month when I would be discussing the book with my 'Morning Book Discussion Group.'

Oprah Winfrey would make *The Heart is a Lonely Hunter* her new book club selection in April 2004.

"She is too fond of books, and it has addled her brain."

~ Louisa May Alcott

JUNE 2002: Plain Truth by Jodi Picoult

Prolific author, Jodi Picoult, was chosen for a second time following our selection of Salem Falls in August 2001. When we read Plain Truth, the compelling story of the death of an infant among the Amish, our discussion was neither politically charged nor religiously centered. 'The Literary Gallery' was made up of both men and women, Democrats, Republicans, Liberals, Catholics, Jews, Protestants, and Jehovah's Witnesses.

We talked at great length about the culture of the Pennsylvania Dutch Amish and about what a mother would do to save her child. Our meeting was most informative and enlightening.

I don't know exactly when I gave up the hurt, the anger, and the bitterness I felt toward my Mother, probably sometime after I became a parent myself, but I did "Let It Go!" just as Elsa, the Ice Queen in "Frozen," had to do. And just as Elsa had her sister, Anna, I, too, had the help and the love of my sisters. I found that it took too much energy to be angry. I learned to channel my thoughts and concentrate on making myself the best mother, the image of what I thought a mother should be.

When Dani and Brett were born, my in-laws became YaYa (YiaYia, Grandma in Greek), and TaTa, Big Ed became Papa Ed and my Mom, Delores, became Grandma Dee.

We had a big Perlman Cousins' Picnic at the park in Bolton Landing in August of 1977. Everyone was there, poised, and ready to perform. Diane did her giggling headstands, Mom rocked the hula hoop, and a towel-draped Karyn acted out her famous Bert Lahr routine as the cowardly lion from the Wizard of Oz.....\"If I were King of the Forest...not Duke, not Earl, not Prrrrince." Dani, two and ½ years old, sang "It's a Small World," with Kirsten and Ali and my ever hilarious Saturday Night Live (SNL)-imitating nephew, Craig, made faces at the camera while Ted took motion pictures of our antics with his cumbersome, oversized video camera that sat on his shoulder.

I was minding my own business, tending to my four-month-old little boy, when Mom, egged on by the others, threw a perfectly delicious chocolate cream pie in my face. Yes, it's all on film, preserved for the ages, my shock, then pure delight, as I licked the cream from my lips. How can you top that? We tried by taking on the von Trapp Family singers in our own rendition of, "So long, Farewell," (auf wiederschen, adieu, adieu, adieu, to yuh and yuh and yuh!).

And that's all I have to say about that!

194

*"Tenderness and kindness are not signs of
weakness and despair, but manifestations of
strength and resolution."*

~ *Kahlil Gibran*

JULY 2002: Women of the Silk by Gail Tsukiyama

Twenty people attended our book club in July 2002. Our
original, long-standing members, Ellen Davis, Elvira
Lubrano, Connie Sabatino, and Rita Silver were there and my
sister, Diane, was visiting from Florida.

Women of the Silk, by Gail Tsukiyama, was the second book we
would read by this author, (we read *The Samurai's Garden* in
December 2000), who has said that she writes "to explore her
dual heritage." (30) Tsukiyama was born in San Francisco to
a Chinese mother and an Americanized Japanese father from
Hawaii.

The story of Pei, as told in Women of the Silk, takes place in
rural China in the early 1900s and spans several decades. At
the age of eight, Pei was given to the silk factory by her
father, a peasant farmer in South China. There Pei and the
other women would forge a sisterhood amidst the noise of
the machines and the exhaustion of the long fourteen-hour
days. In a time when women didn't have much, the "women
of the silk" could achieve freedoms, like going to the opera,
sending money home to their families and meeting other
women throughout China. They would unite because of their
ambition and dreams and lead the first strike the village had
ever seen.

I created 'Questions for Discussion' based not only on the
story but on my own recollections of having visited China in
the late 20th and early 21st centuries. Ted had called it

"Donna's Big Adventure" when he first took me to Taiwan and Mainland China in 1992. My travel experiences and those of several of the members enhanced our discussion of *Women of the Silk.*

AUGUST 2002

"The Literary Gallery" did not meet in August of 2002. Ted and I, Dani, Greg, and Brett were in San Diego, CA at the wedding of Frank & Libby Canova's son, Christopher, a grand event.

SEPTEMBER 2002: Nine Parts of Desire: The Hidden World of Islamic Women by Geraldine Brooks

Exactly one year after the horrific attacks on our country on September 11, 2001, we gathered together to discuss then prize-winning foreign correspondent for the Wall Street Journal, Geraldine Brooks's work, Nine Parts of Desire: The Hidden World of Islamic Women, and to pay tribute to our country and to the men and women who heroically sacrificed or lost their lives one year ago. We wanted to make a donation to a charitable organization, to the FDNY or NYPD. We agreed that we would send our contributions to the FDNY. Several of the members had a father, a brother, an uncle, or a son in the fire department, and I had a personal interest, myself. My grandfather, Nathan Perlman, was Fire Chief of New York City back in the 1950s. I was proud to donate in his name.

In 2012 my son-in-law, Greg, joined the Plandome Volunteer Fire Department, much to the delight of us all, especially his four girls, Dani, Lily, Lauren and Alice during the Christmas season. (Love those candy canes the elves threw from the fire truck).

Prior to delving into the book, we talked about other books that we have read in the last six years that illustrate how life can be changed in the blink of an eye.

Several examples of this are:

> ➢ *The Deep End of the Ocean*, by Jacquelyn Mitchard
> ➢ *The Pilot's Wife*, by Anita Shreve
> ➢ *Midwives*, by Chris Bohjalian
> ➢ *While I Was Gone*, by Sue Miller

Geraldine Brooks spent six years covering wars, insurrections, and upheaval in the Middle East. When she first arrived, she felt cut-off from much of Muslim society as a female correspondent. She turned that liability into an advantage when she donned the "hijab," (the black veil worn by most Muslim women in the Middle East), and thereby enabled herself to penetrate the cloistered world of Muslim women.

The title, *Nine Parts of Desire*, comes from an interpretation of the Koran offered by the Shiite branch, "Almighty God created sexual desires in ten parts; then he gave nine parts to women and one to man." As Laura Shapiro, writing for *Newsweek* commented, "Good enough reason to keep women under wraps."

More than twenty-five people attended our discussion. We had become very relaxed, talking about books that were "out of our comfort zone" from both a religious and political perspective. (Refer to my Tip #6 - Religion & Politics).

That's another reason why we were all caught off guard by the random men and women who raucously "invaded" our discussion of Dan Brown's, *The Da Vinci Code*, the next year.

"He who rides the sea of the Nile must have sails woven of patience."

~ William Golding

OCTOBER 2002: The True Sources of the Nile by Sarah Stone

Border's Books & Music gave "The Literary Gallery" rave reviews in their October 2002 Newsletter when they wrote:

Monday, October 14, at 11am

DONNA DIAMOND'S LITERARY GALLERY

Book Discussion Group

The Literary Gallery is a long-standing discussion group at Border's Commack since 1996. The group consists of mothers and daughters, men and women, from varying backgrounds, ages, and interests all coming together once a month to share a love of reading (and talking!). Literary tastes of the group run the gamut from Pulitzer Prize winners to NY Times bestsellers, tales of dysfunctional families to home-on-the-range cowboy yarns, and they have a good time dissecting the books and offering up their different opinions. This month's selection is The True Sources of the Nile, by Sarah Stone. Join Donna Diamond this morning for this lively and topical discussion.

The True Sources of the Nile, by Sarah Stone, is a story of passion, of love and betrayal between Annie, an American working for peace and democracy in Central Africa, and Jean-Pierre, a Paris educated, high ranking member of the Tutsi ruling class. The book received mixed reviews from the group. Thereafter, I decided that it would be a good idea to give each book that we read a rating.

Based on a scale of 1-5 (with #5 being the best!) have each member grade the book that you are currently reading based on the following criteria:

1. Author's style of writing
2. Plot/storyline
3. Characters
   a. Were they likable? (Does that matter?)
   b. Could you relate to them?
   c. Did you care what happened to them?
4. Would you recommend this book to someone else?

Bookmarks Magazine gives the following Star * Ratings:

***** CLASSIC: A timeless book to be read by all

**** EXCELLENT: One of the best of its genre

*** GOOD: Enjoyable, particularly for fans of the genre

** FAIR: Some problems, approach with caution

*POOR: Not worth your time

It became a tradition for Ted and me to host our annual Thanksgiving feast. Having grown up with fond memories of Thanksgiving dinners with Grams and Pop, long tables with holiday tablecloths set up in the basement of their Bayside home with all the Perlman cousins, it was important for me to instill similar rituals with our Diamond children.

Our Thanksgivings were usually a three-day marathon event. On Wednesday evening, November 27, 2002, we started with a wine tasting presentation. Each guest, Mom and Luke, Diane and Chris, Kirsten, her husband, Steve, and their children, Brendan and Morgan, and Diane's sons Adam and Josh, Dani, Greg and Brett, (YaYa and TaTa were now living in Tarpon Springs, a large Greek community in Florida), would be required to purchase one bottle of wine and then "sing its praises." The region, the grape, the taste or aftertaste, and the aroma would need to be described in a humorous or theatrical way. A rating would, subsequently, be given to both "performers" (c'est à dire, to the person acting out his/her scenario and to the particular wine being described).

I chose to go with a gallon jug of 'Diana' California white wine purchased at Costco for $5.99. I won the 1st Place prize for "Best Demonstration." The wine garnered the last place for taste.

A new post-Thanksgiving tradition had also been established by Brett and his Georgetown buddies. Every year since they graduated in 1999, on the Saturday after Thanksgiving, each of the ten or twelve boys would escort his parents to a delectable dinner in a private room at a New York City restaurant. At the table, we very proud mothers of our Georgetown sons would discuss books and politics and our lives.

I introduced the ladies to a book that we had read at Harborfields Library called, The Georgetown Ladies Social Club: Power, Passion, and Politics in the Nation's Capital, by C. David Heymann. Thereafter, we would refer to ourselves as "The

Georgetown Mother's Social Club." We Georgetown Mothers, Linda Pines, Robyn O'Neill, Ann Hopwood, Joan Mitchell, Aferdita (Dita) Daerti, Tina Mattimore, and Annette Pizirusso are still friends rallying around our boys and their families today.

"No matter what you do, someone always knew you would."

~ Ami McKay, The Birth House

NOVEMBER 2002: Empire Falls by Richard Russo

From the moment I opened this book about life in a small, decaying, fictional town in Maine, I was hooked. Having spent so much of my childhood in Bolton Landing (although far from decaying) on Lake George (NY), I was quickly immersed in the quotidian lives of Russo's quirky, but very believable and relatable characters.

Russo won the 2002 Pulitzer Prize in Fiction for *Empire Falls*. It was made into a two-part miniseries that aired on HBO Memorial Day Weekend, 2005. An incredible cast poignantly portrayed by Ed Harris (Miles Roby,) the "nice guy" manager of the Empire Grill, Helen Hunt (Janine Roby,) Miles's estranged wife, the perpetual yo-yo dieter/exercise fanatic, Paul Newman (Max Roby,) Miles's outspoken, roguish father, Aidan Quinn (David Roby,) Miles's younger brother, the diner's cook and Joanne Woodward (Francine Whiting,) the manipulative town matriarch, explored themes of family, disappointment, love in all of its disguises, loss, bullying and redemption.

Richard Russo, likewise, grew up in the small town of Gloversville, NY. A former English professor at Colby College in Maine, the author often explores these recurring themes in his books.

'Empire Falls,' the HBO miniseries, would go on to win the Golden Globe and be chosen by NBC for their on-air book club. I would select *Empire Falls* again for our 'Morning Book Discussion' at Harborfields Library, also in November 2002 and for our 'Page Turners' Group in Northport in October 2012.

"Peace is its own reward."

~ *Mahatma Gandhi*

DECEMBER 2002: Peace Like a River by Leif Enger

"Hailed as one of the year's top five novels by *Time* and selected as one of the best books of the year by nearly all major newspapers, a national bestseller, *Peace Like a River* captured the hearts of a nation in need of comfort...."

- Marta Salij, Detroit Free Press

Enger tells the story of eleven-year-old Reuben Land, an asthmatic, who, along with his father, Jeremiah, and sister, flees Minnesota and treks West in search of Reuben's "outlaw" brother. Their journey "is at once a heroic quest, a tragedy, a love story, and a haunting meditation on the possibility of magic in the everyday world." (Grove Press)

Leif Enger took the title, *Peace Like a River*, from the lyrics of the hymn, "It is Well with My Soul," which was performed at his wedding. He wrote the novel to amuse his family and took their plot suggestions. He gave his lead character, (Reuben) asthma to encourage one of his sons who also suffers from this ailment.

Our book club joined the legions of newspapers that applauded this heartwarming novel.

1977, 1979, 1981, 1983, 1988

Some years are memorable because of a happy occasion, like a wedding or the birth of a child. Others are seared in our memories because of a tragedy or a loss of some kind, an accident or an outstanding current or historical event, such as JFK's assassination, (November 22, 1963) or the First Moon Landing, (July 20, 1969), the O.J. Simpson acquittal ("not guilty") trial, (October 3, 1995), or the Terrorist Attacks on our nation, (September 11, 2001).

When my body first fell apart a few months after Brett was born in 1977, I unconsciously began to divide my life into MS exacerbations, when they took place and what I lost. Before my MS diagnosis, I was adventurous, almost fearless, looked forward to new experiences, tried different things. Now I found myself shying away from a change of any kind. Maintaining the status quo worked for me just fine. I guess that's why I always cry on New Year's Eve. I know what I have and where I've been. The daunting, unknown future frightened, rather than excited, me now.

We were in Disney World, Florida, with the kids in the spring of 1979, when suddenly I was overcome with a severe case of dizziness, light-headedness or vertigo so overwhelming that I had to scramble to sit down. Danielle was four, Brett just two years old. We have a photo album filled with pictures of them shaking hands with Mickey Mouse and hugging Cinderella.

My dizziness and disorientation persisted the next day, so we flew home with me on a stretcher in the back of the plane. I went straight to Huntington Hospital, where I began my two week - twice-daily injections of ACTH (ACTHAR) to help quiet my symptoms. By then, my eyes had begun to blink uncontrollably, and I felt nauseous. I threw up violently, more than fifteen times a day and, although I was starving, I couldn't keep anything down. Saltine crackers and sips of ginger ale were all that I could tolerate.

206

(To this day, the sight or smell of either one makes me gag).

I was weak and frightened, unable to sleep or focus. My hospitalization would last a full two weeks before I was sent home on an oral regimen of prednisone to help reduce the flare-up of my Multiple Sclerosis. Fortunately, for "Lucky Me", my body always responded positively to both the ACTH injections and the heavy doses of oral prednisone and, although the recuperation period seemed interminable, and the pins and needles were excruciating, I was ultimately able to regain the use of any limb (or my eyesight) that was affected.

My at-home recovery was slow, but I was able to function in 1979 with the aid of a health care worker for the next 6-8 weeks. Thank heavens for family and good friends who took turns carpooling and arranging play dates for my two young children, and for looking out for my husband, who was caught in the crossfire.

I can recall being obsessed with the fact that I needed to buy a pair of purple moccasins for Danielle. (My dear friend, Ellen Marino, eased my mind and purchased a pair for both my Dani and her Lisa).

Diane and Renee (remember, her real name is Doreen), both living in Glens Falls, Big Ed and Sharon, YaYa and TaTa, all pitched in. Our neighbors were irreplaceable. How blessed and how very fortunate I was, and am, to have such kindness surrounding me. Our lifelong friendship with Pat and Al Fusaro, the parents of Dani and Brett's early childhood friends, would eventually lead to our 25+ year love affair with the island of Aruba in the Dutch West Indies, and our purchase of a timeshare property. (The third generation of Diamonds and Westfalls have now become regulars in seeking the sun and glorious trade winds of our very "Happy Island").

From Dani's dance classes, flute playing and four year stint as a cheerleader, to Brett's soccer, Little League and football, plus religious instruction, (CCD) for both, Ted's and my life during the 1970s, 80s and 90s was centered in the wholesome community of Elwood, with our PTA and dinner dates, sleepovers and holiday parties. I played tennis weekly, (both "singles" and later "doubles" as both age and MS exacerbations started to catch up with me), and threw a wicked curveball in the bowling alley to match my 126 point average, (my personalized 10 lb. red and gold bowling ball still sits with my bowling shoes in my purple bowling bag, on the top shelf, next to my one-armed 3rd place tennis trophy, drawing dust in my husband's precious "man cave" garage).

Dani and Brett went from Nursery School to Kindergarten, to Middle School and High School, with many of their first BFFs. Dani's Kindergarten buddy, her partner in crime, painting our bathrooms in nail polish red and storefront Christmas windows with "potty words," Lisa Marino, would go on to med school at U Penn, be Dani's Maid of Honor and Godmommy to Lily, Dani's firstborn. Lisa would forever be our heartbeat and inspiration, dwarfing any complaints or triumphs I would have with my MS. Lisa was diagnosed with Cystic Fibrosis at a very young age; yet, she would bravely plunge forward after every setback, after every cold or infection forced her to be hospitalized. While the other kids were playing, Lisa was having her lungs palpitated so that she could breathe. She is a petite, (in stature), young woman with long dark hair, crater dimples like my granddaughter, Brielle, and laughing brown eyes that twinkle with mischief and cut to the chase.

In 2013, Lisa was formally and officially heralded among the Cystic Fibrosis, "40 Under 40," who have left their mark on the world. She is my daughter's best friend, my granddaughter's Godmother, and today, my pain management doctor. I love her and thank her so very much.

1981

There's an advertisement for Bayer Low Dose aspirin, (July 2014), in which a man reads a note: "John's heart attack didn't come with a warning."

AND NEITHER DID ANY OF MY SUBSEQUENT MS EXACERBATIONS!!!!!

*I could be walking down the street, or waking up in the morning, to find that my eyes were blurry or that I couldn't raise my right hand or that I'd be dragging my left leg. My face, fingers, and toes would tingle with an almost Novocain-like sensation. "**BAM!**", as Emeril Lagasse would say. But, unlike Emeril, I couldn't "Kick it up a Notch!" I'd be stopped dead in my tracks, dizzy, light-headed, double vision.*

I began to develop some kind of pattern, having relapsing-remitting flare-ups every 1-1/2 - 3 years. The procedure was always the same. Dr. Mortati would put me in the hospital for another two-week regimen of twice-daily ACTH injections. In 1981, it started with weakness on my right side. I couldn't hold a pen to write or a brush to style my hair. I am right-handed, but I had to learn to lift a fork with my left hand.

Dani was now six, and Brett four years old. I was thirty-five, Ted, 359 days younger. Of course, I couldn't know the outcome or IF I would return to a "healthy" state once, or IF, the symptoms had subsided. But, thankfully, I did progress, and our lives moved forward, and for every MS exacerbation, there was a silver lining and a pot of gold waiting at the end of the rainbow. Ted's export business partnership with my Dad was doing well, and our children were happy and healthy. We took summer vacations on the Jersey Shore, (Avalon), and Ted continued his world travels.

Between exacerbations, no one but an ophthalmologist, (looking closely with a magnifying glass to see the damage to the optic nerve in my left eye), could tell that I had a chronic disease. Visibly my speech, my gait and my overall demeanor belied the fact that I had Multiple Sclerosis. My new morning ritual began with a fervent, "Thank you, God," when I could wake up symptom-free until the next time.

Most of my attacks occurred either during the hot summer months or during the Christmas season, two of my favorite times of the year. The doctor said that these were particularly stressful periods, but I didn't see it that way. When I tried to buy the "perfect" Christmas gift for my family, find the "perfect" Christmas tree, make the most "perfectly delicious" Christmas cookies, or decorate our home the "perfectly Dickensian" way, (I have a charming Charles Dickens', "A Christmas Carol" Village from Department 56 that I set up every year, with Ebenezer Scrooge, Tiny Tim, Jacob Marley, Bob Cratchitt, Fezziwig, and the gang), I didn't realize that internally I was activating those crazy jumping beans/pins and needles.

I remember spending New Year's Eve, 1981 in Huntington Hospital, wearing the 'Burger King Crown' that Ted and our friends brought for me. ("Queen for a Day," or maybe for the Eve).

I remember being on Tegretol and Phenobarbital for my seizures another time. The doctor said that one of the side effects could be increased facial hair. So, not wanting to miss an opportunity to playfully make fun of me, my sister, Renee, came down from Glens Falls with her two daughters, Allyson and Jaime, grabbed my Dani, and paid me a visit in the hospital sporting moustaches of their own to complement the one they were sure they would find growing under my nose. Dr. Mortatii was in my room at the time. He took a double-take when he saw these four mustachioed girls enter the room, unsure of what my reaction would be.

Laughter truly is the best medicine.

210

Reading has always been my outlet, my escape, my portal to new adventures. I suppose that's why it was hardest for me to find that my eyes were affected with each MS exacerbation.... dizziness, excessive blinking, blurry or double vision. I had permanently lost 20% of the vision in my left eye, but my right eye more than compensated for the loss. There were times when I had no peripheral vision, and times when I couldn't drive. But my vision always did come back, slowly, much too slowly, and "Lucky Me" did turn out to be truly blessed.

1983

By 1983 we were living high and savoring the success of our export business. Ted had purchased a silver Ferrari from François's California friend. We had a 36 ft. Sea Ray that we christened, the 'Son of a D,' (in recognition of my in-laws' 42 ft. Chris Craft named, the 'Mr. D'). We started construction to expand our home on Carrol Place, and we rented an octagonal beach house on the water in Bridgehampton for the summer of 1983. Everyone shared in our joy, Diane's family, Renee's family, YaYa and TaTa, (Uncle George and Aunt Bev were the next town over at a rented cottage in Southampton), François, Libby and their sons and other college friends and their families, came for a visit.

We threw a Surprise 60th Birthday Party for my Dad and invited almost one hundred people to celebrate with us. What a joyous affair it was and one that, in hindsight, we were grateful to have hosted. (Big Ed Perlman never lived to see his 65th birthday. He died of a massive heart attack moving into his new home in Florida on August 13th, just nine days shy of his 65th birthday).

We had our expensive toys in 1983, living "A Wonderful Life." Ronald Reagan, The Great Communicator, was our 40th President and there seemed to be a lot of everything....

211

Until our bubble burst.

We had a very big job pending in the Philippines. I can recall sitting on the porch of our rented home on the south fork of Long Island, Ted and me talking about all of the "what ifs" hanging on this huge business deal.

But, once again, an assassin's bullet altered the course of history and made an abrupt change in our lives. Persuaded by the deterioration of political and economic conditions in his country, and Ferdinand Marcos's declining health, Benigno ("Ninoy") Aquino and his wife, Corazon, decided to return to the Philippines after a three-year self-exile for medical treatment in the United States. Aquino was shot in the head and killed as he was escorted off an airplane at Manila International Airport on August 21, 1983. In the blink of an eye, we went from riding high on the waves of the 'Son of a D' to bailing out the overflow on the raft that barely kept us afloat.

Construction on our house came to a grinding halt. We sold the Ferrari first and then the boat. To supplement our dwindling export business, we began to manufacture wooden crates, built and assembled in our Farmingdale warehouse. There was a staff of maybe fifty people now working with Ted and Dad (among them, my nineteen-year-old brother, Chris, working part-time).

I lost a child that year, brought on by what I thought was a never-ending MS exacerbation. The symptoms that I was by now used to experiencing lasted for a longer period of time and became so much more intense. I didn't know that I was pregnant. I was on medication that would have been dangerous to my unborn fetus and life-altering to my family and me.

Still, I mourned the loss of what I knew in my heart was another baby boy.

1988

Some years are memorable because of a happy occasion, while others are seared in our memories because of a tragedy, or a loss of some kind. 1988 is my stand-out year.

According to Wikipedia, the free encyclopedia, "Murphy's Law is an adage or epigram that is typically stated as: "anything that can go wrong will go wrong." Theories still persist as to the actual derivation of this so-called law. From mathematician, Augustus De Morgan's writing, (37) to John Sack's mountaineering epigraph, (38) and Anne Roe's quote regarding an unnamed physicist who described Murphy's law or the fourth law of thermodynamics, (39) I, myself, favor the argument that "it was named after Capt. Edward A. Murphy in 1949, an engineer working on an Air Force Project MX981, (a project) designed to see how much sudden deceleration a person can stand in a crash. One day, after finding that a transducer was wired wrong, he cursed the technician responsible and said, "If there is any way to do it wrong, he'll find it." (40)

But I wasn't thinking about Murphy's law or the origins of the adage back in 1988 when my Theo (Ted) and I had to make some hard choices about our future.

As the export market continued to plummet, it was difficult for us to make the mortgage payments on our home. The kids were older now, in middle school. I thought it might be a good time for me to go back to college and learn a new profession. I applied for and received, a graduate assistantship to work in the Circulation Dept. at Long Island University, at the Palmer School of Library Science. I would start by taking two courses.

How difficult could it be? Weren't libraries all about books? If that was true, then wasn't the study of Library Science also about the study of books? And weren't books meant to be read? Why didn't I think of majoring in Library Science sooner, if that's what it was all about?

I set out with the best of intentions. I was eager to become a student again. And while I studied (or tried to), our children did the typical things an average pre-teen and thirteen-year-old Elwood student did in 1988.

Ted labored over trying to save the family business. By now, Big Ed and Sharon had sold their home on the south shore and moved into their "vacation home" in Florida. Our failing/ flailing business couldn't support both our family and Dad and Sharon. Things were stressful. The bills still had to be paid, and mortgages met in a timely fashion. Nasty bill collectors and creditors called multiple times a day, using threatening language. We didn't have Caller I.D., if it even existed in the late '80s, and I was afraid to pick up the phone. Then our downward spiral began, and Murphy's Law set in, in rapid succession.

The first thing to go was my eyesight, leaving me totally blind, while I sat in Professor Morriss's, 'Intro to Library Science' class. Suddenly, I was dizzy and extremely nauseous. Then everything went black. When our class ended, I asked the woman seated next to me if she would walk me to the telephone booth in the lobby so that I could call my husband. She was patient and solicitous and insisted on driving me home (although it was very much out of her way). I thanked her and told her that I preferred to wait for my husband to pick me up.

One hour later, the troops arrived. An outwardly calm Theodore Arthur Diamond and visibly shaken, Danielle and Brett, pulled up in our famous station wagon, affectionately termed the "Diamond Mobile," "The Woody," and later, with other models of the same beloved car, the "Shaggin' Wagon." I don't think any of us quite

214

knew what to say. Dr. Mortati said this attack was concentrated solely on my eyes. My limbs and extremities remained untouched.

The Bottom Line: *With the exception of a tiny pinprick of light, I remained totally blind for slightly more than six months. The irony was, I felt pretty good this time around. I just couldn't see.*

Murphy's second pin was the next to drop. At last, unable to meet our monthly mortgage, we sadly and reluctantly agreed to put our beloved, half-finished, architecturally designed, dream home up for sale. YaYa and TaTa would provide a temporary safe haven for us.

Leaving Elwood and all of our friends, packing up our furniture to be put in storage, was a difficult and painful thing for us to have to do. We were in our prime, me and Ted, still young and strong, but Dad and Sharon were in their '60s and our children just thirteen and eleven. Is it possible to know who suffered the most? Would we all be scarred for life, or could we get past this?

As we tearfully drove away from the place, we called home for thirteen years, Danielle, in her child's optimistic voice, said, "It'll be OK, Mom. It's just a house, and a house isn't a home. We're together. It'll be OK".

And I knew somehow it would be, as long as I had my frat boy on the left and our two healthy, funny children beside me.

Sharon's phone call late at night was the last straw. Big Ed Perlman was dead. Dead of a heart attack, just like his parents and his brother before him. DAMN that dreaded "Perlman Curse!"

I've heard people say that tragedy and adversity make us stronger, make us better people. I'm not sure that I agree. I didn't think that we were bad people to begin with.

215

My husband always says that I live in the past, but I guess that only applies to our happy past, which constitutes 95% of my life. Writing all of this down isn't cathartic for me. I don't want to go back to 1977, 1979, 1981, 1983 and 1988. I've/we've gone so far from there.

Barry Manilow sang, "I Made It Through the Rain," and so did we.

"Some memories remain close; you can shut your eyes and find yourself back in them. These are first-person memories --- I memories. But there are second-person memories, too, distant your memories, and these are trickier: you watch yourself in disbelief…"

~ Beautiful Ruins, by Jess Walter (page 259)

Chapter 7

Donna's Big Gaff! (Among Other Things) 2003

Ted and I, Dani and Greg, departed from LGA airport on Thursday, September 11, 2003, en route to my nephew's wedding in Seattle, WA. We were a bit apprehensive about flying on that particular day, but our fears were allayed at the thought of visiting a city we had never been to and reuniting with family members for such a happy occasion.

I was particularly eager to ferry out to Bainbridge Island, site of David Guterson's evocative novel, Snow Falling on Cedars, (the first book I would discuss in May of 1996 in my new role as a book discussion facilitator). The breathtaking Bainbridge Island was where their rustic nuptials were held on Saturday, September 13, 2003. I was anxious to smell the cedar and feast my eyes on the natural beauty of this place that didn't disappoint. It was exactly the way I had imagined it, the way Guterson had so vividly depicted it.

Having the opportunity to meet Nancy Pearl, the Executive Director of the Washington Center for the Book at the Seattle Public Library at the time, founder and pioneer of the much-imitated "If All Seattle Read the Same Book" Project, the author of several books and the prototype for the librarian action figure doll with shushing motion, was another reason I looked forward to this trip. I hadn't made any advance arrangements to meet Ms. Pearl, but we were fortunate enough to find that she was available and willing to meet with us. The others held back and allowed me the time to talk books with this brilliant, friendly, and outgoing woman. We asked each other what was the current "hot book" for discussion, what genre of book we most preferred to read, and how (and if) our book clubs in New York differed from hers in Seattle.

She took me into her office. I asked if I could purchase her book, Book Lust: Recommended Reading for Every Mood, Moment and Reason, and her action figure doll that I'd heard so much about and was most anxious to show my fellow librarians.

Ted and I, our daughter and son-in-law, had enjoyed a very full morning ogling and tasting many of the delectable products to be found at the famous Pike's Market. And, of course, gulping a soup-size bowl of Starbucks coffee at its original home. We loved the walking and munching as we dug into some juicy, ripe peaches. I had the bag of peaches in my hand when I entered Ms. Pearl's office. I was so caught up in the magic of the moment, the mere exchange of "book talk" with this very engaging woman, that I put my brown bag of peaches on her desk. Our conversation and a brief tour of the library followed. When we returned to her office, I picked up the brown bag that I believed contained my succulent Pike's Market peaches.

It didn't.

As Dani and Greg, Ted and I continued our walk down the hill from the library, I opened MY BROWN BAG and looked inside. And what to my wondering eyes should appear but a HAM AND CHEESE SANDWICH and an apple instead!!! Horrors!!! While Agatha Christie's artful detective, Hercule Poirot, might have said, "Sacrebleu," les Français ne disent jamais ça. Hercule Poirot was, after all, Belgian. I, however, exclaimed in disbelief, "Qu'est-ce que j'ai fait?" (What have I done)?

What was I to do? I was mortified. I had just spent a delightful hour with Nancy Pearl, and as thanks for her time, what did I do but steal her lunch? We were now more than a mile from the library. I kissed everyone good-bye and hurried back from whence I had come.

Too embarrassed to confront Nancy Pearl with my gaff, I left HER BROWN BAG at the information desk and asked the person seated there to return the lunch bag to its rightful owner, aka Nancy Pearl, Executive Director, with my deepest apologies. I wondered if I had made a "good" first impression. "Memorable," I'm sure. "Good" is questionable.

THE YEAR 2003

According to my notes and year end recap, "we encountered some very interesting and a few dysfunctional characters in 2003 ---- a neighborly talk show hostess and her family and community of friends, a slain fourteen-year-old girl looking down from her Heaven at her grieving family and the man who murdered her, a British piano tuner, (an Erard specialist,) and his musical, savage, jungle surgeon in Burma, (reminiscent of Rudyard Kipling and Joseph Conrad), an immigrant family seeking to find its way in America, a Depression era horse that won the hearts of America, ("the little horse that could"), an angry and secretive French family during WWII, a fictional portrayal of the attack on Pearl Harbor and the events and actions of FDR and Churchill that preceded it, a soprano, a Japanese businessman and some terrorists at a birthday party, a charming local vintner and her perils in creating an American family winery, the blockbuster, page-turner of the year, discussing hidden secrets and clandestine societies, Leonardo Da Vinci and the relationship between Jesus Christ and Mary Magdalene, a cruel and precocious thirteen year old girl who committed a crime that was destined to haunt her family for decades, and the secret life of bees, the Black Madonna and the Divine Feminine."

"Why are there so many songs about rainbows,
And what's on the other side? Rainbows are
visions, but only illusions, And rainbows have
nothing to hide…"

~ *Kermit the Frog, The Rainbow Connection*

JANUARY 2003: Standing in the Rainbow by Fannie Flagg

The lovable, unflappable, Fannie Flagg, caught our fancy in January with her delightful novel, *Standing in the Rainbow*, a slight deviation in the genre for us, but most welcome and highly received. We all delighted in her authentic characters, Neighbor Dorothy, with her friendly local news broadcasts, Norma and Macky Warren, their eighty-nine-year-old Aunt and the other friendly folks of Elmwood Springs. I love a book like this where the worst thing to happen is to have your cake fall coming out of the oven, or your icing melting prematurely. In this fast-paced world, it's always a breath of fresh air to read such a feel-good book, a sort of *Chicken Soup for the Soul*, Jack Canfield's tender take on the subject.

Standing in the Rainbow follows Flagg's successful Fried Green Tomatoes at the Whistle Stop Café, which thrilled as both a book and a Hollywood movie.

"When the Fox hears the Rabbit, scream, he comes a-runnin', but not to help."

~ Thomas Harris, The Silence of the Lambs

FEBRUARY 2003: The Lovely Bones by Alice Sebold

"Sleeper hit of 2002, took off when Anna Quindlen proclaimed it the hottest book of the summer. It's Sebold's only novel. A murdered girl peers down from heaven to narrate the story". (31)

I was reluctant to read this book because of the nature of the subject matter. I don't do well with cold-blooded reality novels, or movies, because I'm squeamish and often have nightmares. But this novel, The Lovely Bones, kept calling out to me. Everywhere I turned, the hype and word of mouth, the advertisements and the book lists, all pointed to Alice Sebold's debut novel. 'Good Morning America' chose it for its book club in August 2002 but, as cited previously, what catapulted it to another level, was "the Anna Quindlen moment." Within hours, advance orders drove it up Amazon's Bestseller List. Rave reviews followed, including one from Janet Maslin of the New York Times on CBS' Sunday Morning." (32) Bookstore promotions and an excerpt in the July 2002 issue of *Seventeen Magazine*, made it the fastest-selling debut novel in memory. Sebold, herself a rape victim, said she didn't "fully understand why her novel was so popular. But she said readers she had met at bookstore signings suggested several reasons:

1. It resonates with those who have lost a relative or a friend and stimulates others to ponder: "What would

it be like if I lost someone?" "What would their heaven be like?" Lots of readers use the word "healing" when they discuss the novel, Sebold said.

2. It triggers ways of dealing with Sept. 11, when, as one reader told Sebold: "America came to understand that the worst thing that 'could happen,' could happen here."

3. It appeals to teens – girls and boys – who identify with the quirky adolescent narrator who never gets to grow up." (33)

There were numerous negative reviews as well, but whether positive or negative, I felt I had to read *The Lovely Bones* and make it one of our monthly selections, (unlike, *Fifty Shades of Grey*, by E.L. James, which I believed I was compelled to read because of all the hype but DIDN'T choose to impose on our book club members. Now, *Fifty Shades of Chicken*, by F.L. Fowler, with its "dripping thighs, sticky chicken fingers, mustard-spanked chicken and chicken with a lardon," that was another story.

As Kathleen Bouton wrote in her review of *The Lovely Bones* for the *New York Times* Book Review, Sunday, July 14, 2002 (page 14,) "This book happens to have been published at a moment when a real-life kidnapping of a fourteen-year-old girl, Elizabeth Smart, taken from her comfortable middle-class bed in the dead of night, haunts the news. The very idea of Sebold's subject matter might make a reader queasy. But there's nothing prurient or exploitative in "The Lovely Bones." Susie's story, paradoxically, is one of hope, set against grim reality." (34)

Note: On Wednesday, April 30, 2003, Elizabeth Smart and her parents, Ed and Lois, gathered at the White House to watch President George W. Bush sign a law establishing a nationwide "Amber Alert" System to thwart kidnappings.

The Amber Alert is named for Amber Hagerman, a Texas nine-year-old, who was kidnapped and killed in 1996. (35) (USA Today, Thursday, May 1, 2003, page 2A, by Richard Benedetto).

"The piano ain't got no wrong notes."

~ *Thelonious Monk*

MARCH 2003: The Piano Tuner by Daniel Mason

We 'marched' through 19th century British dominated Burma in Daniel Mason's, *The Piano Tuner*, a debut novel set in the jungle, with a middle-aged protagonist, Edgar Drake, commissioned by the British War Office to repair a rare Erard grand piano belonging to Surgeon-Major Anthony Caroll. The story, reminiscent of Joseph Conrad's, *Heart of Darkness*, in its gloomy, stifling sense of place, received mixed reviews from the men and women who joined us at Border's on Monday, March 3, 2003. At that meeting, we also extended our condolences to one of our original, long-time members, Elvira Lubrano, whose husband had recently died after a long illness. Elvira, who had never missed a meeting in seven years, was awarded the "Perfect Attendance" honor and presented with a copy of our next book selection, *How the Garcia Girls Lost Their Accents*, by Julia Alvarez.

"The accent of one's birthplace remains in the mind and in the heart as in one's speech."

~ *Francois de La Rochefoucauld*

APRIL 2003: How the Garcia Girls Lost Their Accents by Julia Alvarez

It snowed quite heavily on April 7, 2003. We were forced to postpone our gathering until the following Monday, April 14th. Julia Alvarez's, *How the Garcia Girls Lost Their Accents*, was the book chosen by the Long Island Reads Committee, and thus, by me, to be discussed at Nassau Community College and libraries throughout the Island. The very charming, Julia Alvarez, addressed a large audience of college students, faculty and guests, who eagerly queried her on her book and her writing. A book signing and light lunch followed.

This was just the second year of a shared project for libraries in Nassau and Suffolk Counties. The year before, (2002), the inauguration of the Long Island Reads Celebration, the Committee explored the world of *The Great Gatsby*, by F. Scott Fitzgerald. I joined the Long Island Reads Committee, immediately following the Julia Alvarez event at Nassau Community College.

*"There is something about the outside of a horse
that is good for the inside of a man."*

~ Winston S. Churchill

MAY 2003: Seabiscuit: An American Legend by Laura Hillenbrand

I chose *Seabiscuit: An American Legend*, by Laura Hillenbrand for our discussion in May 2003. A work of non-fiction, released in 2001, and on the New York Times Bestseller List for more than 57 weeks, *Seabiscuit* tells the story of "the little horse that could." It is a Depression-era story of an unlikely champion, an "undersized, crooked-legged racehorse," as Hillenbrand has dubbed him in her book.

Seabiscuit was the perfect title to discuss for all thirty of us in "The Literary Gallery," who met on Monday, May 12, 2003. May is always Kentucky Derby month, (the first Saturday in May) and that year, 2003, and on that day at Churchill Downs, May 3rd, Jockey José Santos, rode his horse, Funny Cide, to victory at the 129th Run For The Roses. But, the unlikely story of *Seabiscuit*, like the scrutiny over Santos's victory, were quickly dispelled.

The story of *Seabiscuit's* scribe, Laura Hillenbrand, is as much a heartwarming and triumphant victory of spirit as was Seabiscuit's or Funny Cide's. Diagnosed with a debilitating illness while a sophomore at Kenyon College in Ohio, Chronic Fatigue Syndrome has rendered the author housebound with overwhelming exhaustion, extreme dizziness, and severe joint and muscle pain. She said in an interview with *People Magazine*, dated August 11, 2003, (Page 71), that Seabiscuit's story "kept me going. It's all about trying your hardest." Hillenbrand, a former sports fanatic, (an equestrian, tennis player and competitive swimmer,) successfully did just that during the years it took to write about the iconic 1930s racehorse, who became an American legend. For the adaptation of her book, Laura Hillenbrand turned to filmmaker Gary Ross, a fellow horseracing fan.

The successful film starred Tobey Maguire as the jockey, Red Pollard, Chris Cooper as the trainer, Tom Smith, and Jeff Bridges as Charles Howard, Seabiscuit's owner.

In 2010 Laura Hillenbrand wrote a book which depicted the life of another hero, Louis Zamperini, a former Olympic track star, who survived a plane crash over the Pacific, afloat on a raft for 47 days, and then held prisoner for more than 2-1/2 years in multiple Japanese internment camps. *Unbroken: A World War II Story of Survival, Resilience and Redemption,* was as overwhelmingly received in my three book clubs in 2011 as *Seabiscuit* was received in 2003. Both non-fiction works generated a 5+ Rating from the group, the highest honor accorded an author.

Louis Zamperini died of pneumonia on July 2, 2014, at the age of 97 years. He lived long enough to partially see his life story re-enacted in a film produced by Angelina Jolie that opened with mixed reviews on Christmas Day 2014.

"Some books you read. Some books you enjoy. But some books just swallow you up, heart and soul."

~ Joanne Harris

JUNE 2003: Five Quarters of the Orange by Joanne Harris

Joanne Harris was born in Barnsley, the United Kingdom, of a French mother and an English father.

Perhaps best known for writing about her passion for chocolate, *Chocolat* became a bestseller, was nominated for the Whitbread Award, one of Britain's most prestigious literary prizes, and was made into an Oscar-nominated film starring Juliette Binoche and Johnny Depp.

Our selection of *Five Quarters of the Orange* is the third novel in the loosely termed "food trilogy" that included, *Chocolat* and *Blackberry Wine*. The author's emphasis on the importance and significance of food, provoked a lively discussion, especially among the cooks and foodies of the group.

*"The reading of all good books is like conversation
with the finest men of past centuries."*

~ Rene Descartes, Discourse on Method
(1639)

JULY 2003: A String of Pearls: From Infamy to Victory, a WWII Series – Book One by Benedict Baglio

A fellow Long Islander and Adelphi University alum, Benedict Baglio joined us in July to discuss his work of historical fiction, *A String of Pearls: From Infamy to Victory, a WWII Series – Book One*. Equipped with the melodic CD, "String of Pearls," by Glenn Miller, the author wowed our World War II buffs and charmed us all with his thoughtful discussion of Franklin D. Roosevelt, the USS Arizona and the events of December 7, 1941.

Ultimately, Dr. Baglio would follow-up, *A String of Pearls*, with three other books that formed his four-book series of WWII.

(Note: In December 2013, we discussed a work of non-fiction, another WWII story titled, *The Girls of Atomic City: The Untold Story of the Women Who Helped Win WWII*, by Denise Kiernan. Just as Dr. Baglio had augmented his book discussion by playing Glenn Miller music, I ,too created a similar atmosphere by softly playing background tunes that the women of Oak Ridge, TN, working on the "gadget" for the Clinton Engineering Works, might have been listening to....."I'll Be Seeing You," "Praise the Lord and Pass the Ammunition," "You'll Never Know," "As Time Goes By," and Johnny Mercer's, "Accent-tchu-ate the Positive." (Refer to my Tip #22 in back of the book).

"Without music, life would be a mistake."

~ Friedrich Nietzsche

AUGUST 2003: Bel Canto by Ann Patchett

Ann Patchett took us into the world of opera and terrorism, in an unnamed South American country, in *Bel Canto* in what the *New Yorker* termed, "Glorious" and the San Francisco Chronicle called, "Blissfully romantic… a strange, terrific, spellcasting story."

Awarded both the Orange Prize for Fiction and the PEN/Faulkner Award for Fiction, Ann Patchett's novel is lyrical, its characters unforgettable. The sound of music pervades every page of *Bel Canto*, as we cheer for the men and women whose lives become joined by the power of that same music that has become their sole means of communication.

From Roxanne Coss, the American soprano, to the Japanese industrialist, Mr. Katsumi Hosokawa, and the young terrorist female, Carmen, this beautifully evocative novel was loosely inspired by an event of December 1996, when fourteen members of the Tupac Amaru guerrilla group entered the Japanese Ambassador's residence in Lima, Peru, seized nearly 600 hostages and demanded the release of numerous political prisoners.

I had obtained a copy of Ann Patchett's audio interview with Diane Rehm of National Public Radio, to augment our discussion. It only added to our already unanimous enjoyment of this truly evocative novel.

"You can make anything by writing."

~ *C. S. Lewis*

SEPTEMBER 2003: The Vineyard: The Pleasures and Perils of Creating an American Family Winery by Louisa Thomas Hargrave

Lenn Thompson, interviewing for Appellationamerica.com on March 29, 2006, called Louisa Thomas Hargrave, "Long Island's Founding Mother."

In 1973, Louisa Thomas Hargrave and her husband, Alex Hargrave, founded Hargrave Vineyard, Long Island's 1st modern commercial vineyard on Route 48 in Cutchogue. The couple produced vintage wines similar to those of France's wine regions, (Chardonnay, Cabernet Sauvignon, Merlot and Cabernet Franc). They launched a successful wine industry, primarily on the Island's North Fork, with several located in the area of the Hamptons, as well.

The Hargraves divorced in 1999 and sold their vineyard to Ann Marie and Marco Borghese. Today it is known as Castello di Borghese Vineyard and Winery. (36)

Louisa spoke about her book, about grape production on Long Island, about the choices we make in life and the careers we choose, about family and spouses working together in the same business, about how physical strength relates to mental and emotional strength and about the sheer joy of drinking fine wine, when she joined us at Border's Books & Music on September 8, 2003.

Louisa was ebullient and chatty, intelligent and knowledgeable, and she seemed to truly love everything about the wine industry she represented. Before I extended

233

an invitation to Louisa to join our book club, I had a chance to talk privately with her a few months prior at the Book Revue, (Huntington), as she prepared to do a book signing. Our conversation was easy, and I found that the two of us had much in common.

I often think about the questions you ask a person that somehow lead to unexpected answers, and then to further questions, as the conversation changes gears in totally unexplainable ways.

As we discussed different wine regions, I mentioned that I had gone to school at Keuka College, in the heart of the Finger Lakes area of New York State, where Louisa, herself, had done research. Somehow, in our talk about loving to drink wine, we discovered a shared pleasure in singing French drinking songs:

"Chevaliers de la Table Ronde, goutons voir si le vin est bon."

(It's a French drinking song. No need for any translation).

And how we got on this topic, I cannot begin to imagine, but somehow, someway, somewhere, I obviously told Louisa that I had Multiple Sclerosis. She said her father had MS, too.

Louisa Thomas Hargrave is a writer, columnist, wine judge, and consultant. In October 2004, she was named Interim Director of the Stony Brook University Center for Wine, Food, and Culture. She retained the position as Director through 2009.

She is the current President of Winewise, LLC, consulting for the wine industry, 1999 – present.

"The book to read is not the one that thinks for
you but the one which makes you think."

~ Harper Lee

OCTOBER 2003: The Da Vinci Code by Dan Brown

"The Hottest Book of the Year!"

"Who Was Mary Magdalene?"

"Does The Da Vinci Code Crack Leonardo?"

Such were the headlines in the book world with the publication of Dan Brown's, *The Da Vinci Code* in 2003. What is 'The Priory of Scion,' 'Opus Dei' and 'The Knights Templar?' Readers wanted to know.

"An almost unheard-of 10,000 galleys were printed, more than any of Brown's previous books had sold." (41) (*Digital Fortress*, (1996), *Deception Point*, (1998) and *Angels and Demons* (2000). "In its first week on sale, *The Da Vinci Code* achieved unprecedented success when it debuted at # 1 on the *New York Times* Bestseller List, simultaneously topping bestseller lists at the *Wall Street Journal, Publisher's Weekly*, and *San Francisco Chronicle.*" (42).

Dan Brown is a graduate of Amherst College and Phillips Exeter Academy, (New Hampshire), where he spent time as an English teacher before turning to write full-time. "The son of a Presidential Award-winning math professor and a professional sacred musician, Dan grew up surrounded by the paradoxical philosophies of science and religion. His wife, Blythe, - an art historian and painter – collaborated with him on his research and accompanied him on his frequent research trips, the latest to Paris, where they spent time in the Louvre for his new thriller," (43) today's book discussion, *The Da Vinci Code* (Dan Brown Website (5/7/03). Described as "a riddle wrapped in a mystery inside an enigma," as Sir Winston Spencer Churchill once wrote, The Da Vinci Code is filled with intrigue, science, technology, romance, religion, murder, cryptology and mysticism and is set in picture-perfect places such as Paris, my all-time favorite city, Rome and Seville.

We were a large group of twenty-seven to assemble at Border's Books and Music that day, including my die-hard regulars, Rita Silver, Connie Sabatino, Ellen Davis, Elvira Lubrano, and Jackie Metzger. As our book discussion was about to begin, we were halted by a loud disturbance in the store. Fifteen or twenty people clamored to hear what was being said about Mary Magdalene purportedly being the wife of Jesus Christ. "Are there any Catholics here today?" "How do you feel about Dan Brown's contention that Jesus Christ sired a child with Mary Magdalene?" "What does the Catholic Church have to say about this book?" "Has it been banned by the Church?"

Loud questions were being shouted out…. rude, intrusive remarks. A chaotic, free-for-all situation was about to erupt. Who were these people so eager to voice their opinions and disrupt what is, ordinarily, such a civil discussion of our monthly book selection? One of our faithful, I think it was Big John McGuinness, laughingly quipped, "Hey, Donna, what did you do to draw so many people off the street …….post a placard outside or get a hook to reel them in?"

It was difficult to maintain order, stay on track, and hear above the fracas. Our normal hour and a half discussion extended to two hours before I was finally able to wrap it up with a firm, definitive statement that sounded more like a snarl. "*The Da Vinci Code*, by Dan Brown, is a NOVEL! YES, it's a page-turner, and YES, it's about art, architecture and religious history BUT, when all is said and done, IT'S STILL JUST A N O V E L !!!"

I had violated my own Tip #6 about avoiding any discussion of religion or politics and Tip #7 of staying clear of any "personal" subjects. But what I didn't expect is that I would need a cowbell, a judge's gavel or a bull horn (or, perhaps, a fragile tinkling crystal bell,) to maintain order in the room. (Refer to my Tip #23)

"If a book is well written, I always find it too short."

~ Jane Austen

NOVEMBER 2003: Atonement by Ian McEwan

We quietly convened in November to discuss Ian McEwan's, *Atonement*, a blockbuster, tour de force, Booker Prize Finalist, in its own right --- totally different in subject and scope from Dan Brown's, *The Da Vinci Code*, but, nonetheless, as brilliant and thought-provoking.

Atonement "a beautiful and majestic fictional panorama" - John Updike, *The New Yorker* (New York Times Book Review, Sunday, March 2, 2003).

Having previously read, *Amsterdam*, (May 1999), nineteen of us were accustomed to McEwan's psychological approach to his storytelling. Luminous in its characterization and profoundly gripping in its themes of class differences, love and war, individual vs. collective responsibility, and a child's vs. an adult's sense of judgment, *Atonement* is a compelling read with plot twists and surprises best left up to the reader to discover.

SPOILER ALERT: For those who like to read the ending before they read the first chapter…. D O N 'T!!

*"I'm not the same reader when I finish a book as
I was when I started."*

~ Will Schwalbe, Books for Living

DECEMBER 2003: The Secret Life of Bees by Sue Monk Kidd

I never made it to our discussion of Sue Monk Kidd's, *The Secret Life of Bees*, nor to our 8th Annual Holiday Luncheon at the Greek Village in Commack. The night before, on Sunday evening, December 7th, around 6:00 PM, I fell down the stairs and fractured my left ankle. "Oh, that was a pain that would surely linger well into next year," (to paraphrase Martin Short's, Ed Grimley). I was feeling really good and thought I was on the last step. I wasn't. There were still two more steps to reach the bottom.

I was really disappointed because I had articles and pictures and other material related to Sue Monk Kidd's successful debut, coming-of-age, civil rights era novel, and I was all set to bring in a beehive that I had found under our patio umbrella that summer.

Good Morning America had selected the book for its *Read This!* Book Club and Book Sense named *The Secret Life of Bees* as one of the finalists for its Book of the Year Award in the Adult Fiction Category.

The story revolves around strong, southern women, fourteen year old, Lily Owen, a white girl raised by her elderly African American nanny, Rosaleen, after her mother's accidental death, and the three bee-keeping Boatwrights, "The Calendar Sisters," August, May and June, who provide shelter for Lily and Rosaleen following a racial disturbance in Tiburon, SC.

According to the phone calls and get-well cards I received from the members of 'The Literary Gallery,' *The Secret Life of Bees*, was a huge success, with which I wholeheartedly concurred.

Chapter 8

Why Thaddeus Named Me the Ultimate Hard-core, High-handed, Card-carrying Bibliophilist (2004)

Thaddeus, (Ted) named me "The Ultimate Hard-Core, High-handed, Card-carrying Bibliophilist," he said, because of my overzealous tactics in signing my books out to my family and friends. Just because I kept a very official-looking "sign out" log or asked that borrowers NOT dog-ear the pages of my books; just because I asked that my books be returned without a trace of coffee or chocolate stains; and just because I didn't tolerate any passing of my books to third parties, certainly isn't cause for name-calling. The "Ultimate Hard-core, High-handed, Card-carrying Bibliophilist," indeed!

I had very lenient policies regarding due dates. NO DUE DATE as long as my book was returned ("the rules are there are no rules!") That's fair, don't you think?

I also never imposed any fines for overdue books, (well, maybe just once when my indomitable sister, Diane, still hadn't returned my copy of The Death and Life of Charlie Saint Cloud, by Ben Sherwood after 3-1/2 years).   Really, and to make matters worse, she insisted on calling me, 'Marion, the librarian,' (a reference to the prim and persnickety librarian in Meredith Wilson's,' The Music Man'). After all, "Nobody puts Baby in a corner" or pushes me, "Marion, the Librarian/Donna the "Ultimate Hard-core, High-handed, Card-carrying Bibliophilist" into a library carrel"!

Do you remember the Soup Nazi from Seinfeld? ("NO SOUP FOR YOU!") Well, I had to say to my big sister, "NO BOOKS FOR YOU!"

My librarian friend, Deborah Clark Cunningham, once shared a very interesting quote with me regarding the lending of books. She said she had been watching an old movie the other night, 'Out of Africa', and thought of me. In the story, Isak Dinesen, (the Baroness Karen von Blixen-Finake character, played so beautifully by Meryl Streep,) discusses how Robert Redford, (Denys Fitch Hatton in the movie,) also loved and collected books. Like me, he would lend, but you damn well better return the book, or you wouldn't be his friend. His friend is telling this to Meryl Streep (Dinesen). She exclaims, "You mean Denys would lose a friend forever over a book?"

Response: "No, Denys's friend would."

Think about it.

But, in this case, it wasn't a friend. My own strong-willed sibling, Diane, was the culprit and she had to be cut off. Apparently, my recriminations were so intimidating that my equally opinionated fair-haired sister, Renee, said she'd rather buy her own books than risk incurring the wrath of "The Ultimate Hard-core, High-handed, Card-carrying Bibliophilist."

In 2013 we chatted with the author, Denise Kiernan, about her fascinating work of non-fiction, The Girls of Atomic City: The Untold Story of the Women Who Helped Win WWII. During our SKYPE talk, we discussed the General who worked on "The Project" at Oak Ridge, TN. Apparently, he, too, was accused of employing "Gestapo" techniques (page 53).

There are those misinformed borrowers of my books who felt justified, (however misguided), in calling me, "The Ultimate Hard-core, High-handed, Card-carrying Bibliophilist," and, like the said General, I felt I was doing what was necessary considering the circumstances

And so, it goes.

THE YEAR 2004

*"I am no bird; and no net ensnares me: I am a
free human being with an independent will."*

~ *Charlotte Bronte, Jane Eyre*

JANUARY 2004: The Eyre Affair by Jasper Fforde and Jane Eyre by Charlotte Bronte

2004 was a mixed bag of surprises… some wonderful, like celebrating baby brother Chris's (Cubby's) 40th Birthday, and reading a dual entry, *The Eyre Affair*, by Jasper Fforde, and *Jane Eyre*, by Charlotte Bronte, which combined the clever literary secret agent, Thursday Next, with the classy and classic Jane Eyre. In *The Eyre Affair* Thursday Next is in hot pursuit of Acheron Hades, who has stolen the manuscript of "Martin Chuzzlewit" and is plotting to kidnap the character of Jane Eyre. If Hades cannot be stopped, Jane wouldn't become a governess at Thornfield Hall and Mr. Rochester, and the mysterious attic dweller, might not have become figments in the mind and imagination of Charlotte Bronte.

Do check out *The Eyre Affair* and help Thursday Next save the classic Jane Eyre.

(See my Tip # 24 re Dual Titles)

….and others not so wonderful, like receiving the news that, after two arthroscopic surgeries on my right knee, the MRI showed that I had "bone-on-bone" degeneration and loss of cartilage and would ultimately require a complete right knee replacement. I wasn't quite ready to think about that yet. I was still doing PT for my fractured left ankle and had previously been receiving SYN VISC injections into both knees. That used to be my panacea. Like prednisone, my

244

miracle drug, the SYN VISC shots made my entire body feel good, temporarily erased the constant pain of my osteoarthritis. Now, what would I do?

"Do it with passion, or not at all."

~ Rosa Nochette Carey

FEBRUARY 2004: The Passion of Artemisia by Susan Vreeland

Going to Aruba always seemed to make everything alright...Pina Coladas, warm trade winds, saltwater, good-bye aches and pains on our 'Happy Island.' Before our family departed in February, we had the most colorful, artistic discussion of Renaissance/Baroque, father-daughter painters, Orazio and Artemesia Gentileschi, followers of Caravaggio, famous for "chiaroscuro" – the subtle balance of light and shadow. Susan Vreeland deftly portrayed their lives and Artemesia's struggles in her novel, *The Passion of Artemesia.* This work provoked a resounding thumbs-up by both the wishful and the tried-and-true artists in the group.

"We are all born ignorant, but one must work hard to remain stupid."

~ Benjamin Franklin

MARCH 2004: Benjamin Franklin by Walter Isaacson

I loved reading, *Benjamin Franklin*, by Walter Isaacson in March 2004. I felt so smart, so full of facts and little tidbits of trivia that I would, most surely, use against Ted in our nightly competitions watching **JEOPARDY!** (Category: Famous Quotes. Answer: He said: "Early to bed and early to rise makes a man healthy, wealthy, and wise." Question: "Who is Benjamin Franklin?")

Benjamin Franklin was born on January 17, 1706, in Boston, MA. He died in Philadelphia, PA on April 17, 1790. He was an American polymath and one of the Founding Fathers of the United States. Franklin was a leading author, printer, political theorist, politician, Freemason, postmaster, scientist, inventor, humorist, civic activist, statesman, and diplomat. But of all that he was, and all that he said, my husband will always remember Benjamin Franklin as being the man who uttered the old truism (from *Poor Richard's Almanack*), "Fish and visitors stink after three days." My Theo decreased the time to two days.

*"There are 10,000 books in my library, and it
will keep growing until I die. This has
exasperated my daughters, amused my friends, and
baffled my accountant. If I had not picked up this
habit in the library long ago, I would have more
money in the bank today; I would not be richer."*

~ Pete Hamill

*~ Donna Diamond, The Ultimate Hard-core,
High-handed, Card-carrying Bibliophilist has
embraced this quote and made it her own.*

APRIL 2004: Snow in August by Pete Hamill

For our third annual Long Island Reads – "One Island-One
Book" Selection in April, the Committee chose *Snow in
August*, by an established writer, journalist and former editor
of the *Daily News*, Pete Hamill.

Why *Snow in August?*

The author was born in Brooklyn and is a true New Yorker
and library lover.

(<u>Note</u>: This was before the L.I. Reads Committee narrowed
its author search to those authors who specifically come from
Long Island or whose book takes place on Long Island).

The author/name recognition provided a special appeal that
attracted new library users, especially the men in our
communities. The combination of mysticism and reality in
Snow in August appealed to young adults, as well as adults, and
the book is on school reading lists. It is a coming-of-age
story that shows the power of reading, and how a child's
imagination is stimulated by reading Captain Marvel comics.

I met Pete Hamill on two occasions, at Flushing Library in November 2003 and again at Northport Library in April 2004. Both times the author praised libraries because they "help you dream." He, likewise, gave credit to J.K. Rowling for what she did to get children reading *Harry Potter*.

"I've never quite believed that one chance is all I get."

~ Anne Tyler

MAY 2004: The Amateur Marriage by Anne Tyler

Anne Tyler's books always seem to "hit the nail on the head" when it comes to targeting a particular subject with a keen, unprejudiced eye. Her novels usually take place where she resides, in the Roland Park neighborhood of Baltimore, Maryland. This one, her 16th, begins, "Anyone in the neighborhood could tell you how Michael and Pauline first met."

Michiko Kakutani, writing for *The New York Times*, has called *The Amateur Marriage*, "An ode to the complexities of familial love." It is December 1941, and parades still marked the excitement of the Second World War, especially to Pauline Barclay, the exotic, non-Catholic lady in the red coat, who jumped off the streetcar and collided with a lamppost. Pauline sets Michael Anton's Polish world aflutter when she bursts into the family grocery store, that Michael works with his mother, complaining of a slight cut to her head. That's all that I will write on this book jacket. You, the reader, must decide for yourself if you will follow this couple's courtship and marriage.

Anne Tyler does not do book tours, and she rarely gives interviews. She won the Pulitzer Prize for Fiction with *Breathing Lessons* in 1989 and was a finalist for the Pulitzer in 1982 with *Dinner at the Homesick Restaurant* and *The Accidental Tourist* in 1985.

Nick Siciliano led the discussion of Anne Tyler's, *The Amateur Marriage*, in May 2004. I was in Huntington Hospital, having

250

a total right knee replacement. I would much rather have been in Baltimore with Tyler's Pauline and Michael as they tried to maneuver their way through the pretense of a marriage.

I wasn't getting any better. I don't want to say that the knee replacement was a "piece of cake," but, in retrospect, the pain I experienced from the knee surgery was nothing compared to the overwhelming trauma and re-awakening of my MS symptoms, which were now in full-blown attack mode. No part of my body escaped the wrath of the pins and needles, the excruciating tingling, the dizziness, and the numbness. I was assigned a pain management specialist to help me monitor and get a grip on the pain. I tried to be present in the moment, but I couldn't focus. I was on Oxycontin, and my doctor even considered me as a possible candidate for medical marijuana. My children laughed at the thought of me playing mah jongg with my Aruba pals as we passed the pipe? the joint? the lollipop? across the table.

It didn't happen.

But I can tell you what did happen in my medical life between May 2004, and March 2005. My family encouraged me to seek out a new doctor, a neurologist. I hadn't been seeing any specialists for years for my chronic disease because I had been feeling so well. There is an MS Support Group called, "But You Look So Well." That was me, poster child and president. No one would ever guess just by looking at me that I suffered from Multiple Sclerosis. I was blessed. I didn't limp or walk with a cane. My eyesight (between attacks) was fine, and my memory, like an elephant's, seemed to be intact and, although I had frequent urinary tract infections, I wasn't incontinent.

But I was in terrible pain.

In June 2004, I made an appointment to see an MS specialist at NYU Hospital. We were starting from scratch again with my medical history. Dr. Joseph Herbert asked me questions, observed my gait, and performed a litany of neurological tests. He called for lab work and an MRI of the brain and cervical spine.

252

In July 2004, I underwent a five-day infusion of Solumedrol at Huntington Hospital, but that had no effect. I started a high dose of oral prednisone. My eyeballs hurt, and my vision was blurry. I was dizzy, and my legs felt as if I was dragging concrete weights.

I returned to Dr. Herbert, who watched me walk again, and said he believed that I was suffering from more than just Multiple Sclerosis. He wanted me to see a neurosurgeon because the MRIs that were taken showed signs of acute stenosis of the cervical spine and would require immediate surgery.

And, he wanted me to start taking Avonex, one of the common 'ABC' drugs (as they are called), for MS patients. I was to begin a regimen of weekly injections into my thigh. The Avonex regimen came with several pamphlets and a video that described the bad side effects (flu-like symptoms, depression, thoughts of suicide), as well as the good health that would result, (fewer and less severe exacerbations).

After three months of taking the Avonex injections and suffering debilitating side effects and great sadness, I decided to take my chances and take myself off further treatments.

I went to an orthopedic specialist at Mount Sinai Hospital in New York who, in turn, took four more MRIs (cervical spine, thoracic spine, lumbar spine, brain) to corroborate his diagnosis of severe stenosis. From the pain management doctor to my two neurologists, my GP, orthopedist, and neurosurgeon, all doctors agreed that I should have surgery to fuse vertebrae C3-C7.

Instead, I turned to prayer. People of science don't give much credence to miracle cures, but I became walking proof. My brother-in-law, Jim D'Amico, had special "Healing Masses" said for me and added my name to a prayer circle, so that a rosary was said on my behalf. My pal, Libby Canova, did the same for me with her prayer group.

253

Our prayers were answered.

From May 2004 to March 2005, I can sum up my (medical) life in the following way:

Pain	*Tingling & Numbness*
Doctors	*Blood work*
MRIs	*Pain*
Avonex	*Sleep*
Pain	*Duragesic/Fentanyl Patch(es)*
Spinal Stenosis	*Dizziness*
Depo Medrol Infusions	*Multiple Sclerosis*
Pain	*Pain*
Pins & Needles	*Overwhelmingly tired*
Prednisone	*Eyeball pain*
Urinary Tract Infections	*SADNESS (never the "D" word = depression)*

"MY MIRACLE AT ARASHI"

The next year I would read Jacqueline Mitchard's, The Breakdown Lane, which aptly describes the sudden and paralyzing fallout of an exacerbation of Multiple Sclerosis and its repercussions.

We, in 'The Literary Gallery,' welcomed back one of our most dedicated members, John McGuinness. After a debilitating car accident and long hospital stay, our big, strapping Irishman, returned to our monthly gatherings at Border's Books & Music. During his lengthy recuperation, we tried to keep both his spirits and his reading up by sending him cards, balloons, and the current books that we were discussing.

John would return the favor in May 2004 when he visited me at St. Charles Hospital, where I was convalescing from a total right knee replacement. Big John was among the first to put a smile on my face post-op. The knee surgery was a complete success; however, the trauma of the operation led to one of the worst exacerbations of

254

my Multiple Sclerosis that I had experienced since my attack in Disney World (Florida) in 1978 when Dani was three, Brett one.

I was totally brazen back in those days of 2004, completely forgetting that I had a chronic condition and talking myself into believing that I was invincible, that I was cured. I hadn't seen a neurologist since the mid-1990s. My gentle hand-holder, "I don't want you to go on any of the ABC drugs for MS because you are not a viable candidate," specialist, Dr. Mortati, was slowly easing himself out of the practice and heading for retirement. Besides, I had been practically asymptomatic for so many years. Why would I even suspect for a moment that I wouldn't glide through my surgery the way one breezes through the drive-in of a fast-food chain? But, when the anesthesia and the morphine wore off, the painful pins and needles, the facial neuralgia and the crazy jumping beans that maniacally danced on my chest and pirouetted over my extremities, had taken up full-time residence in my body. Montel Williams, in one of his books, I think it was Living Well Emotionally: Break Through to a Life of Happiness, co-written with William Doyle, so aptly described the pressure and the palpitations around my heart as the "MS hug."

I was placed on a self-administering morphine drip, and a pain management doctor was assigned to my case. I was on so many drugs (uppers, downers, sleep aids, and pain killers), they would have made an addict grin and say, "Thank You." My unrelenting MS attack would last almost one- and one-half years, (so much for relapsing-remitting Multiple Sclerosis). The severe Spinal Stenosis, which the doctor said I probably had had for more than twenty years, mimicked many of my MS symptoms, (tingling, pins, and needles of the feet).

I was completely oblivious to this new illness, living in "Donna Land" again, (but oh, what a wonderful place to be!)

255

I was so sick, so tired and ready to give up, just get the operation over with. Every one of the six doctors who reviewed the seven or eight MRIs that I had taken of the spine and neck agreed that, if I didn't go forward with the surgery, then I would end up in a wheelchair. I had lost a good deal of weight (an ironic twist for me, the eternal dieter, the perpetual Jenny Craig, Atkins, Slim-Fast, Neutra System, Weight Watchers yoyo poster girl,) and had trouble walking and standing for any length of time. Ted, my very necessary "patient advocate," urged me to procrastinate, hold off with this "irreversible" operation until we returned from our beloved Aruba, "Our Home Away from Home."

Looking back at those dreadful days of 2004-2005, I'm happy and relieved that I agreed to wait.

"On a scale of 1 — 10, (with 10 being the worst pain,) what is your pain level?" I was asked daily. For months my reply was 11+. Then I experienced "My Miracle at Arashi" within days of our arrival in Aruba, this very "Happy Island" of sun, sand, saltwater beaches, and Pina Coladas. My scheduled operation was canceled, thanks to the love and perseverance of my family and to my new-found author, "psychic" friend, Saralee Rosenberg, (Dear Neighbor, Drop Dead, Fate, and MS Fortune,), (ironic how the MS in Saralee's title had so aptly pertained to my illness,) Claire Voyant, and A Little Help From Above). Saralee and I met over lattes at Barnes & Noble (Huntington) and discussed the possibility of her coming to our book group, 'The Literary Gallery,' to talk about her new novel. During the course of our impromptu "get-to-know-you" conversation about books and writing and family, Saralee told me that she often "hears" voices in her head, telling her what to do. She asked if I would be receptive to these directives. Then she "listened" to the voices that would direct me to

the "right" doctor, (Donald? Donaldson? Ronald?) She "heard" that I might have to travel to reach this doctor, (perhaps as far as Massachusetts). The sounds in my friend, Saralee's head, would not be silenced. The very next day, she called me early in the morning and told me to sit down. She had found him, my Donald/ Donaldson/ Ronald, and I didn't even have to go very far. The Massachusetts she had distinctly heard in her ear was where this doctor Donald/ Donaldson/ Ronald had interned, Mass General Hospital. And best yet, he was a neurosurgeon currently practicing at a very prestigious New York City hospital. Sacre Bleu!!!! Eureka!!! Bingo!!! I don't know which one of us was more excited about this news. We laughed at this very special moment that we had shared. I knew I would make an appointment to see this doctor, but how would I respond when his receptionist/secretary asked who had referred me to Donald/Donaldson/Ronald? Do I say my "psychic" recommended him? Or do I say that my friend "heard a voice?"

Just think about that, dear reader, and what you might think my answer was. In any case, I can never thank her enough for what she "heard," my very funny, clever friend, Saralee Rosenberg, with the sardonic wit, whose books capture the very essence of what it means to be human and living on Long Island, what it means to deal with the day- to- day tedium of life. She is a veritable modern-day Irma Bombeck.

Oh, and another thing I forgot to tell you. Saralee had a pounding headache from all that she "heard" about me. As we exchanged family pictures, she nonchalantly asked, "Who is the twin?" Gasp! "It's me," I mumbled. And then she looked at a photo of Lily, my first-born granddaughter. She looked hard at the picture and then told me Lily was an "old soul." The next day my daughter, Dani, found just a single "onesie" at 'Baby Gap' in a six-month-old size. Written across the front were the words, "Old Soul."

257

"The bad news is time flies. The good news is you're the pilot."

~ Michael Althsuler

JUNE 2004: Aloft by Chang-Rae Lee

I returned to 'The Literary Gallery' in June to talk about Chang-Rae Lee's third novel, *Aloft*, a Long Island story that details the mid-life crisis of 59-year-old protagonist, Jerry Battle, whose Italian predecessors changed their name from Battaglia "for the usual reasons." My daughter, Dani, was present to cheer me on, along with Barbara Golden, Mary O'Donnell, Marie Mastellon, Diane McCarthy and Jill Mancini.

This was our second book by Korean American novelist, Chang-Rae Lee. We had previously discussed, *A Gesture Life*, in March 2000. A Professor of Creative Writing at Princeton, Lee introduces us to his retired, narcissistic Battle as he flies his single-engine plane (Donnie) over Long Island, and ruminates on the vicissitudes of life, on aging, youth, and death, on aloneness and human behavior. One reviewer called *Aloft* a "satire of family friction in the suburbs."

Lee published several books in the late 1990s and early 2000s which explored themes of identity and isolation. (Note: In April 2008, *Aloft* would become the unanimous choice of the Long Island Reads Committee because of its specific, map-located and referenced Long Island sites. It was our pleasure to host Chang-Rae Lee, an extremely intelligent and personable gentleman.)

"Most things break, including hearts. The lessons of life amount not to wisdom, but to scar tissue and callus."

~ *Wallace Stegner*

JULY 2004: Angle of Repose by Wallace Stegner

Wallace Earl Stegner was an American novelist, short story writer, environmentalist, and historian, often called "The Dean of Western Writers." He won the Pulitzer Prize for Fiction in 1972 for *Angle of Repose* and the National Book Award for Fiction in 1977 for *The Spectator Bird*.

But, for me, there was no *Angle of Repose* as there was for Wallace Stegner, our pick for July 2004. The group was divided in its enjoyment of this novel, which deals with wheelchair-bound, Lyman Ward, his estrangement from his family, and his decision to write about his frontier-era grandparents. The Atlantic Monthly described *Angle of Repose* as a "superb novel with an amplitude of scale and richness of detail altogether uncommon in contemporary fiction," and the Los Angeles Times wrote: "Two stories, past and present, merge to produce what important fiction must: a sense of the enhancement of life." *Angle of Repose* was selected by the Board of the Modern Library as one of the hundred best novels of the 20th century. Not so for me. It provided no comfort, no sense of peace nor eagerness to get back to the reading of it. I was still hurting. I needed a "comfortable read," a Rosamunde Pilcher or an Adriana Trigiani, a Fanny Flagg or a Ruth Reichl. (Refer to my Tip #10 - re Timing!)

"People perish. Books are immortal."

~ Robert Harris, Pompeii

AUGUST 2004: Pompeii by Robert Harris

Kristine Huntley, writing for *Booklist*, had the following to say
about *Pompeii*: "Popular thriller writer Harris (*Enigma*, 1995)
sets his sights on one of the most famous natural disasters in
history: the eruption of Mount Vesuvius in A. D. 79. It starts
innocently enough: two days before the eruption, Marcus
Attilius Primus, the engineer in charge of the massive Aqua
Augusta Aqueduct, is summoned to the estate of Ampilatus.
He is in the process of executing a slave for killing his fish.
Attilius finds sulfur in the water and immediately realizes the
problem is bigger than a few dead fish. With the approval of
the famous admiral Pliny, Attilius sails to Pompeii and treks
to the heart of the Aqua Augusta at the base of Mount
Vesuvius. Attilius discovers the blockage that threatens to
deprive a large chunk of the empire of water, but he is also
troubled by the strange natural occurrences that may portend
something far more serious than a blocked water supply.
With rich historical details and scientific minutiae, Harris
vividly brings to life the ancient world on the brink of
unspeakable disaster."

The book, *Pompeii*, for me, for Judy Phillips, Jackie Metzger,
Mary Ellen Hofmann, Carolyn Sciortino, and the others who
joined our discussion at Border's, was a difficult read,
ponderous and dense and easy to put down. Our meeting,
however, was enhanced by the many people who had traveled
to this buried city in Italy and brought this forgotten place
back to life. Ted and I would take a Mediterranean cruise in
2008 with my sister/cousin Karyn Connolly, and her
husband, Jim, (my cousin-in-law), Lynne and Paul Carlson

and Marlene and Stu Silbergleit. One of the stops took us to the ancient city of Pompeii to glance first-hand at these famous ruins. (Refer to my Tip #12 - re Travel/Destination Books).

"Two beheadings out of six wives is too many."

~ Henry VIII of England

SEPTEMBER 2004: The Other Boleyn Girl by Philippa Gregory

Power, incest, scandal, sisterly rivalry, beheadings in the court of Henry VIII of England, such is the stuff of *The Other Boleyn Girl*, by Philippa Gregory, "The Queen of Historical Fiction." In 2002, *The Other Boleyn Girl* won the Romantic Novel of the Year Award from the Romantic Novelists' Association and had been adapted into two separate films.

Mary, the sweet, blonde sister, portrayed by Scarlett Johansson, wins King Henry's favor when she is just fourteen and already married to one of his courtiers. Sister Anne, (Natalie Portman), will have none of it, and brother, George, joins in on the unscrupulous machinations that take place daily in the Tudor court.

I had completed a tapering down of my oral prednisone and ratcheted up the dosage of my Fentanyl (transdermal) patch, as we read and frolicked through *The Other Boleyn Girl*. Traipsing through court life with all of its restraints and demands, tight-fitting corsets and devious calculations, was a royal romp through history for all seventeen of us in 'The Literary Gallery.'

"Do yourself a favor. Before it's too late, without
thinking too much about it first, pack a pillow
and a blanket and see as much of the world as you
can. You will not regret it. One day it will be too
late."

~ *Jhumpa Lahiri, The Namesake*

OCTOBER 2004: The Namesake by Jhumpa Lahiri

In October we discussed *The Namesake*, by Jhumpa Lahiri, a compassionate story of the Ganguli family, as they moved from Calcutta, India to America, (Cambridge, MA, and ultimately to New York), after an arranged marriage back home, seeking acceptance and assimilation into their new culture. Originally published as a novella in the *New Yorker*, this first novel explores the clash of cultures, the diaspora of Bengalis living in America, and the parent-child relationship. The *Namesake* is a compelling look at a family trying to "fit in" while still retaining its heritage, much like "Doc" Hata in Chang-Rae Lee's, *A Gesture Life* (March 2000).

The book was widely received by the group.

Jhumpa Lahiri won the Pulitzer Prize for Fiction and the Hemingway Foundation/Pen Award in 2000 for *Interpreter of Maladies*, her collection of nine stories.

"For years I would get up every day and go back (in imagination) to rubble-torn Berlin, little suspecting that I would see it in my own city."

~ *Joseph Kanon*

NOVEMBER 2004: The Good German by Joseph Kanon

The Good German is Joseph Kanon's third novel. Set in Berlin in the late 1940s, following the collapse of the Third Reich, Jake Geismar, former Berlin correspondent for CBS, has secured one of the coveted press slots for the Potsdam Conference. The book opens with a graphic tour of the bombed-out city. I read that the irony of that wasn't lost on Manhattanite Kanon, who lives only a few miles from the destroyed World Trade Center.

Kanon turned to fiction-writing after a long career as an executive in the publishing industry. His novels are primarily set in the late 1940s and early 1950s, a period that fascinates him, and combine elements of the crime novel and suspense and deal with issues of individual and collective moral conflict.

Joseph Kanon's, *The Good German*, (November 2004) was "a great read about post-WWII Berlin on four levels: suspense, history, mystery, and romance…." (42) The movie adaptation of *The Good German* starring George Clooney, Cate Blanchett, and Tobey Maguire, however, was as disappointing on four levels: suspense, history, mystery, and romance, as the book was a great read.

In June, 2012, 'The Literary Gallery' was asked by Hillary Tisman, Marketing Manager, Atria Books, (a Division of

Simon & Schuster Publishing), to write a "Reading Group Guide" for Joseph Kanon's, *Istanbul Passage*, (a "fin de guerre thriller," according to Jason Goodwin writing for the *New York Times*, Sunday Book Review and published on June 1, 2012), in exchange for free ARCs ("Advance Reader's Copy") of the book. What fun it was for sixteen of us: Elvira Lubrano, Deb Cunningham, Barbara Golden, Judy Phillips, Ruth Ann Trimarco, Helaine Bank, Michele Bisom, Kathy Kreytak, Jill Mancini, Maureen Spisak, Ellen Davis, Pat DeSilva, Kathy Dreschler, Mary Ellen McCarthy, Belle Baxter, and me, to brainstorm over coffee and cookies at the Elwood Library and create 'Questions For Discussion.' I must say, we were quite clever, indeed!

"No act of kindness, no matter how small, is ever wasted."

~ Aesop

DECEMBER 2004: Before You Know Kindness by Chris Bohjalian

I'd like to tell you, dear reader, what an amazing person, as well as author, Chris Bohjalian is and how Border's Books & Music made it possible for us each to have a personalized, signed copy of *Before You Know Kindness*. I had made arrangements to have a telephone conference call from the author's home directly to the store in Commack during our discussion on Monday, December 13, 2004. We collected $21.75 from every person who was interested in receiving a personal, autographed copy. We would then purchase the books from Border's, and Border's would handle the postage and shipping to and from Chris Bohjalian's home. He, in turn, would address a greeting to every one of the seventeen people (moi, inclue) who requested one. From Connie Sabatino and Elvira Lubrano, Rita Silver and Ellen Davis, to Judy Phillips and Barbara Golden, from Mary Ellen Hofmann and Kathy Drechsler, to Carol Sciortino and Mary O'Donnell, to Jill Mancini and Mary Ellen McCarthy and from Nick Siciliano and John McGuinness, and my own Danielle Westfall, money was collected and books were signed. We were given more than one month to read Bohjalian's novel of the Seton Family, three generations who met annually at their home in New Hampshire to play tennis and swim and try to "just be." (Quote from *Before You Know Kindness*).

Before You Know Kindness is trademark Bohjalian, all the way from the family squabbles and discord to the attention to

266

current divisive issues in America, such as gun control, animal rights, and vegetarianism. Our discussion was lively, and our telephone chat with the author reinforced his appeal to the many avid and intelligent readers in our group.

What a delightful way to close the calendar on our reading year 2004!

Chapter 9

Of Kites and Plots and Crows and Devils (2005)

"Quiet is turning down the volume knob on life.
Silence is pushing the OFF button."

~ *Khaled Hosseini, The Kite Runner*

JANUARY 2005: The Kite Runner by Khaled Hosseini

The Kite Runner became a favorite of reading groups with the release of the paperback edition in 2004. Set in Afghanistan and California, it focuses on the friendship between its two protagonists, Hassan and Amir. Hassan is the young hair-lipped kite runner of the title, the Hazara servant of Amir's wealthy father. The story spans several decades and became part of a growing list of popular novels and non-fiction on Middle Eastern cultures. It is Hosseini's debut novel and topped the *New York Times* charts for more than two years.

The author, an Afghan immigrant who became a doctor in California, wrote the story after he learned that the Taliban had outlawed kite flying in Afghanistan. Having grown up with the sport, he found the ban to be particularly cruel.

The Kite Runner is a story of friendship, father/son relationships, love, betrayal, and loss, not just of innocence but of a country so once beloved. While it garnered rave reviews in the United States, parts of the plot were subjected to controversy in Hosseini's former country.

Many pages in my copy of the book still display traces of the tears I shed while reading this beautifully written, poignant "love story." Hosseini's characters live with me still.

The Kite Runner was made into a movie in 2007.

"....nor had I understood til then how the
shameless vanity of utter fools can so strongly
determine the fate of others."

~ *Philip Roth, The Plot Against America*

FEBRUARY 2005: The Plot Against America by Phillip Roth

"Phillip Roth's huge, inflammatory, painfully moving new novel draws upon a persistent theme in American life: "It can't happen here." .....*The Plot Against America* brings the sum of Roth's books to more than two dozen. It may well arouse more controversy than all the rest combined."

- Jonathan Yardley, *The Washington Post*

"A terrific political novel.... sinister, vivid, dreamlike.... creepily plausible.... You turn the pages, astonished and frightened."

- *The New York Times* Book Review ("What If It Happened Here?" by, Paul Berman,) Oct. 3, 2004.

"Too ingeniously excruciating to put down.... Intimately observed characters in situations fraught with society's deepest, most bitter tensions."

- *Newsweek*

In *The Plot Against America*, Roth has created an alternate universe, a revisionist look at history, as Dr. Ben Baglio has done in his book, *A String of Pearls*, (July 2003). It was chilling and frightening to read about an America where the anti-Semitic, Hitler-loving, Charles Lindbergh, was President of the United States. It was difficult and painful to envision our country as a place where Fascist propaganda, in the guise of

270

patriotism, was flaunted and paraded on the same streets where the Jews of Weequahic in Newark, New Jersey, walked.

The Plot Against America was readily received in our book clubs as a defined example of the writings of one of America's foremost and critically acclaimed authors, Phillip Roth. On another level, it left each of us with a dread that such events could actually exist in "The Home of the Brave and the Land of The Free."

"Laurie (Pye) was just one more dropped stitch in
a family tapestry already full of holes."

~ Mary Lawson, Crow Lake

MARCH 2005: Crow Lake by Mary Lawson

Set in rural Ontario, *Crow Lake* is narrated by Kate Morrisson, one of four siblings who try to navigate her isolated farm life after the death of her parents in a car accident.

In a home where understatement was the rule of the house and "thou shall not emote" was the Eleventh Commandment, Lawson's story of sibling rivalry and misunderstanding, of coming to terms with change and finding peace and closure, is a beautifully written tale of the choices we make and the roads we choose to walk. Any reader of *Crow Lake* will feel the chill of the Canadian winter, and the heaviness of things left unsaid. Mary Lawson has written a very unsettling yet compelling debut novel.

"Books are the plane, and the train, and the road.
They are the destination and the journey."

~Anna Quindlen

APRIL 2005: Travels with Charley: In Search of America by John Steinbeck (* A Long Island Reads Selection)

We, the Long Island Reads Committee, chose *Travels with Charley: In Search of America*, by John Steinbeck as our pick for all of Nassau and Suffolk Counties to read in April 2005, during National Library Week. In our Program Guide, we wrote:

"In one of his last works, the Nobel Prize-winning author recounts his trip across the United States with his Standard Poodle, Charley, in a custom-made camper named Rocinante. Setting out from Sag Harbor, L.I., Steinbeck is determined to travel across the continent in an attempt to regain the understanding of the land and people he wrote about so intimately and felt he had lost touch with over the years. Travel with the author and his engaging dog and discover how much and how little has changed."

We held a special all-day event at Nassau Community College, which featured a short film about John Steinbeck in Sag Harbor. I moderated a panel of friends who knew Mr. Steinbeck while he lived on Long Island, as they reminisced about the author.

We took a culinary tour as Chef Charlie taught us how to make a variety of regional American cuisine from the Pacific Northwest to the Florida Keys.

Other programming events included "traveling with your digital camera," which gave tips for capturing lifetime moments from professional photographers.

I hope the late, great author, John Steinbeck, would have appreciated how much we tried to recapture his one-man, one-dog account of his trans-American expedition.

"Books may well be the only magic."

~ Alice Hoffman

MAY 2005: The Devil in the White City: Murder, Magic, and Madness at the Fair That Changed America by Erik Larson

The New York Times Book Review noted on Sunday, March 30, 2014, page 24, "Larson's true-crime account of the 1893 World's Fair has been a best-seller since 2003; after 292 weeks on the paperback non-fiction list, it's at No. 12."

QUESTION:

What do the following have in common?

1. Chicago circa 1893
2. The Ferris Wheel
3. *Daniel H. Burnham (de facto Ambassador of the fair)
4. Buffalo Bill Cody and Annie Oakley
5. Belly Dancers
6. Aunt Jemima's Pancakes
7. Shredded Wheat
8. Pabst Blue Ribbon Beer
9. Juicy Fruit Gum

10. Melvil (Melville Louis) Dewey's Vertical File and the Dewey Decimal System
11. Thomas Edison
12. *Dr. H.H. Holmes (Herman Webster Mudgett, the titular "devil" in Burnham's "white city").

ANSWER:

They all existed simultaneously at the 1893 World's Columbian Exposition, the great architect, Daniel H. Burnham, creating, while serial killer, H.H. Holmes, savagely murdered between twenty and two hundred young women in his "Hotel of Horrors."

The Devil in the White City is filled with a plethora of information on the latest inventions, styles, foods, and dances. Reading this book made us all feel intelligent.

Note: In 2010, Leonardo DiCaprio and Production Companies, Appian Way and Double Feature, acquired the rights to Erik Larson's 2003 blockbuster, *The Devil in the White City*. Deadline.com reported in August 2015 that DiCaprio and director Martin Scorsese would team up on a film version after securing a deal from Paramount. DiCaprio will take on the role of the diabolical yet charismatic serial killer, Dr. H. H. Holmes.

Tip #25 - Deciphering the Title

Try to decipher the title of the book that you are discussing. Do you think the title aptly describes the story contained therein? YES! to *The Devil in the White City: Murder, Magic and Madness at the Fair That Changed America*, by Erik Larson and years prior, a resounding YES! to *Atonement*, by Ian McEwan and *Wait Till Next Year*, by Doris Kearns Goodwin. Sometimes the title is appealing but quite misleading, for example, *The Master Butcher's Singing Club*, by Louise Erdrich (title not discussed here). And sometimes you have to wait a long time until you discover the meaning or find a clue to the title, (i.e., *Snow in August*, by Pete Hamill).

"Your library is your paradise."

~ *Desiderius Erasmus*

JUNE 2005: Paradise Alley by Kevin Baker

Set in Ireland and New York in 1863, *Paradise Alley* is an example of historical fiction at its best. In this follow-up to Dreamland, the second book in his "City of Fire" Trilogy, Kevin Baker methodically researched a "tumultuous moment in the record of the Civil War: The 1863 New York riots that followed President Lincoln's decision to create a draft." (Tom Keogh for Amazon.com.) The National Conscription Act required that all able-bodied men be drafted but simultaneously made provisions for any rich man's son with $300.00 to buy an exemption from services in the Union Army. "As many of the Irish saw it, poor white workingmen like themselves were being forced to fight for the freedom of blacks, who would then come north and take their jobs. They burned federal property and attacked Republican newspaper offices, looted stores and wrecked private homes, killed policemen and soldiers who tried to stop them -- and beat or butchered any African-American men, women or children who happened to cross their path." (43)

Kevin Baker, who was born in New Jersey in 1958, but grew up mostly in Massachusetts, and now resides in New York, has painted a vivid picture of the worst civil disturbance in American history, (with the exception of September 11, 2001). One hundred nineteen people died in three days (Monday-

Wednesday, July 13-15, 1863.) The movie, *The Gangs of New York*, captures some of that chaos and bloodshed.

Paradise Alley is a terrific read for any man or woman looking for a bit of New York City and American history and wanting to pit well-known Americans against fictitious Irish and Black men. Baker's characters are vividly drawn and hard to forget.

"A word is dead when it is said, some say. I say it just begins to live that day."

~Emily Dickinson

JULY 2005: Vanishing Act by Jodi Picoult

In *Vanishing Act*, Jodi Picoult once again tackles controversial issues: parental and platonic love, alcoholism, prison conditions, self-identity, and memory. She is a master (or rather, mistress) at presenting various points of view and shades of gray, producing a novel approximately every nine months.

Critics were mixed in their appraisal of this tale of the kidnapping of a child by one parent, who then disappears from the other parent. Our book group, likewise, was split about 50/50 in their like/dislike of this novel. (Refer to Jodi Picoult, Aug. 2001, June 2002.)

"Tears are words that need to be written."

~ Paulo Coelho

AUGUST 2005: Nightfall by Nelson DeMille

As a fellow Long Islander who appreciates Nelson DeMille's wit and dry humor, I was invited by Harborfields Library, specifically by my very knowledgeable, ever set-for-an-adventure, quick-witted, Teddy Roosevelt scholar, equestrian extraordinaire, and mutual Syosset High School graduate, Deborah Clark Cunningham, to do a Retrospective on the author on August 16, 2007. My presentation would serve as a prelude to the library's 'Writer's On The Vine' trip to Palmer Vineyards, on the North Fork of Long Island, at the conclusion of their 'Summer Reading Club.' I had devoured almost every book DeMille had ever written and was pleased to present a slide show of his life...." So Far." I say, "So Far" because, when I contacted Mr. De Mille's office regarding my invitation to hold a retrospective discussion of his life, he apparently chuckled and said, "usually a retrospective of one's life is done when that person is dead, and I AM VERY MUCH ALIVE!" He then generously wrote a letter to me, and to the other librarians at Harborfields Library, thanking us for our interest in his work and sent inscribed copies of *Plum Island* to each of us. (Refer to Nelson DeMille, July 1997).

My selection and discussion of *Nightfall* in August of 2005, however, was neither witty nor reflective. It was a stark and objective review of the events that surrounded the disappearance of TWA Flight 800.

In an exclusive interview with the "Literary Guild World of Authors" Newsletters in 2004, Nelson DeMille responded to the question: "When did you become interested in TWA Flight 800 as the subject of a potential book?" (*Nightfall*). His response: "I was on the east end of Long Island that night it happened, July 17, 1996. I didn't hear or see it, didn't know anything about it until about an hour later. In a chilling turn of events, my daughter had been on the same flight two nights before. Coincidentally, I had met the pilot a few years before. I was writing *Plum Island* at the time of the tragedy." DeMille then goes on to explain how he interviewed NYPD and FBI members who were on the Joint Terrorist Task Force and had worked the case. Two versions of what actually happened to TWA Flight 800 on July 17, 1996, emerged: the eyewitness and conspiracy group's belief that a rocket shot down the plane, and the official declaration that a malfunction, a spark in the central fuel tank, ignited the vapors and caused the explosion.

On that August Monday in 2005, our book discussion group was honored to host my late, dear friend, XE (Chi Sigma), retired Detective Lieutenant, Richard Mueller, from the Nassau County Police Dept., his partner, (and their spouses, which included my longtime friend, fellow XE wife and Aruba pal, Carol Mueller). As President of the New York State – Eastern Canada Chapter of the FBI National Academy, Rich had a first-hand personal relationship with fellow chapter members who were directly involved in the initial and ongoing investigation of Flight 800. The Chapter's Annual Conference at the Marriott's World Trade Center Hotel concluded at noon on the day of the Flight 800 disaster. "No one expected to be meeting each other again in less than eight hours," Rich said.

Questions still abound regarding the fatal crash of TWA Flight 800. As recently as 2013 (Sat., July 20, 2013,) the Stony Brook Film Festival aired a feature film, "TWA Flight 800," produced by print and broadcast journalist, Kristina Borjesson.

"Write it on your heart that every day is the best
day in the year."

~ *Ralph Waldo Emerson*

SEPTEMBER 2005: McNally's Bluff by Vince Lardo *(Guest Author)

My Godchild, Kirsten Elizabeth Francis Lamb O'Brien (frequently known as KEFLO), was responsible for bringing author, Vince Lardo, to Border's Books and Music to speak about his sixth Archy McNally mystery. *McNally's Bluff* was the latest in a long-running series Lardo had taken over from original author, Lawrence Sanders. Kirsten had read the book and promptly decided it would be a fun read from "Lardo Palm Beach's discreet inquirer." (The Palm Beach Post, Sunday, Aug. 1, 2004,) Arts & Entertainment, pg. 20, by Paul Lomartire, Palm Beach Post Staff Writer.

My sisters, Diane and Renee, joined in on the fun and, although we didn't serve cocktails or secretly dine in a famous Palm Beach restaurant, (your book club may want to,) we thoroughly enjoyed spending time with Vince Lardo, who was as charming and entertaining as his wealthy Floridian, "non gumshoe" investigator, Archy McNally.

"It was good to walk into a library again; it
smelled like home."

~Elizabeth Kostova, The Historian

OCTOBER 2005: The Historian by Elizabeth Kostova

Newsday proclaimed it, "the blockbuster book of the summer starring everyone's favorite vampire." (44) *USA Today* said, "First-time author sinks teeth into the legend of Dracula." (45) And the *New York Times Book Review* claimed Elizabeth Kostova was in search for the truth about Vlad the Impaler, the *Dracula of Myth*. (46)

Elizabeth Kostova spent more than ten years studying Dracula, doing much of her research at the University of Michigan's Hatcher Library. Inspired by childhood 'happily horrid' tales her father told her during trips to Europe, Kostova decided to write a fictional story about Vlad the Impaler, the erstwhile sadistic 15th-century Romanian prince. The completed manuscript created a publishing frenzy and media blitz, a substantial monetary advance, foreign rights, and multi-language printings.

The Historian is a dense, informational travelogue that takes the reader into libraries throughout Europe, from Amsterdam and Romania to Istanbul and Hungary. And Dracula lives on still 'Stayin' Alive' as he surveys his lands from the castle tower. (47) (Ibid.)

Our overall opinion of the book was that it was good, but not great. After all, compared with that other summer blockbuster in 2003, *The Historian* is about Kostova's search for a vampire, (like Bram Stoker's, *Dracula*), not Dan Brown's search for Jesus or The Holy Grail!!

Your book club might want to watch a Bela Lugosi 'Dracula' movie after your discussion of *The Historian* or, perhaps, create a creepy, hair-raising mood by playing the music from a horror movie, such as Bernard Herrmann wrote for, (the 'Shower Scene') in Alfred Hitchcock's, *Psycho* or Andrew Lloyd Webber's music to *The Phantom of the Opera*.

AND DON'T FORGET TO DIM THE LIGHTS!!

"Every dog must have his day."

~ *Jonathan Swift*

NOVEMBER 2005: The Cruelest Miles: The Heroic Story of Dogs and Men in a Race Against an Epidemic by Gay and Laney Salisbury

The time was 1925. The place was Nome, ("The town that wouldn't die") Alaska, a diphtheria epidemic, a life-saving serum, a blizzard and teams of dogs racing against time.

Freelance journalist, Laney Salisbury, and her cousin, Gay Salisbury, a former publishing executive, have written a fast-paced, heartwarming story of courage, canines and cold competing in a race that would ultimately be the precursor to the famed, 'Iditarod,' (the annual sled race commemorating the courageous Siberian Huskies who led dog teams in the famous 1925 Serum Run.) It's the story of three-year-old Balto, the lead dog on that grueling trek, that reached Nome first. A bronze statue honoring Balto can be found in New York City's Central Park.

Although somewhat slow starting, with background history of Alaska and the Gold Rush, the native population and Eskimo traditions, *The Cruelest Miles* is a book for travelers, dog lovers and readers who enjoy medical thrillers, (such as those Robin Cook has so deftly written: (i.e., *Coma, Shock, Toxin* or *Chromosome 6*), only the Salisbury cousins have chronicled actual events and not hypothetical scenarios.

Our book club gave Gay and Laney Salisbury's, The Cruelest Miles   4**** out of a possible 5*****).

285

"No dumb bastard ever won a war by going out and dying for his country. He won it by making some other dumb bastard die for his country,"

~ George S. Patton

DECEMBER 2005: 1776 by David McCullough

We concluded another year of great reading with *1776,* written by the distinguished historian, David McCullough. Within the pages of this compact historical gem, we encounter some of the colorful characters who marched for freedom, who fought and stood tall in the year of our nation's birth. We meet George Washington and George III, General Howe, Henry Knox, and Nathanael Greene, farmers and blacksmiths and a gang of ragamuffin recruits who had no uniforms, who wore shoes with holes, (if they wore any shoes at all,) the lot of whom suffered from the cold, hunger and disease. Desertion, cowardice, and defeat were rampant, and wooden teeth were "de rigueur."

McCullough paints from a vivid palette in *1776,* the book that was originally issued as the companion to his *John Adams.* (Cross Reference December 2001.)

Chapter 10

Jump Start Your Book Club & Literary Terms, Nancy Pearl's 'RULE OF 50', A Few of My Favorite Books

The Year I Became Mimi (2006)

I was the keynote speaker at two Book Club Summits in January 2006, compliments of the Long Island Reads Committee. Heralded at libraries throughout Nassau and Suffolk Counties as "JUMPSTART YOUR BOOK CLUB!"- Donna Diamond will provide you with the necessary tips and tools to do so.

I went to the Riverhead Library on Long Island on Tuesday, January 24, 2006, and followed up with the same presentation at the Bryant Library in Roslyn on Saturday, January 28th. The auditorium quickly filled with ladies and gentlemen who love to read, some of whom were already in book clubs but needed a little "oomph" and others who were eager to get some ideas on how to start a book club.

Deborah Clark Cunningham (Deb), (Head Reference Librarian at Harborfields Library in Greenlawn), worked with me in assembling a display of recommended books. I distributed handouts with tips I considered to be helpful. I talked about how I got started leading book discussions in 1996, about Oprah's influence and the fun of inviting an author to speak or do a telephone chat with the group.

We joked about the cartoon I passed out, "When Book Clubs Go Bad," and discussed some of the pitfalls of a bad book selection.

This was also the perfect opportunity for me to discuss literary terms and devices that have frequently plagued me during the course of my reading, for example:

1. **BILDUNGSROMAN** – (German): a novel concerned with the education, psychological and moral development and maturing of a young protagonist or a "coming-of-age" story in which character change is very important. The bildungsroman confronts its protagonist with views and dreams that are in marked contrast to those of the other characters in the story, then waits for him (i.e., Theo Decker in Donna Tartt's, *The Goldfinch* or her, (i.e., Scarlett O'Hara in Margaret Mitchell's, *Gone With the Wind*,) to navigate the wider world to achieve them.

2. **COZY MYSTERY** - Often referred to as "Cozies," are considered gentle books, a subgenre of crime fiction. According to both Nancy Pearl (Book Reviews KUOW Soundfocus@KUOW.org (1/12/09) and Cozy-Mystery.com), whatever blood and gore is, is minimal and always takes place off the page.

   The "Cozy Mystery" is most often set in a small town or village which makes it believable that the suspects know each other. It's the polar opposite of "noir" fiction, and there's usually an amateur female sleuth (à la Jessica Fletcher (Angela Lansbury), in 'Murder, She Wrote').

   According to Nancy Pearl, someone, she's not sure who, defined this type of book as "murder in a teacup."

The Brits were the first to perfect the "cozy mystery," most famously in the series of Miss Marple mysteries by Agatha Christie (or P.D. James's Inspector Adam Dalgliesh series).

3. **EPISTOLARY NOVEL** - Wikipedia, the free encyclopedia, states that an epistolary novel is a novel written as a series of documents. The usual form is letters, although diary entries, newspaper clippings, and other documents are sometimes used. Recently, electronic documents, such as recordings and radio, blogs, and emails, have also come into use.

The Guernsey Literary and Potato Peel Pie Society, by Mary Ann Schaffer and Annie Barrows, is a perfectly enjoyable epistolary novel, but it has a bit of the cozy mystery in it, too.

4. **ROMAN A CLEF** – (French) Literally, novel with a key. Dictionary.com defines roman à clef as a novel in which real people are depicted under fictitious names, for example, *Girl in a Blue Dress: A Novel Inspired by The Life and Marriage of Charles Dickens*, by Gaynor Arnold.

Wikipedia further states that the fictitious names in the novel represent real people, and the "key" is the relationship between the non-fiction and the fiction. This "key" may be produced separately by the author or implied through the use of epigraphs or other literary techniques.

I was exposed to the roman à clef during my courses in French Literature in college. The roman à clef, which was often used in writing satire, was created by Madeleine de Scudéry in the 17th century to provide a forum for her thinly veiled fiction featuring political and public figures. George

Orwell and Victor Hugo occasionally used the roman à clef format in their writing.

5. **DOPPELGANGER** – A ghostly double or counterpart of a living person. Also called "doubleganger" (Dictionary.com). Literally, a "double goer" is a look-alike or double of a living person who is sometimes portrayed as a harbinger of bad luck. (Wikipedia, the free encyclopedia). A doppelganger may be an evil twin, unknown to the original person, who causes mischief by confusing friends and relatives. (wisegeek.org). A famous example of a doppelganger in literature is Robert Louis Stevenson's, *The Strange Case of Dr. Jekyll and Mr. Hyde.*

*"It was the best of times, it was the worst of times,
it was the age of wisdom, it was the age of
foolishness, it was the epoch of belief, it was the
epoch of incredulity, it was the season of Light, it
was the season of Darkness, it was the spring of
hope, it was the winter of despair...."*

~ *Charles Dickens, A Tale of two Cities*

'The Literary Gallery' was on the move again in 2006. We
were welcomed by Debra Gaynor at the new Barnes & Noble
in Huntington and given the use of the very private meeting
room that was strictly reserved for author talks and book
signings.

Debra quickly became a book-loving friend and advisor,
introducing us to authors and providing books that we sold at
our yearly AAUW (American Association of University
Women) Book & Author Luncheons or author appearances
at the libraries I represented. It was the lovely Debra, in
beautiful sartorial garb, who made us aware of Book Expo
America, the four-day book fair held each year at the Jacob
Javits Center in New York City, and which became an annual
outing for me and Deborah Clark Cunningham (Deb). Book
Expo America (BEA) became a veritable feast for us, two
book-loving, suitcase-toting fanatics as we filled our satchels
with signed ARCs (Advance Readers Copies) from some of
our favorite authors and sat in on various book-related
seminars.

"Money can buy you a fine dog, but only love can make him wag his tail."

~ Kinky Friedman

JANUARY 2006: Sweetwater Creek by Anne Rivers Siddons

The first book selected at our new venue was *Sweetwater Creek*, by Anne Rivers Siddons, one of South Carolina's favorite low country authors. Sweet Water Creek tells the tale of eleven-year-old Emily Parmenter and her bond with a legendary spaniel, a Sweetwater Boykin named Elvis, after her mother disappears and her older brother dies. Perhaps, as memorable for its sense of place as much as for its storyline, Pat Conroy, himself a South Carolina author, wrote, "*Sweetwater Creek* made me laugh out loud and cry in secret, the way great literature always does when it is written with passion and flair."(47)

It was a fitting choice for us as we settled down after the holiday hustle and bustle.

The blizzard of snow and ice in February 2006 forced us to cancel our regularly scheduled gathering in favor of nestling close to home and curling up with a good book by the fire.

NOTE: Our baby shower for my Dani at Divino's on New York's east side on that snowy, February Saturday afternoon, quickly became a fabulous three-day event as we frantically searched for hotel rooms for our out-of-town guests and snowed-in family members looking to take the Long Island Expressway home.

"War is cruelty. There is no use trying to reform
it. The crueler it is, the sooner it will be over."

~ *William Tecumseh Sherman*

MARCH 2006: The March by E. L. Doctorow

So, when we marched into March to discuss E. L.
Doctorow's *The March*, we were prepared for General William
Tecumseh Sherman's march through the south in 1864.
Doctorow's ignorance of quotation marks, and insertion of
quirky fictional characters, side by side Civil War legends,
makes for an interesting in-depth critique of this National
Book Critics Circle Award Winner and Pen/Faulkner Award
Winner.

"Babies are bits of stardust blown from the hand
of God. Lucky the woman who knows the pangs
of birth, for she has held a star."

~ *Larry Barretto*

It was a joyous time for our family in the spring of 2006-- the
birth of our first grandchild, a blue/green-eyed, fair-haired,
chubby-cheeked beauty, a baby girl named Lily Diamond
Westfall. Crying loud and clear, despite the two fingers
(pointer and middle) that she placed in her mouth upon her
arrival, she would quickly follow in her Grand-mère,
"Mimi's" footsteps being already blessed with a library of her
own Golden Books.

293

"That's the thing about books. They let you travel without moving your feet."

~ Jhumpa Lahiri

APRIL 2006: Amagansett by Mark Mills *(A Long Island Reads Selection 2006)

Mark Mills, a British citizen who lives happily across the pond, easily won the hearts of our Long Island Reads Committee Members when he wrote about a people and a place so close to home for all of us.

Not quite a love story or a crime thriller but, perhaps, a little of both, in his debut novel Mills has created a study of an old community, a fishing village in the years immediately after WWII. History is important, as well as a sense of place. Relationships are explored, and class and prestige impact events in the novel. Who are the "outsiders" and can justice prevail in a town so intent on maintaining the status quo?

Mills wrote his story over three years and at least five lengthy "research trips," a phrase which invariably drew a wry smile from his wife. (from L.I. Reads 2006 Reader's Guide--- "A Message from Mark Mills.") The South Fork of Long Island, the omnipresent ocean, the geography and the isolation of the area filled him with a sense of calm. Any reader of *Amagansett*, be it fisherman or boatman, Long Island history buff or crime aficionado, will be drawn into this small fishing community on the South Fork (of L.I.) where "his characters are buffeted by the elements of nature, class, war and their personal memories and demons." (48)

"Snow Flower was my old same for life. I had a greater and deeper love for her than I could ever feel for a person who was my husband."

~ *Lisa See, Snow Flower, and the Secret Fan*

MAY 2006: Snow Flower and the Secret Fan by Lisa See

My reading mirrored my life in May of 2006. My new granddaughter shared the same name (Lily) as the protagonist in Lisa See's novel, *Snowflower and the Secret Fan*. Lily shared a silk fan, a friendship and a poem in "nu shu" (women's writing), with Snowflower as they became "laotongs" (old sames) at the delicate age of seven.

Nineteenth-century China, Ted's ninety or more business trips to Mainland China, and Lisa See, a very receptive author, who chatted freely with us from her home in California, all converged in *Snowflower and the Secret Fan*. This author quickly became a favorite of our and other reading groups. We discussed foot-binding and mother love, atonement and regret, and learned a lot about 19th-century matchmakers. We compared the phonetic nature of "nu shu" and how it could easily be taken out of context and misunderstood, just as our present-day use of email and instant messaging, because of a lack of tone of voice or facial and body gestures, can be misconstrued.

Lisa See, well-spoken and very intelligent, a petite redhead with freckles and one-quarter Chinese, proudly writes and talks about her family heritage. We followed up our first telephone call with the author, who so graciously accommodated us with a SKYPE chat from her home on the West Coast. She had just come off the tennis court. It was

12:00 Noon for us in New York, just 9:00AM California time. Thank you, Lisa.

When we read *Snowflower and the Secret Fan*, I brought in fortune cookies from the Chinese restaurant and served tea on placemats that described each of the Chinese symbols and the corresponding year of birth. Mood music played softly in the background. (Refer to my Tip #9 - Contact an author, Tip #21 - Food and Tip #22 - Mood music).

> *"You know you've read a good book when you turn the last page and feel a little as if you have lost a friend."*

JUNE 2006: Lucia, Lucia by Adriana Trigiani

She isn't easy to forget, this powerful "force of nature," this "larger than life" personality, this generous beyond everything else, funny, kind, good-hearted, smiling woman with big hair and an even bigger heart. Critics from the *Washington Post* to the *New York Times*, to *People Magazine,* have described Adriana's novels as "tiramisu for the soul," "sophisticated and wise," and "dazzling."

I first met this very prolific author at a book signing at the Smithtown Library on Long Island where she had come to speak about her newest work…. or so we thought. A packed audience consisting of men and women, young and old, filled the seats and crowded into the standing room only aisles. She told jokes, she kibitzed with people and asked about their families, and after more than an hour, finally began to talk about her books. When people lined up for the book signing, the library personnel, who were instructed to close by 8:45PM, finally relented and succumbed to the flow of Adriana's warmth and determination to address each and every person who took the time to wait in line to talk to her about their life, their children, their parents or their enjoyment of her many books, *Lucia, Lucia, The Queen of the Big Time, Rococo*, and *Cooking with my Sisters*. They came to hear her talk about Big Stone Gap, the small coal-mining town in southwest Virginia where she was raised in a big Italian family. *Big Stone Gap* would be the first of a planned trilogy of novels that revolve around her strong central character, Ave Maria Mulligan, and her love interest, Jack MacChesney, and her quirky friends, sexpot Iva Lou, the chain-smoking Bookmobile librarian, big-hearted Fleeta Mullins and her musical friend, Theodore Tipton. Subsequent to *Big Stone Gap, Big Cherry Holler*, and *Milk Glass Moon*, were released. *Home to Big Stone Gap* turned her trilogy into a quartet.

I remember what I was wearing as I stood in line to meet Adriana that night. A crème colored suede blazer and matching slacks, a black turtleneck sweater, and black suede shoes completed my ensemble, which Adriana perused with a critical eye. She called me a model and asked how she could inscribe my book. I told her my name was Donna Diamond, and for the last ten years, it has been my great pleasure to lead monthly book discussion groups at Barnes & Noble and at Harborfields Library in Greenlawn. I also told her that I was a long-standing and proud member of the Long Island Reads Committee. Then I asked if she would consider doing a telephone chat with one or both of my book clubs. She politely declined, citing prior engagements, then promptly invited my book clubs and me to join her for lunch at Valdino's, one of her favorite little Italian restaurants in the West Village. I told her that each of my two book clubs consisted of almost thirty people. That large number neither intimidated nor deterred her from extending an invitation to join her for lunch on Sunday, December 17, 2006.

Thirteen of us "girls" happily sat around the table sipping wine and savoring a five-course spread personally arranged by our hostess. In *Big Stone Gap*, the author discusses the 'Chinese Art of Face Reading.' We had so much fun as Adriana went around the table examining this one's nose or lips and that one's chin and eyebrows, and then explaining what characteristics each facial feature represented. I came well prepared with photos of George Clooney and Angelina Jolie. How we laughed! About two and ½ hours later and well into our fourth course, our gracious hostess, Adriana, told us that she had another engagement at the 92nd Street "Y" but insisted that we stay and eat the assorted pastries she had ordered for dessert.

Adriana nicknamed me "The Catherine Deneuve of Book Clubs" that day, a compliment I hope to live up to given my college adoration of the French film, "Les Parapluies de Cherbourg," the young and beautiful Catherine Deneuve and the movie's timeless love song, "I Will Wait For You."

Looking back now, almost ten years and seven books later, Adriana continues to write lovingly about her family, about the people she knows and the traditions they've introduced her to, traditions she continues to maintain and carry forth for the next generation. She has said that she writes for her fans, her readers, who simply adore her. And she shows her appreciation by giving back to them. I have had so much fun, gotten so much enjoyment out of attending two of Adriana's "World's Biggest Book Club" Events with members of my own book clubs, at the Sacred Heart of Mary School in New York City and at a country club in New Jersey for her "WBBCII," where book groups from all over the country came to hug her and hear her joyous storytelling.

After graduating from Saint Mary's College in South Bend, Indiana, Adriana moved to New York City to become a playwright. She did stand-up with the all-female comedy troupe she founded called "The Outcasts." She was writer/producer on 'The Cosby Show,' 'A Different World,' and executive producer/head writer for 'City Kids' for Jim Henson Productions. Ms. Trigiani is married to Tim Stephenson, the Emmy Award-winning lighting designer for the 'Late Show with David Letterman.' They are the proud parents of a daughter, Lucia Bonicelli Stephenson.

I have often said to my book groups that writers need us "readers" to validate their work, for "the baby" they have created over the course of months and years of toil. Likewise, I have recited Nancy Pearl's "Rule of 50" (see below) to determine whether or not they should continue to read a given book, one that hasn't grabbed them from the start.

Your/Our reading time is valuable. You don't necessarily have to follow Woody Allen's twenty-minute speed reading of *War and Peace*, to know that it's about Russia. One of my favorites, the late Nora Ephron, said it well, "Reading is everything. Reading is bliss." And Alice Hoffman said it quite simply, "Books may well be the only true magic."

'RULE OF 50'

"Time is short, and the world of books is immense. If you're 50 or younger, give every book about 50 pages. If you're over 50, (which is when time gets even shorter), subtract your age from 100 – the result is the number of pages you should read before deciding. At 99, that first page would be all-important."

~ Nancy Pearl (Executive Director of the Seattle Public Library) "First Lines to Remember" from Book Lust

"That's Venus, September thought. She was the
goddess of love. It's nice that love comes on first
thing in the evening, and goes out last in the
morning. Love keeps the light on all night."

~ Catherine M. Valente, The Girl Who Fell
Beneath Fairyland and Led the Revels There
(Fairyland #2)

JULY 2006: The Birth of Venus by Sarah Dunant

Lorenzo de Medeci, Ruler of Florence and Art Patron (1449-1492) (15th Century Florentine Renaissance,) Girolamo Savonarola, religion, love, art, violence and betrayal, *The Birth of Venus* has it all. From Botticelli's illustrations of *The Divine Comedy* to the agonizing death at the convent of St. Vitella, of her narrator, the dutiful Sister Lucrezia, Sarah Dunant's historical novel remained on the New York Times Book List for nine weeks in 2004. It is highly recommended for art lovers and art historians, women's study groups and lovers of Italian history and politics.

Fans of George R.R. Martin's *Game of Thrones* will delight in some of the high jinx.

"I went to the hotel of the Violet Hippopotamus
and drank five glasses of good wine."

~ *Anton Chekhov, The Prank: The Best of*
Young Chekhov

AUGUST 2006: The Tender Bar by J.R. Moehringer

When I chose *The Tender Bar* for our discussion in August
2006, it was because I was drawn to this coming of age work,
this non-fiction novel, set here on our Island, in the
picturesque town of Manhasset, on a barstool at Dickens
Pub. My daughter, Danielle, son-in-law, Greg and ten month
old granddaughter, Lily, would move from their New York
City apartment to this Norman Rockwell inspired village,
where *The Tender Bar*, the title itself a clever play on words, is
a love story between a boy and his mother, and the men he
meets along the way, who raised him up and taught him how
to chug 'em down.

J.R. Moehringer's novel is written with a journalist's eye for
detail and a novelist's capacity to evoke unbridled emotion.
When our Long Island Reads Committee chose *Sutton* for our
"One Island-One Book" title in April 2013, J.R. Moehringer
charmed the audience with his glib stories of Willie, "the
actor," Sutton and reminiscences about his boyhood days in
Manhasset, now so far from his present home in Oregon.

You don't have to have a particular reason for reading *The
Tender Bar*. Just saddle up, sit down and enjoy this delightful
read.

Note: Real Estate brokers teasingly told Dani & Greg that
one of the requirements for buying a home in Manhasset is to

read *The Tender Bar.* They had both already done so, without any coaxing or pressure.

STOP End of page

Below quote starts above Sept. 2006

*"Books break the shackles of time. A book is
proof that humans are capable of working magic."*

~ Carl Sagan

SEPTEMBER 2006: Time and Again by Jack Finney

Jack Finney's *Time and Again* features prominently on the *New York Times Book Review*, 'A Literary Map of Manhattan' (where imaginary New Yorkers lived, played, drank, walked and looked at ducks) by, Randy Cohen and Nigel Holmes, (Sunday, June 5, 2005.) The character, Simon Morley, hears about the Dakota, the time-traveling apartment building on 72nd Street and Central Park West, and is intrigued. Ralph Ellison's *Invisible Man*, Tom Wolfe's, *The Bonfire of the Vanities*, Truman Capote's, *Breakfast at Tiffany's*, Philip Roth's, *Portnoy's Complaint*, Edith Wharton's, *The Age of Innocence*, Caleb Carr's, *The Alienist*, Michael Chabon's, *The Amazing Adventures of Kavalier and Clay*, and Emma McLaughlin and Nicola Kraus's, *The Nanny Diaries*, among others, are also pictured there.

Simon Morley, a young Manhattan illustrator, has been selected by a secret government agency, presumably to test the theory that the past actually co-exists with the present. Since its publication in 1970, *Time and Again* has become a timeless cult classic with a loyal following. Its sequel, *From Time to Time* (Time #2), was written twenty-five years later and was published a year after the author's death in 1996 at age 84.

If futuristic time travel à la Audrey Niffenegger's *The Time Traveler's Wife*, is your reading preference, you will certainly not be disappointed reading Jack Finney's, *Time and Again*.

"Reading is a conversation. All books talk. But a good book listens as well."

~ *Mark Haddon*

OCTOBER 2006: Fate and MS Fortune by Saralee Rosenberg *(Guest Author)

Have we spoken yet about how to draw the timid and the quiet members of your book club out? Have we discussed "dead air" and pregnant pauses? You can start by reading Susan Cain's *Quiet*. After that, you might want to invite an author like Saralee Rosenberg to come to your group. She can help make even the timid find their voice.

Saralee wanted to include a "kitchen table" chat with herself, the author, when she was in the process of designing her website in 2006. Ten years prior, she had no idea that there was an emerging new genre called "Chick Lit" to which she was proud to be a card-carrying member.

Fate and MS Fortune, like her previous novel, *A Little Help From Above*, focuses on contemporary issues with great humor, finding love and responding to that knock on the door, not timidly but brashly, like the Patrick Dennis character, socialite Auntie Mame, so perfectly portrayed by Rosalind Russell on Broadway and in the Warner Brothers film.

I wrote the following testimonial for my friend, Saralee, in 2009:

"Saralee Rosenberg is glib and witty. She speaks just as she writes, bringing joy and laughter to "everyday events" and human foibles. Saralee is a modern-day Erma Bombeck and how lucky are we to hear her voice."

Tip #26 -You can have your timid or shy members write their questions or comments on a piece of paper and have it read aloud anonymously. OR For those members who may not be comfortable speaking in front of a group, ask them to take one question from "The Reading Group Guide" and ask the person seated next to them to respond. You can then pass the "Reading Group Guide" around the table, and the next person and the next will have the opportunity to be heard.

Sometimes the timid or quiet would like to simply listen to what is being said by the group. It isn't always necessary to speak.   In the book, *The Art of Racing in the Rain*, by Garth Stein, there is a paragraph on this listening business. Narrated by a dog, it reads "I never deflect the course of the conversation with a comment of my own. People, if you pay attention to them, change the direction of one another's conversations constantly…. Pretend you are a dog like me and listen to other people rather than steal their stories." (http://tinybuddha.com/blog/how-to-help-someone-without-saying-a-thing).

"Death toll: About 35,000 people died during
Krakatoa's two major days of 1883 eruptions
(after water from tsunamis pushed inland)."

NOVEMBER 2006: Krakatoa: The Day the World Exploded by Simon Winchester

Our book club took a geological turn in November 2006 with the reading of Simon Winchester's *Krakatoa: The Day the World Exploded.*

Winchester describes, in breath-taking detail, one of history's most notorious volcanic eruptions off the island of Krakatoa along the Indonesian arc, between the much larger islands of Sumatra and Java. He is the author of several other books, including one of my favorites, *The Professor and the Madman: A Tale of Murder, Insanity,* and the *Making of the Oxford English Dictionary,* the true story of Dr. W. C. Minor, a convicted murderer, who provided more than 10,000 definitions for the Oxford English Dictionary from his book-lined cell at England's Broadmoor Lunatic Criminal Asylum.

Winchester, himself a geologist, provides an in-depth account of seismic shifts and excavations. But beyond scientific explanations and blood-curdling descriptions, more than anything else that I've read about Krakatoa is the indelible image I have of Edvard Munch's blood-red sky in "THE SCREAM." In the graphic photo, "The Scream," East of Krakatoa – Why did Munch Paint the Sky Blood Red? Because It Was. (*The New York Times*, Sunday, Feb. 8, 2004, Art, Richard Panek, in his byline story, writes, "Three researchers report in Feb. issue of *Sky and Telescope* that it would have been the color Munch saw as he took a sunset stroll along the Ljabrochausseen Road (now Mosseveien) in the port city of Christiania (now Oslo) in late 1883 or early

1884. At that time the detritus from the eruption of the Indonesian volcano, Krakatoa, on August 27, 1883, had just reached Norway."

Such a vivid image evoking the horror of what Munch saw.

"There's no such thing as bad publicity."

~ P.T. Barnum

DECEMBER 2006: Water for Elephants by Sara Gruen

Although we didn't discuss Canadian author, Sara Gruen's, *Water for Elephants*, until December 2006, early book buzz proclaimed this heavily researched historical novel as the '2006 Summer Sleeper Hit.'

Water for Elephants is a tale about a Depression-era traveling circus, as an aging Jacob Jankowski reminisces from his nursing home. It is a love story about a loyal elephant named Rosie. Danger and cruelty to people and animals mingle to tell the story of Jacob, orphaned when his parents were killed in a car accident, aimless and broke, catches a ride on a train that co-exists with a shabby circus.

Rich in historical detail and as colorful as the sequined gowns sported by Marlena, the glamorous performer and abused wife of the circus owner, August, *Water for Elephants* was well received by book clubs and hit the big screen in April 2011, starring Reese Witherspoon and Robert Pattinson. Your book club may want to view the movie after your book discussion. And, be sure to bring some peanuts and cotton candy.

I am often asked if I have a favorite book. The truth is, I have about three hundred favorite books of all time. Each cheered me up when I was feeling low or put a smile on my face or taught me something new.

Reading has taken me on incredible adventures and opened the doors to learning about a place or a people or a language or religion. With reading, I can explore unknown worlds, journey into new territories, delve into hidden mysteries. Watching JEOPARDY! at night, as we eat dinner, provides that same "aha" moment as Ted and I challenge one another to see who will be the first to answer the question, and who will respond correctly to the greatest number of questions.

There has never been any rhyme or reason to my taste in books. I guess you can say I am an eclectic reader. Yes, I generally favor fiction, especially historical fiction, but that doesn't preclude me from reading anything and everything I can get my hands on.

You won't find a "List of Duds" on these pages, books that were given a negative rating by the group. Every book, regardless of the writing, the content, or the characters, is capable of generating good conversation. As a book club facilitator for almost twenty years, I have learned that some book clubs will enjoy a particular book on a particular day, while others will absolutely abhor that very same book on another day.

C'est la vie!

Remember: "You can please some of the people some of the time......," et patati et patata (etc.) And I do always propose using Nancy Pearl's 'Rule of 50' because our reading time is so precious.

There have been times when members came to book club but hadn't read or hadn't liked, the selected book. Their participation was vital, nevertheless, because they contributed to the conversation by

310

telling us about their travels to a country or a state described in the book, (i.e. Shanghai Girls, by Lisa See or New York, by Edward Rutherfurd,) or because they have lived through a particular period of time and were familiar with the protagonist, (i.e., Willie, the actor, Sutton in J.R. Moehringer's Sutton).

Through the years, these are but a few of the many books that I have loved, and which have provided me with hours of pleasurable companionship. ..... and in no particular order:

- *A Tale of Two Cities, by Charles Dickens (for the French Revolution, 'Liberté, Egalité, Fraternité,' and for Sydney Carton doing "a far, far better thing....").*
- *Death Be Not Proud, by John Gunther. (Growing up Renee and I were hypochondriacs, imagining that we had every illness that we read about. Sadly, John Gunther's poignant story had us imagining that we, too, had a brain tumor).*
- *Pillars of the Earth, Kane and Abel, and 'The Century Trilogy' by Ken Follett (chivalry, rivalry).*
- *A Woman of Substance, and Voices of the Heart, by Barbara Taylor Bradford*
- *Gone with the Wind, by Margaret Mitchell (because of Scarlett O'Hara, "I'll think about it tomorrow," and for Rhett Butler, "Frankly, Scarlett, I don't give a damn," Civil War history).*
- *The French Lieutenant's Woman, by John Fowles*
- *Midwives and The Double Bind, by Chris Bohjalian*
- *The Winds of War (Trilogy), by Herman Wouk*
- *The North and South (Trilogy), by John Jakes*
- *Big Stone Gap, (Quartet) and Valentine (Trilogy), by Adriana Trigiani (for the love and the laughter, and most particularly because her character, Bret Fitzpatrick, (Valentine) reminded me of my Brett (handsome, intelligent, sensitive, loving, "family-oriented").*

311

- *Green Mansions: A Romance of the Tropical Forest,* by William Henry Hudson *(had me at "hello" when I was in high school, starry-eyed, romantic, fateful)*
- *The Physician,* by Noah Gordon
- *Sleepers,* by Lorenzo Carcaterra
- *Knock on any Door,* by Willard Motley
- *Flags of our Fathers,* by James Bradley *(because he made me cry thinking of my own Father, Big Eddie Perlman, and the role he played on the European stage and for helping to liberate a German concentration camp. He was so young)*
- *The Shell Seekers and Coming Home,* by Rosamunde Pilcher *(always a warm and fuzzy, just because...)*
- *The Kite Runner,* by Khaled Hosseini *(a historical tear-jerker)*
- *Little Black Sambo,* by Helen Bannerman *(because my grandfather (Pop) Perlman always called Grams "Sambo" and she was the first to introduce me to this beloved book)*
- *Snowflower and the Secret Fan,* by Lisa See *(for the friendship and "sister love" between Lily and Snowflower and because of my husband Ted's travels to the Far East and my own two trips to Taiwan & Mainland China)*
- *Dancing on Broken Glass,* by Ka Hancock *(for the "Sister Love," three fairytale princesses, like the Perlman Girls, whose father knew them so well.)*
- *The Book Thief,* by Marcus Zusak *(made me cry and feel proud of my German heritage)*
- *Snow Falling on Cedars,* by David Guterson *(because it was my first book discussion, like the birth of a first-born child)*
- *The Light Between Oceans,* by M.L.Stedman *(although I would like to change the ending)*
- *Clan of the Cave Bear, etc. (The Earth's Children series),* by Jean M. Auel

312

- *Team of Rivals: The Political Genius of Abraham Lincoln and No Ordinary Time: Franklin & Eleanor Roosevelt: On the Home Front, by Doris Kearns Goodwin*
- *Seabiscuit: An American Legend and Unbroken: A WWII Story of Survival, Resilience, and Redemption, by Laura Hillenbrand*
- *Bel Canto, by Ann Patchett*
- *Cutting for Stone, by Abraham Verghese*
- *And Ladies of the Club, by Helen Hooven Santmyer*
- *Forever, by Pete Hamill*
- *Nancy Drew Mysteries, by Carolyn Keene (the original books- Diane, Renee, Karyn and I poured through them every summer in Bolton Landing (Lake George). A special thank you to the Bolton Free Library for introducing us young readers to Nancy's adventures......pre-feminism).*
- *The Devil in the White City: Murder, Magic, and Madness at the Fair That Changed America, by Erik Larson*
- *Protect and Defend, by Richard North Patterson (controversial, thought-provoking)*
- *84, Charing Cross Road, by Helene Hanff (I see only Anne Bancroft and Anthony Hopkins)*
- *Le Petit Prince, par Antoine de Saint-Exupéry*
- *The Ingenious Gentleman Don Quixote of La Mancha, by Miguel de Cervantes Saavedra*
- *Les Miserables, par Victor Hugo et Madame Bovary, par Gustave Flaubert (tous les deux en français, naturellement)*

"So please, oh PLEASE, we beg, we pray,

Go throw your TV set away,

313

And in its place, you can install,

A lovely bookshelf on the wall."

~ Roald Dahl, Charlie and the Chocolate
Factory

Chapter 11

Back by Popular Demand (2007)

2007

My reading pleasures expanded in many ways. I joined 'The Folio Society' and began my collection of beautifully embossed, leather-bound classics from Great Britain. Arrowsmith, by Sinclair Lewis, The Picture of Dorian Gray, by Oscar Wilde, In Cold Blood, by Truman Capote, Rebecca, by Daphne du Maurier, The Brothers Karamazov, by Fyodor Dostoevsky, Dubliners, by James Joyce, Travels With Charley: In Search of America, by John Steinbeck, The Pilgrim's Progress, by John Bunyan, Animal Farm, by George Orwell, Carson McCullers -Complete Novels, The Greek Myths, Volumes I and II, Love Poems and Sonnets of William Shakespeare.

I bought the complete tales of Hans Christian Anderson, Volumes I and II, for my "Lilylicious" Easter girl.

And Ted bought me bookcases to accommodate my newly created loft/library. The shelves were a deep cherry, the books duly arranged in alphabetical order according to the author's last name, separating Fiction from Non-Fiction.

Melvil (Melville) Dewey would have approved. "The Ultimate Hard-Core, High-Handed, Card-Carrying Bibliophilist," if that was really me, was proud.

"Have you ever lost someone you love and wanted one more conversation, one more chance to make up for the time when you thought they would be here forever? ..."

~ Mitch Albom, For One More Day

JANUARY 2007: For One More Day by Mitch Albom

We read a variety of outstanding books in 2007 and were introduced and/or re-introduced to many of our favorite authors.

Mitch Albom started us off in January with *For One More Day*, a spiritual "if only" book, on the order of *Tuesdays With Morrie* (Cross-reference June 2000), that was well-received. Full of longing and regret and time lost, *For One More Day* is the story of a mother and a son, a philosophical novel that will leave the reader pondering many things...

"It's such a shame to waste time. We always think we have so much of it."

"Sometimes, love brings you together, even as life keeps you apart."

"The more you defend a lie, the angrier you become."

"I like myself better when I'm with you."

"Memory is a way of holding on to the things you love, the things you are, the things you never want to lose."

~ *Kevin Arnold*

FEBRUARY 2007: The Memory Keeper's Daughter by Kim Edwards

The Memory Keeper's Daughter, by Kim Edwards, begins on a cold and snowy night (refer to *Midwives*, by Chris Bohjalian, Cross-reference Nov. 1999). It tells the story of a doctor, who gives his newborn daughter, who has Down Syndrome, to a delivery nurse working with him. This haunting tale of love and lies and deceit sparked a very lively discussion of how much or how little to tell your spouse or how much to hide in order to "protect" them. We talked about the moral responsibility to tell the truth. (Cross-reference *The Pilot's Wife*, by Anita Shreve (September 1999 and *The Light Between Oceans*, by M. L. Stedman, Feb. 2013).

"Good friends, good books and a sleepy conscience:
this is the ideal life."

~ Mark Twain

MARCH 2007: The Double Bind by Chris Bohjalian

One of my favorite books, by one of my favorite authors, is
The Double Bind, by Chris Bohjalian. The author sent galley
copies to me and to several members of the L. I. Reads
Committee for consideration as our 2007 pick. Although it
was not chosen for Long Island Reads that year, (*The Color of
Water: A Black Man's Tribute to His White Mother*, by James
McBride, was, cross reference March 1998), *The Double Bind*
quickly became a book club favorite.

The novel opens and closes with a bang! From the brutal
attack of a young (girl) bike rider to a look into the
fascinating past of a homeless man, photographer, Bobbie
Crocker, to a treatise on mental illness, Betsy Willeford,
writing for *The Miami Herald*, has described Bohjalian's work
as, "Artfully constructed and fiercely felt…Bohjalian…has
deliberately wandered into thriller territory, rearranging our
previous assumptions, producing the sense of shock we felt
viewing *The Sixth Sense*. He's playing with our minds in a way
that ultimately evokes not Fitzgerald but that master of
deviousness, Alfred Hitchcock."

You'll stay up all night reading this highly researched, gem-of-
a-novel.

SPOILER ALERT: Oh, that ending!

"My alma mater was books, a good library.... I could spend the rest of my life reading, just satisfying my curiosity."

~ Malcolm X

APRIL 2007: Striver's Row by Kevin Baker

Striver's Row completed Kevin Baker's "City of Fire" Trilogy and presented a novelist's view of Malcolm X and the world of Harlem in the 1940s. In this work of historical fiction, we meet the Reverend Jonah Dove (fictitious) as he encounters the future Malcolm X on a very disturbing train ride. It is a period of personal and racial unrest, at a time, and in a place (Harlem), so cleverly portrayed by this social historian, Kevin Baker. *Striver's Row* was enjoyed by the group; however, it would have been a better selection for February, Black History Month. (See my Calendar of Book Recommendations).

"The thing women must do to rise to power is to redefine their femininity. Once, power was considered a masculine attribute. In fact, power has no sex."

~ Katharine Graham

"In politics, nothing happens by accident. If it happens, you can bet it was planned that way."

~ Franklin D. Roosevelt

MAY 2007: The Georgetown Ladies' Social Club: Power, Passion, and Politics in the Nation's Capital by C. David Heymann

Even though our son, Brett, had graduated from Georgetown in 1999, my heart was still there among the brownstones and boutique shops on Wisconsin and M Streets. I loved the stories of Katherine Graham's elegant soirées and dinner parties, her famous quotes: *"A mistake is simply another way of doing things,"* "News is what someone wants suppressed. Everything else is advertising", as captured so vividly in biographer, C. David Heymann's *The Georgetown Ladies' Social Club: Power, Passion, and Politics in the Nation's Capital.* Earlier I mentioned the dinner parties that our Georgetown sons, (and us parents), held for 5 years in a private room of a New York City restaurant on the Saturday after Thanksgiving. After having read this book, I renamed us mothers, 'The Georgetown Mothers' Social Club.' We Georgetown Mothers loved our name; the book was not as favorably received.

"Children of the same family, the same blood, with the same first associations and habits, have some means of enjoyment in their power, which no subsequent connections can supply...."

~ *Jane Austen, Mansfield Park*

JUNE 2007: The Glass Castle by Jeannette Walls

The ultimate in dysfunctional families.... stories too unbelievable to be true, and yet they are. A three-year-old child burning herself while cooking her own meal, children being left hungry and alone, living in fecal conditions for days on end. This 2005 memoir by American author and journalist, (formerly gossip columnist for MSNBC), Jeannette Walls's "outrageous misfortune", (*The New York Times Sunday Book Review*, *"The Glass Castle: Outrageous Misfortune"* by Francine Prose, March 13, 2005), blockbuster remained on the New York Times Bestseller List for more than 421 weeks (as of June 3, 2018), and was made into a 2017 movie starring Brie Larson, Woody Harrelson and Naomi Watts. Your group can talk about parenting and family dynamics, or you can discuss the relevance or importance of "finding yourself." (See Making Toast by Roger Rosenblatt and Room by Emma Donoghue, Sept. 2011 and *Eat, Pray, Love*, by Elizabeth Gilbert, June 2008).

You can follow the author's family in her prequel, *Half Broke Horses* and in The Silver Star, her first exploration into fiction.

"Have you read anything beautiful lately? Do make sure somehow to get hold of and read the books by (George) Eliot, you won't be sorry."

~ Vincent Van Gogh, Letter to Theo Van Gogh

JULY 2007: The Last Van Gogh by Alyson Richman

Alyson Richman joined us in 'The Literary Gallery' at Barnes & Noble to discuss her beautifully written, extensively researched novel, *The Last Van Gogh*. Her subject matter was my "cup of tea," … France, Art, History. Alyson is soft-spoken and affable, with a powerhouse of knowledge, and a deft hand. She had us all imagining what life was like in Auvers Sur Oise with the tender Vincent and his melancholy "healer," Dr. Paul Gachet.

Give this book a read if painting and art history interests you. You won't be disappointed.

Our Long Island Reads Committee chose Alyson Richman's, *The Lost Wife*, in 2012 as our featured book.

"I can shake off everything as I write; my sorrows disappear, my courage is reborn."

~ *Anne Frank*

AUGUST 2007: One Thousand White Women: The Journals of May Dodd by Jim Fergus

Jim Fergus's first novel, *One Thousand White Women: The Journals of May Dodd*, written in epistolary form, was hailed by many as being brilliant and satisfying. His premise, based on fact, the covert "Brides for Indians" program proposed by the Administration of Ulysses S. Grant, had us cheering for incarcerated women, some unjustly held prisoner, such as May Dodd, some ne'er- do- well -thieves and murderers, as they head west to marry Indians of the Cheyenne Nation in exchange for 1,000 horses. What follows is a portrait of the West in 1875 and May Dodd's adventures living her life between two worlds, as the blue-blood wife and mother of two she left behind, and as the Cheyenne squaw who came to love and cherish both the "sisters" who took that fateful train ride west with her, and the Cheyenne Indians they mated with.

Our discussion was lively and thought-provoking, as we considered the basic premise of the book, and all of the "can you just imagine what if's?" that followed.

"A library is not a luxury but one of the necessities of life."

~ Henry Ward Beecher

SEPTEMBER 2007: The Gods of Newport by John Jakes

The Gods of Newport, by John Jakes, gave us an intimate look into the wealth and opulence of this small Rhode Island town, known as America's 'Queen of Resorts,' in the 1890s. It is a fast, easy read that your book club might select to read during the summer months, or during the December holidays when more demands are placed on your time. My family and I spent Thanksgiving weekend 2005 in Newport, RI, and although it was cold and damp, we found warmth and comfort dining at *The (historic) Canfield House*. We returned to this landmark classic with our college friends, Libby & Frank Canova, years later, as we searched for the "BEST" cup of New England Clam Chowder soup from Newport Rhode Island to Boston, MA and every small town on the Cape (Cod), MA.

Note: We voted for:

~ Skipper Restaurant and Chowder House in Yarmouth, MA

~ The Chowder House in Webster, MA

~ 1908 Public House in Newport, RI

"A library is a good place to go when you feel unhappy, for there, in a book, you may find encouragement and comfort. A library is a good place to go when you feel bewildered or undecided, for there, in a book, you may have your question answered.

~ E. B. White

OCTOBER 2007: Nineteen Minutes by Jodi Picoult

This book is relevant and timely, conversational and controversial and a "must-read" for every parent and school-age child. It is a story of bullying and of being an outsider, not one of the "cool kids," written post-Columbine, but before the Virginia Tech Massacre or the Sandy Hook School shootings. It is a story of secrets kept and of often never really knowing someone close to you. It is a chilling page-turner of a novel that will open up your eyes and ears to the cruelty and revenge retaliation of those children "hidden" on the sidelines and in the background of society.

"In nineteen minutes, you can mow the front lawn, color your hair, watch a third of a hockey game. In nineteen minutes, you can bake scones or get a tooth filled by a dentist; you can fold laundry for a family of five…. In nineteen minutes, you can stop the world, or you can just jump off it. In nineteen minutes, you can get revenge."

(Taken from the Book Jacket of Nineteen Minutes, by Jodi Picoult).

- In 2016 the Broadway Play, *Dear Evan Hansen*, won the Tony Award for Best Musical. Like *Nineteen*

Minutes, Dear Evan Hansen deals with bullying and social networks.

"Books are the quietest and most constant of friends; they are the most accessible and wisest of counselors, and the most patient of teachers."

~Charles W. Eliot

NOVEMBER 2007: A Thousand Splendid Suns by Khaled Hosseini

Spanning a period of over fifty years, Afghan American author, Khaled Hosseini, once again captured our hearts and the spirit of his former homeland in creating two memorable characters, Mariam and Laila. With the gentle stroke of his pen, Hosseini weaves this unforgettable mother-daughter story and captures the lives of these "invisible," burqa-clad women, who try to find their place in a male-dominated society.

A Thousand Splendid Suns is a poignant and beautiful read, historically correct, enlightening and sad. With *The Kite Runner*, (Jan. 2005), we book clubs were drawn into the tortured friendship between Amir and Hassan and shed many tears over their misunderstandings and "lost time." We, likewise, succumbed to the power of this perfectly titled, although not immediately understood, historical novel.

"In the end, both sides wanted what the Pilgrims
had been looking for in 1620: a place unfettered
by obligations to others."

~ Nathaniel Philbrick, Mayflower

DECEMBER 2007: Mayflower: A Story of Courage, Community, and War by Nathaniel Philbrick

I hosted our book club's 12th Annual Holiday Party (chez moi) in 2007. Twenty-one people from "The Literary Gallery" were present as we sipped wine, indulged in mini "bagel sandwiches" and home-baked cookies and talked about our forebears who came to America aboard the Mayflower. Published by Penguin Books in April 2007, *Mayflower* was the *New York Times Book Review* Finalist for the Pulitzer Prize in History. This was our second foray into Nathaniel Philbrick's world. (Cross-reference: In the Heart of the Sea: The Tragedy of the Whaleship Essex (Feb. 2002). This time Philbrick attempts to answer the question, "How did America begin?"(Refer to my Tip # 11- Celebrate!)

Ten days later, we boarded a plane for Aruba, "Our Home Away From Home," Dani, Greg, eighteen month old Lily, Brett and his fiancée, Rebecca, the dark-haired beauty, star of FOX TVs, The Happy Hour, Ted and me.

I hand-carried the books I would read on the beach for fear they might get lost: Run, by Ann Patchett, On Chesil Beach, by Ian McEwan and World Without End, by Ken Follett. Ted called the latter, 'BOOK WITHOUT END.'

<u>Note</u>: (Depending on your copy, the hardcover edition had 1014 pages, the paperback edition 1024 pages.)

Chapter 12

Authors, Fraternities, Sororities, and a Wedding at the Plaza (2008)

Some years are memorable because of a happy occasion, like a wedding or the birth of a child. The year 2008 was one of those happy years for my family and me.

We spent a sparkling New Year's Eve celebrating on the very happy Dutch island of Aruba where Lily had her first official taste of 'CRASH, BOOM, BANG!' No, it wasn't her PopPop playing his drums. It was the sound of fireworks exploding over the water. We laughed and made light of the noise, as we held our Lily close, making sure she knew she was safe.

"All happy families are alike; each unhappy
family is unhappy in its own way."

~ *Leo Tolstoy, Anna Karenina*

JANUARY 2008: Loving Frank by Nancy Horan

In January 2008 'The Literary Gallery' read, *Loving Frank*, by Nancy Horan. This re-imagined historical novel captured a period in the life of the famous architect, Frank Lloyd Wright, and his tempestuous affair with the erudite beauty, Mamah Borthwick Cheney. Book Clubs everywhere embraced this story which, in turn, led to field trips to Taliesin (East) in Wisconsin and the Guggenheim Museum in New York City, both structures imagined and built by the famous architect, himself.

Eli Manning and the New York Football Giants beat Tom Brady and the New England Patriots 17-14 in Super Bowl XLII on Sunday, February 3, 2008. By now, our son Brett had taken over the traditional nose-bleed seats so coveted by his grandfather, Big Ed Perlman, and moved to better viewing thanks, in part, to PSLs ("Personal Seat Licenses") and funding for the new stadium.

"Half the night I waste in sighs, Half in dreams…"

~ Alfred Tennyson

FEBRUARY 2008: Bridge of Sighs by Richard Russo

A real favorite of mine, Richard Russo once again captured the essence of small-town living and painted lifelike portraits, warts and all, of his very human characters. In *Bridge of Sighs*, written six years after winning the Pulitzer Prize for *Empire Falls*, Russo extends his reach to Italy, as his main character, Louis Charles, ("Lucy"), and his wife, Sarah, endeavor to find answers about themselves and about Noonan, their childhood friend, who abandoned small-town life in search of something else. Russo's work grabs a piece of your heart and opens it up for close examination and scrutiny. Any book by Richard Russo always garners a # 5 rating from me. (Cross Reference: November 2002 – *Empire Falls*, by Richard Russo).

"Silence and a deeper silence when the crickets hesitate."

~ Leonard Cohen

MARCH 2008: When Crickets Cry by Charles Martin

Our friend, and fellow book club aficionado, (summers with us in 'The Literary Gallery' on Long Island, NY, and winters with her book club in Hilton Head, SC), Jackie Metzger recommended our March selection 2008, *When Crickets Cry*, by Charles Martin. Jackie had met the author and read the story with her winter book club and thought that we would, likewise, be enchanted by this poignant story of seven-year-old Annie with the weak heart.

We were.

There is much to like about this spiritual novel, categorized as Christian Literature. Although I generally avoid reading any books about religion or politics in my book clubs, *When Crickets Cry* is more of a" feel good" or comfort book to be read over the summer or holidays, than a religious treatise. Using Annie's poor heart as a metaphor, Martin tells a moving story of love and loss. Look for the part when Annie utters the title words, "When crickets cry…".

*Brett, (our son), and Rebecca got engaged on Friday, April 4,
2008, at a vineyard/spa in Georgia. Wanting to be creative, but
not expecting either the sparsity of shrubbery or the torrential rains
that drenched the vines, our boy placed his multifaceted emerald-cut
diamond ring on the mud-stained stub of a passing branch and got
down on one knee. Rebecca didn't see her glittering gem jutting out
from the vine or understand what Brett was doing down on his
knees on such a miserable afternoon. He had to point out the ring
and ask again if she would marry him. She did say, YES! .... the
final rose and the promise of a lifetime, despite Brett's muddled
romantic plans.*

"I don't believe complete assimilation is possible, at least not for anyone who has an active, open mind. Every step, every entry into the flows of existence can be seen as a beginning, a commencement of a brand-new way of seeing oneself in the world. This is the case for everyone."

~ Chang-Rae Lee

APRIL 2008: Native Speaker by Chang-Rae Lee

We read, *Native Speaker*, by Chang-Rae Lee in April. This debut novel focused on Lee's themes of identity and assimilation, just as he did in his subsequent work, *A Gesture Life*, (Cross-reference: March 2000.)

Our Long Island Reads Committee chose Chang-Rae Lee's, *Aloft*, in April 2008 for our Island-Wide Read. Since we had already discussed *Aloft* when 'The Literary Gallery' met in June 2004, rather than rereading the same book, I chose an alternate title by the same author. But, unlike the aforementioned novels by Chang-Rae Lee, *Native Speaker* was not highly received and was only able to garner a 2+ rating from the group. Our discussion, however, did not flounder as we focused on the immigrant experience and assimilation into a new society.

Saturday, April 19, 2008, was such a fun day. Always ready for a "Road Trip," my sister Diane, niece Kirsten and sister/cousin, Karyn drove down from Connecticut, and Albany to meet me in New York City for a show, "Secrets of a Soccer Mom," and author Q & A. Kathy Dreschler and Mary Ellen McCarthy, fellow die-hard bibliophiles always ready for an adventure, also joined us for a day of theatre and writers and soccer and chuckles. My pal, Adri, (Adriana Trigiani), was there to host the event. She introduced me to her friend and fellow author, Meg Wolitzer, who would ultimately take the train to Long Island many times to visit us at Barnes & Noble and at future AAUW Book & Author Luncheons. I bought Meg Wolitzer's new book that afternoon, The Ten Year Nap, which we would discuss with her during her guest visit in September 2008.

*"For one who reads, there is no limit to the
number of lives that may be lived, for fiction,
biography, and history offer an inexhaustible
number of lives in many parts of the world, in all
periods of time."*

~ Louis L'Amour

MAY 2008: The Camel Bookmobile by Masha Hamilton

Books being carried by camel to remote villages in Kenya; the values of one nation being imposed on another, drought, hunger, disease, romance…. such is the stuff of *The Camel Bookmobile*. We were so inspired by the idea of a camel delivering reading material to people thirsting for knowledge and stories of faraway places, that we established a book fund at Harborfields Library and collected money to purchase books to send to Africa, where they were desperately needed.

I would encourage your book groups to read *The Camel Bookmobile* and visit Masha Hamilton's website. It's one step closer to spreading literacy around the world.

* Note on The Camel Bookmobile vs. Donna Diamond, aka "The Ultimate Hard-core, High-handed, Card-carrying, Bibliophilist":

"Because books were rare and precious in the reaches of Africa far from the Safari vacationers, the camel-powered library initiated a severe fine. If even one person lost a book, the bookmobile would boycott that entire village, choosing another to visit instead."

(Taken from The Camel Bookmobile, "The Story Behind the Book," by Masha Hamilton.)

338

Compared to those stringent rules, 'The Ultimate Hard-core, High-handed, Card-carrying Bibliophilist's' demands seemed blissfully benign.

The weekend after we discussed *The Camel Bookmobile*, Diane, Renee, and I took our Mother to Canada to visit her ninety-five-year-old Aunt, our Great Aunt Dorothy, at her farm in Orillia. Surrounded by two of her eight children, Aunt Dorothy, cheerful and sharp as a tack, chatted over salmon sandwiches she had carefully made, (being mindful of cutting off the crusts). She then led each of us into her bedroom where she pulled out a basket of multicolored socks she had nimbly knitted (no arthritis in those fingers!) My sisters and I each selected two pair of her very warm, very special handmade creations.

Note: Aunt Dorothy celebrated her 100th birthday surrounded by loved ones and lived for two more years after. Right up until the end, she was sprite and fit with twinkling blue eyes and snow-white hair.

That May afternoon, after we'd reminisced and walked the beautiful gardens of Dorothy Vivian, we left the farm and headed to the quaint and scenic town of Niagara on the Lake. There, the four of us spent two days laughing, shopping and taking high tea at the Prince of Wales Hotel. It had been many years since we sisters had spent quality time together with our Mother, unencumbered by the daily pressures of work and schedules, husbands and children.

WHAT A SPECIAL TIME IT WAS!

"When the past has passed from you, at last, let
go. Then climb down and begin the rest of your
life. With great joy."

~ Elizabeth Gilbert, Eat, Pray, Love

JUNE 2008: Eat, Pray, Love: One Woman's Search for Everything Across Italy, India & Indonesia by Elizabeth Gilbert

We read *Eat, Pray, Love,* by Elizabeth Gilbert in June 2008, the story of a 30 something woman who has a midlife crisis, and forsakes the life and the person she knew, in search of the woman she was meant to be. Unlike Oprah, the *New York Times Book Review, Time Magazine, Entertainment Weekly, Publisher's Weekly,* and my sister, Renee, we found the book to be a whiney account of a pampered journalist who visited the three countries that satisfied her "I" ego....Italy, India, and Indonesia. We found the movie starring Julia Roberts and Javier Bardem, to be much more enjoyable.

"To acquire the habit of reading is to construct for yourself a refuge from almost all the miseries of life."

~ *Somerset Maugham*

JULY 2008: The Pillars of the Earth by Ken Follett

Although I never like to read a book more than once, ("Quot libros, Quam breve tempus," – "So many books, so little time,") I made an exception with Ken Follett's *The Pillars of the Earth*. Jill Mancini, who, like Elvira Lubrano, had never missed either of my monthly book discussions, asked me one day, "What is your favorite book?" My sister, Diane, and I had always claimed that *The Pillars of the Earth* was outstanding, among our many favorites. Oprah had chosen Ken Follett's historical novel, originally published in 1989, for her Book Club in 2007.

And so, I would read again the tale of Tom Builder and his struggles to construct a cathedral in Kingsbridge, England in the middle of the 12th century. We'd meet personages, real and fictitious, from Thomas Becket to William Hamleigh, the Earl of Shiring, Ellen, Jack, Alfred, and Aliena. We'd travel from England to France and to Spain fighting battles and establishing allegiances. Judy Phillips brought in books on cathedrals and their construction to share with us. We'd learn about the different parts of a cathedral, the nave, the apse, the baptistery, the vestibule, and the transepts.

I enjoyed re-reading *The Pillars of the Earth*. While I knew the story and was familiar with the plot, it didn't alter my feelings or my appreciation of it. The group thoroughly enjoyed being taken back to medieval times, to the knights and the monks and the lords and ladies who populated the small towns and villages.

STARZ aired a mini-series adapted from the book in 2010.

"Laws are a dead letter without courts to expound and define their true meaning and operation."

~ Alexander Hamilton

AUGUST 2008: The Appeal by John Grisham

John Grisham appealed to us in August 2008 with his twentieth legal thriller about Mississippi Supreme Court Justices in, *The Appeal*. As I previously mentioned, it was my policy to avoid political confrontations of any kind (refer to my Tip # 6 re Politics and Religion). This book selection merely piqued our interest in the behind-the-scenes machinations of our justice system. It made for a very interesting discussion.

And on the home front, life went on, with all of its proverbial UPS AND DOWNS. Somehow I managed to slip a disc and got a herniation of the lumbar spine (L4-5); we threw a 90th birthday party for Ted's Mom, my belle-mere, (YaYa); Ted's Dad, (our TaTa), had died earlier in the year at the age of 94 or 91. We never really knew TaTa's true age. He was born in either 1914 or 1917, no one knows for sure because the hospital records were lost in a fire. At the same time my Mom, (Grandma Dee), had stents inserted into her arteries, Brett held his Bachelor Party/Seagirt (NJ) Fishing Weekend, and we threw a bridal shower for Rebecca at Divino's Ristorante in New York City. We went to Washington, D.C., to the Capital, to mark the Grand Finale of Jack Curphey's son, Chris's bike trip across the United States, ("PUSH AMERICA").

All this and more during the month of August alone.

"If a book is well written, I always find it too short."

~ Jane Austen

SEPTEMBER 2008: The Ten Year Nap by Meg Wolitzer

The delightfully "smart," Meg Wolitzer, graced our book club in September 2008. Traveling by train, (the Long Island Railroad) from New York's Penn Station to Huntington, Long Island, Meg spoke to us about her novels, the writing process and about her current work, *The Ten Year Nap*. She was glib. She was knowledgeable. She was personable and entertaining when she spoke about some of the themes in her book, about motherhood, ambitions put on hold, feminism, urban friendships, and jealousies wrapped up in the characters of Amy Lamb, Roberta Sokolov, Jill Hamlin, and Karen Yip. She has been called "a social observer, in the style of Tom Wolfe." Over lunch, we continued our discussion of books. Our guest author told us about one of her personal 'MUST READ' books, Evan S. Connell's, *Mrs. Bridge*, (1959), the story of the failed marriage of India and Walter Bridge, living lives of quiet desperation. She also sang the praises of *Olive Kitteridge*, by Elizabeth Strout, which we would read in November 2009.

Meg would ultimately become a frequent visitor to our book club at Barnes & Noble and guest author at our AAUW Book & Author Luncheon, which was held at the Northport Yacht Club on Thursday, June 18, 2009. We would read *The Uncoupling* in June 2011 and applaud the success of *The Interesting* when it soared to the top of the charts in 2013.

Meg Wolitzer would come to call me "a cheerleader for literature," a moniker I can only hope to live up to.

In September 2008 we celebrated my niece, Kirsten's, 40th birthday at the Blue Fin on Broadway and 47th (New York City) and partied at Judge Jeanine Pirro's home in honor of my nephew's engagement.

Then October came with all of its pleasures: A Chi Sig (XE) Reunion Weekend at Adelphi University, with all of our college friends in tow.....François and Libby Canova came all the way from California, Bonnie and Walter Naef came from Maryland, Jackie and W. Scott Freeman from Virginia, and Randy and Kathy Clifford made it all the way from Arizona. Locally, our pals Mike and Eileen Katz, and Jan and Linda VanderBaan happily joined the party. Like Francois Canova, Jan VanderBaan served as an usher in our wedding. Extraordinary sculptor and artist, Jack Dowd, fashioned a new sculpture for his alma mater, and we all took a stroll down memory lane.

Long Island native, Darin Strauss, was supposed to pay our book club a visit in October to discuss the horrific effects of Munchausen Syndrome By Proxy in *More Than It Hurts You*, a powerful and compelling read, a disturbing and dark novel. Unfortunately, we had a miscommunication, and the author visited us in December instead.

Strauss's work, *More Than It Hurts You*, like other books we have read, illustrates how much or how little we truly know about the people we love and live with. What secrets are hidden? (Refer to: *The Pilot's Wife*, by Anita Shreve, (Sept., 1999), *The Memory Keeper's Daughter*, by Kim Edwards, (Feb., 2007), *Nineteen Minutes*, by Jodi Picoult, (Oct., 2007), *Defending Jacob*, by William Landay, (July, 2012).

Brett and Rebecca wed on Saturday, October 11, 2008, at Saint Vincent Ferrer Church on the Upper East Side, New York City. It was officiated by Father Jonathan Morris, a personal friend of the couple and a frequent contributor of religious news, (from the Vatican in Rome), for FOX TV. Rebecca had spoken of her upcoming nuptials on her FOX Business Show, 'The Happy Hour.'

Their extraordinarily fun-filled reception was held at the Palace Hotel on a glorious fall day. Our daughter, Danielle, pregnant with her second daughter, our sweet Lauren, served as a bridesmaid. Lily, her firstborn, was the flower girl. Rebecca looked magnificent, radiant, beautiful. Brett looked happy but nervous, as any prospective groom (or bride) about to tie the knot, does. They took pictures in Central Park and stopped traffic on Fifth Avenue as the cameras clicked.

There was a Pink Floyd, "The Wall" vodka luge and a chocolate fountain. Italian food and Greek appetizers, Mexican tortillas and seafood canapés were offered to the one hundred twenty-five family members and guests, as our son and his wife danced, sang, and partied all night.

The next day Brett and Rebecca left for their two-week honeymoon in Argentina.

Ted and I, my sister/cousin, Karyn, and her husband, Jim Connolly, our own Coach Jim, and two other couples, Lynne and Paul Carlson and Marlene and Stu Silbergleit, flew to Venice the following week to depart on a Celebrity fourteen-day Mediterranean cruise to Rome, (where Father Jonathan, as promised, gave us a personal tour of the Vatican and invited us all to join him, and an infinite number of seminarians, for dinner at their school's sprawling campus), Croatia, Ephesus, Athens, Barcelona, and for me and my Theo Paris, of course, my Paris, as an add-on, my "I love Paris in the springtime, I love Paris in the fall, I love Paris in the winter when it drizzles, I love Paris in the *summer when it sizzles. I love Paris every moment, every moment of the year. I love Paris, why, oh why, do I love Paris? Because my love is here."*

"Love your neighbor as yourself, but don't take down your fence."

~ Carl Sandburg

NOVEMBER 2008: Dear Neighbor, Drop Dead by Saralee Rosenberg

In November, my author-psychic friend, Saralee Rosenberg, stopped by to talk to us and make us chuckle over nosey neighbors, suburban quarrels, spoiled children and busybody in-laws, *Dear Neighbor, Drop Dead.* It's always a pleasure to welcome this ebullient, warm-hearted, and insightful voyeur of suburbia. (Refer to October 2006, Fate *and MS Fortune*).

"Healing is an art. It takes time, it takes practice.
It takes love."

~ Maza-Dohta

DECEMBER 2008: More Than It Hurts You by Darin Strauss

This bestselling, award-winning author, New York University professor of writing, husband and father of twin boys, spoke with us about a behavioral and psychological disorder, a form of child abuse or medical neglect. Although it was a difficult subject to broach, Munchausen Syndrome By Proxy (MSBP or MSP), our discussion was enlightening and all the more relevant because my visiting friend, a nurse, Libby Canova, was able to lend her professional experience on the topic.

Definitely NOT Tip #27 – "Light Read" or "Comfort Book"

Although we mourned the loss of our inimitable TaTa, my husband, Ted's Father, (Dimon Diamond), our own Zorba the Greek, the year 2008 was, indeed, one of those happy years for our family.

Chapter 13

Playing Tennis, (or not) (2009)

TENNIS

I stopped playing tennis when my legs stopped working. It wasn't a gradual thing. I would simply wake up in the morning, swing my legs out of bed, and crumble like a deck of cards. Despite two arthroscopic surgeries and a total right knee replacement, I was unable to put my (right) foot down on the floor without experiencing excruciating pain and, of course, the requisite tingling and numbness. I never knew when it would happen. I never knew how long it would last.... sometimes a day or two, sometimes longer. You'd think by now I'd have learned to "Expect the Unexpected," but I was constantly surprised by the fickleness and randomness of my disease and my pain.

I described my pain as being akin to being placed on a rack (à la The Inquisition - think Mel Brooks in "History of the World, Part I"), as if I knew what it was like to be stretched on a rack, and being pulled from each end of my body, my head and my feet, stretching me out.

I loved playing tennis. I miss it a lot.

"It goes without saying that Hitler and the Germans supporting him also held a deep, poisonous grudge against the French."

~ Charles River Editors, The Fall of France: The History of Nazi Germany's Invasion and Conquest of France During World War II

JANUARY 2009: Suite Francaise by Irene Nemirovsky

"We shall defend our island, whatever the cost may be, we shall fight on the beaches, we shall fight on the landing grounds, we shall fight in the fields and in the streets, we shall fight in the hills; we shall never surrender."

~ Winston Churchill

FEBRUARY 2009: The Guernsey Literary and Potato Peel Pie Society by Mary Ann Schaffer and Annie Barrows

We read some extraordinary books in 2009. *Suite Francaise*, by Irène Nemirovsky, (January) and *The Guernsey Literary and Potato Peel Pie Society*, by Mary Ann Schaffer and Annie Barrows (February,) took us back to WWII and offered two very different perspectives on that time period. In the former, the first of five stories written by Nemirovsky, a successful writer, a Jew who was arrested and deported to Auschwitz where she died, we encountered men and women

356

fleeing Paris in 1940, on the eve of the German occupation. Sadness pervades this work because we know from the beginning the fate the author faced. It is a very moving paean to the writer and to her fellow Frenchmen.

In the latter, we meet a plethora of quirky but lovable characters, who live in Guernsey, in the Channel Islands, during the German occupation. Written as a series of letters, (epistolary form), the title comes from a clever spur of the moment alibi, when members of a book club are caught late at night, breaking the curfew established by their captors. Funny, and at times extremely sad, *The Guernsey Literary and Potato Peel Pie Society* is a tribute to books and literature and book clubs everywhere. The title alone is worth giving this book a read, although once you meet the pig farmer and his friends, you'll be hooked.

*"I wonder how the book got to Guernsey.
Perhaps, there is some sort of homing instinct in
books that brings them to their perfect readers?"*

~ *From The Guernsey Literary and Potato Peel
Pie Society*

"Sex in the City meets Moonstruck."

~ *People Magazine*

"Snap Out of it!" (I just couldn't)

~ *Donna Diamond*

MARCH 2009: Very Valentine by Adriana Trigiani

In March 2009, Adriana Trigiani treated us to a peek into the
lives of the Roncalli's, a close-knit Italian American family of
shoemakers, *Very Valentine*.

The opening wedding scene at Leonard's of Great Neck
(Long Island) had me almost as fast as Thaddeus's "Crash!
Boom! Bang!" on the drums so many years ago. I flat out
LOVED *Very Valentine*, the details, the visual effects, the
sights, the smells, the laugh-out-loud family squabbles, and
mal à propisms and best of all, the love of family malgré tout.

On Saturday, April 25, 2009, Ms. Trigiani held "The World's Biggest Book Club" Event at the Convent of the Sacred Heart in New York City. Book Clubs from across the country and fans of Adriana Trigiani's books, were invited to eat and drink, take pictures and discuss books, as our hostess regaled us with stories and jokes. As readers, we formed a mutually exclusive group. We "limo-ed" into the city, thirteen ladies from 'The Literary Gallery.' My sister, Diane, Sister/cousin, Karyn and my niece, Kirsten, (ever the adventurers,) my road warriors, drove down for the day to participate in the fun-filled activities.

"The past is not simply the past, but a prism through which the subject filters his own changing self-image."

~Doris Kearns Goodwin

APRIL 2009: Wait Till Next Year by Doris Kearns Goodwin

Wait Till Next Year, by Doris Kearns Goodwin, is a memoir about the author's life growing up on Long Island in the 1950s, and loving her family, and the Brooklyn Dodgers. With tenderness, she takes the reader on a train ride of memories through her mother's debilitating illness and early death, to her play by play recital for her father of every inning of every Dodger game played.

Wait Till Next Year is a keeper for any fan of memoirs (especially by one of America's foremost historians), of a Long Island of yesteryear, and for any lover of America's favorite pastime.

In 2009 the Long Island Reads Committee chose *Wait Till Next Year* for our 'One Island-One Book' Read. Doris Kearns Goodwin graciously accepted our invitation and generously spent more than three hours speaking and signing her book at our Brentwood Library venue. I contributed my son, Brett's, black and white team photo of 'dem bums' which adorned the stage where Doris spoke so fondly of her team……. Jackie Robinson, Roy Campanella, Pee Wee Reese, Gil Hodges, and Duke Snider.

(Note: We have our own "Duke" (Brett) in the family, a childhood nickname we gave our son when he was one year old and crawled onto the great John Wayne's ("The original

"Duke's") handprints at Graumann's (Mann's) Chinese Theatre.

We served peanuts and cracker jacks and played, 'Take Me Out To The Ball Game' as Ms. Goodwin signed her book.

"Between the pages of a book is a lovely place to be."

~ Anonymous

MAY 2009: Revolutionary Road by Richard Yates

A copy of *Revolutionary Road*, the debut novel by Richard Yates, released in December 1961, was presented to me by Nick Siciliano, one of 'The Literary Gallery's' quietly studious and well-informed members. The book, similar in plot and theme to Evan S. Connell's *Mrs. Bridge* and Anne Tyler's *The Amateur Marriage*, is a realistic portrayal/commentary on the devastation of a marriage. With curt, dismissive dialogue and hurtful conversations between suburban husband and wife, Frank and April Wheeler find ways to inflict pain on one another.

Revolutionary Road "locates the new American tragedy squarely on the field of marriage." (Alfred Kazin.)

"a deft, ironic, beautiful novel that deserves to be a classic." (William Styron)

The movie adaptation of the novel starred Kate Winslet and Leonardo Di Caprio.

"You cannot open a book without learning something."

~ Confucius

JUNE 2009: The Story of Edgar Sawtelle by David Wroblewski

Sparse, evocative, elegiac, haunting, these are a few of the adjectives that came to mind when I read David Wroblewski's debut novel. Stephen King said, "I flat out loved *The Story of Edgar Sawtelle*." Oprah chose it for her book club in 2008, and it was a Barnes & Noble "Discover" (Great New Writers) Pick, an Indie Bound # 1 Pick, and an Amazon Significant Seven Selection.

The Story of Edgar Sawtelle received mixed reviews from 'The Literary Gallery,' praised for its lyrical prose and evocation of a weathered landscape—criticized for the slow-moving plot, à la *Cold Mountain*, by Charles Frazier.

"It is not the mountain we conquer, but ourselves."

~ George Mallory

JULY 2009: Paths of Glory by Jeffrey Archer

Historical fiction, my favorite genre, books by Jeffrey Archer, a favorite author. *Paths of Glory*, inspired by a true story, re-imagines the life of George Mallory and his historic climb of Mount Everest. Was he the first to reach the summit of that daunting mountain, every alpinist's dream? Decide for yourself as you choose this selection as a light summer read or a December holiday selection.

"I don't have ugly ducklings turning into swans in my stories..." ~Maeve Binchy

AUGUST 2009: Heart and Soul by Maeve Binchy

Heart and Soul is a lighthearted summer read by the late Maeve Binchy, Ireland's beloved storyteller. Chock full of the familiar characters we have come to know from her books, *Heart, and Soul* vaults us into a hospital setting and anesthetizes us against the harsh realities of life. This is another great choice for a summer or holiday read. (Refer to *Scarlet Feather*, by Maeve Binchy (July 2001).

"Reading makes immigrants of us all. It takes us away from home, but more important, it finds homes for us everywhere."

~Hazel Rochman

SEPTEMBER 2009: Shanghai Girls by Lisa See

Coincidentally, Ted was in Shanghai while we held a telephone chat with Lisa See about her novel, *Shanghai Girls*. Shanghai in 2009, especially along the glitzy Bund, with its opulent shops and tourist attractions, may still resemble the "Paris of Asia" that sisters Pearl and May Chin traversed in 1937.

Blindsided by their father's gambling debts and forced into arranged marriages, *Shanghai Girls* takes the reader on the sisters' journey through war and pain and suffering, through Angel Island (the West Coast equivalent of Ellis Island), and to Los Angeles Chinatown. Lisa See traces historical events and returns again to her themes of sister relationships, love, and rivalry. It is pure joy to read anything by this author, who will enlighten and astound you with her knowledge, in-depth research, and love of her Chinese heritage.

"I do love secondhand books that open to the page
some previous owner read oftenest."

~ Helen Hanff, 84, Charing
Cross Road

OCTOBER 2009: People of the Book by Geraldine Brooks

Passed from hand to hand, transferred from country to country, through centuries of war, religious strife and anti-Semitism, Australian rare-book expert, Hannah Heath, is commissioned to rescue and conserve the famed Sarajevo Haggadah, one of the earliest Jewish volumes to be illuminated with images. Hannah finds clues to a hidden past--- Artifacts: wine stains, an insect wing fragment, salt crystals, a white hair. Immediately fascinated by her discoveries, Hannah plunges into the history and origins of this Sacred Book. An insect wing fragment---from what insect? Wine stains—what kind of wine, dating back how far? Salt crystals? White hair? Impassioned to retrace the footsteps of those who preceded her, Hannah takes the reader along with her as she seeks to explain the manuscript's checkered history. Just as the narrator of *The Guernsey Literary and Potato Peel Pie Society* pondered how the book got to Guernsey, "perhaps there is some sort of homing instinct in books that brings them to their perfect readers." (Quote from *The Guernsey Literary and Potato Peel Pie Society* (February 2009,) Hannah Heath, likewise wonders what channels the Sarajevo Haggadah passed through.

Inspired by a true story, *People of the Book* is a novel of historical fiction, the second work by Geraldine Brooks that we would read and thoroughly enjoy. In September 2002,

'The Literary Gallery' discussed *Nine Parts of Desire: The Hidden World of Islamic Women.*

> *"...., he saw her loneliness as a lesion on her face."*
>
> ~ *Olive Kitteridge by Elizabeth Strout*

NOVEMBER 2009: Olive Kitteridge by Elizabeth Strout

We were introduced to Olive Kitteridge, the prickly and curt, abrasive and heartless, but occasionally sympathetic, Junior High School Math teacher, in November 2009, in the guise of thirteen inter-related stories. It won the 2009 Pulitzer Prize for Fiction and was a finalist for the 2008 National Book Critics Circle Award.

I loved *Olive Kitteridge.* Meg Wolitzer praised *Olive Kitteridge,* and HBO made it into a four-part mini-series in 2014 starring Frances McDormand. Book clubs will talk about *Olive Kitteridge.* For better or for worse, Olive Kitteridge is an unforgettable character.

"There is more treasure in books than in all the pirate's loot on Treasure Island."

~ Walt Disney

DECEMBER 2009: The Lost Symbol by Dan Brown

Dan Brown created another blockbuster thriller with the release of *The Lost Symbol* in 2009. Featuring Harvard symbologist, his recurring character, played so effortlessly on film by Tom Hanks in both 'The Da Vinci Code' and 'Angels and Demons,' *The Lost Symbol* finds the fearless professor in Washington, DC in the midst of a Masonic caper. With each chapter a cliff-hanger, Dan Brown again illustrates his seemingly endless knowledge of symbols, hidden treasures, and mysteries. Dan Brown's novels make you think, make you question, make you wonder, make you mad. His creative imagination is boundless. As Sir Winston Churchill stated in 1939 about the role Russia might play in World War II. I cannot forecast to you the action of Russia. It is a riddle wrapped in a mystery inside an enigma, but perhaps there is a key. (That key is Russian national interest.") A Dan Brown novel is that same riddle/mystery/enigma.

I believe every book club should read something written by Dan Brown. The conversation is always lively; his themes and his plots always generate heated dialogue between members. But BEWARE! You don't want to repeat the fallout I experienced when we read *The Da Vinci Code* in October 2003.

My good friend, Jackie Metzger, gave me a very clever literary towel one Christmas. It was called "A Book Lover's Christmas" and was a take-off on the popular "12 Days of Christmas" song with accompanying cartoon-like characters. It goes like this:

A BOOK LOVER'S CHRISTMAS

A Potter in a Pear Tree

Two Green Eggs and Ham

Three Chilling King Tales

Four Da Vinci Clues

Five Little Golden Books

Six Book Club Meetings

Seven Habits of Highly Effective People

Eight Plots Thickening

Nine Hobbits Dancing

Ten Clancy Heroes Leaping

Eleven Unfortunate Events Unfolding

Twelve Grishams Gripping

Chapter 14

On Breaking the Bank, Chasing Lincoln's Killer and Meeting a Girl with a Dragon Tattoo and a Girl in a Blue Dress (2010)

2010

In January 2010, I was invited to lead a monthly book discussion at Northport Library. 'The Literary Gallery' continued to meet on the second Monday of each month from 11:00AM – 12:30PM at Barnes & Noble. Our Harborfields Library 'Morning Book Discussion Group' (a name I would ultimately change to 'From Cover to Cover'), also met monthly on the third Wednesday of the month from 11:30AM – 1:00PM.

*I had chosen to meet at the main branch of the Northport/East Northport Library on the second Thursday from 2:00PM – 3:30PM. Our new group would be called 'Page Turners' and our first book selection would be Pete Hamill's North River. I would very quickly come to love my 'Page Turners,' men and women, two groups of husbands/wives, best friends. Carolyn Deegan, Carolyn Fricke, Pat Naples, Ed and Doris Nostrand, Phil and Madeline Silver, Mary Danos, Mildred Donelan, Mary Lou Damiano, Matthew Gruen, Diane Ryan, Roberta Kemperle, Deanna Donaldson, Jenn Frost, and many more, some snowbirds, who left us in the fall and returned in the spring, all extremely well-read, highly intelligent bibliophiles, who would challenge me with their questions and urge me to read other authors and search for books to which we could give a 5 Star ***** Rating. We would achieve that when we read, The Book Thief, by Markus Zusak, Unbroken: A WWII Story of Survival, Resilience, and Redemption, by Laura Hillenbrand, and Manhunt: The 12 Day Chase for Lincoln's Killer, by James Swanson. My beloved 'Page Turners,' how we laugh together, and how they keep me book smart!*

Three monthly book discussions, plus my participation/membership on the Long Island Reads Committee, kept me happily entrenched in the world of books.

"I declare, after all, there is no enjoyment like reading."

~ Jane Austen

JANUARY 2010: Breaking the Bank by Yona Zeldis McDonough

A young mother, down on her luck, finds an unexpected life change when an ATM machine gives her free and unrecorded cash.

Networking in the book world is just as important as in any other industry. Through an introduction by Adriana Trigiani, I breakfasted with Yona Zeldis McDonough, a charming and graceful woman who would teach the group and me the meaning and derivation of the word "nitpicker," at a café in New York City. We talked about books. We talked about writing. We talked about book clubs, and we talked family. And then I asked her to join us at Barnes & Noble. Ms. McDonough's presentation was most enjoyable. We placed *Breaking the Bank* into the realm of magical realism so ably characterized by the works of Alice Hoffman.

Yona Zeldis McDonough would speak to us again at my other book clubs and be the central guest at one of our AAUW Book and Author Luncheons at the Northport Yacht Club.

*"Though (Abraham Lincoln) never would travel
to Europe, he went with Shakespeare's kings to
Merry England; he went with Lord Byron poetry
to Spain and Portugal…"*

~ Doris Kearns Goodwin

FEBRUARY 2010: Manhunt: The 12 Day Chase for Lincoln's Killer by James Swanson

Manhunt is a retelling of the assassination of President Abraham Lincoln by John Wilkes Booth on April 15, 1865. In Swanson's deft hands, John Wilkes Booth did not act alone when he shot and killed President Abraham Lincoln.

This non-fiction work, which reads like a novel, a political thriller of sorts, has the reader joining the 12-day chase, on foot and on horseback, of John Wilkes Booth, and the many people, who Swanson claims, aided and abetted him. Swanson's premise is that Booth did not act alone. He opines that many controversial figures, such as Samuel Mudd, the Maryland doctor who set Booth's broken leg, conspired to kill the 16th President of the United States.

My book clubs were unanimous and earnest in their approval and enjoyment of this book. It is a fast-paced history lesson with a familiar ending.

Tip #20 - Re: Rating (Manhunt received a 5***** out of 5 ratings (the highest).

"What really knocks me out is a book that, when you're all done reading it, you wish the author that wrote it was a terrific friend of yours."

~ J. D. Salinger – The Catcher in the Rye
(1951)

MARCH 2010: Brava Valentine by Adriana Trigiani

Book #2 in the continuing saga of Valentine Roncalli, her family, and the Angelini Shoe Company, which Valentine is determined to make successful, a fitting tribute to her beloved grandparents. And I'm happy to say that Bret Fitzpatrick, (like my Brett), is still the main character.

BRAVA, Adriana!

(Cross Reference: *Lucia, Lucia* (June 2006), *Very Valentine* March 2009) *The Shoemaker's Wife* (August 2012). Refer to my Tips in the back of the book.

Tip #12- Travel/Destination Book

Tip #15 – Series Books

Tip #17 – Invite an author

My big sister, Diane, turned 65 on March 25, 2010. We decided to surprise her with a luncheon at the Boathouse in New York City's famous Central Park. It was a beautiful spring day, and the food was delicious, as we laughed and celebrated another milestone together. All was calm. All was bright, when suddenly trench-coat-clad men, with no-nonsense looks on their faces, sealed off the exits and entrances to and from the restaurant. What could be happening? As we gathered close together and studied the anxious faces of those around us, we saw French President Nicolas Sarkozy and his stunning wife, Carla Bruni-Sarkozy, being escorted to a table immediately behind ours.

Quelle surprise! This was way more than we had bargained for. Our surprise for Diane became a most pleasant surprise for all of us. Naturally, my mind was churning, as I searched for something clever, (but not cheeky), to say in French as the famous couple departed. What came out of my mouth was a simple, "Bienvenue à New York, Monsieur le Président!" Welcome to New York, Mr. President!

"Believe you can, and you're halfway there."

~ Theodore Roosevelt

APRIL 2010: The River of Doubt: Theodore Roosevelt's Darkest Journey by Candice Millard

*A Long Island Reads Selection 2010

Our Long Island Reads Selection for April 2010 is a biographical and adventure narrative of Theodore Roosevelt's daring and oft ill-advised exploration of this dark tributary of the Amazon.

This non-fiction work appealed to both men and women, adult and young adult readers. Our TR scholars, like my librarian pal, Deborah Clark Cunningham, enjoyed the biographical details of this period in the life of our 26th President. Adventure seekers could sink their teeth into the poison-tipped arrows of the Indians, who made their homes along the shores, and squeal at the piranhas that slithered through the murky waters of the River of Doubt, (formerly Rio da Duvida).

The very pleasant and intelligent author, Candice Millard, flew to Long Island from her home in Kansas to speak and sign her book at our two venues, one in Nassau County at the Plainview-Old Bethpage Library and the other in Suffolk County at the Westhampton Library.

Book Clubs who choose to read *The River of Doubt* will have a guaranteed, sure-fire hit on their hands.

"I am an invisible man...I am a man of substance, of flesh and bone, fiber and liquids- and I might even be said to possess a mind. I am invisible, understand, simply because people refuse to see me."

~ Ralph Ellison, Invisible Man

MAY 2010: The Help by Kathryn Stockett

The story, set in Jackson, MS, is about African-American maids who work in white households during the early 1960s.

The Help is Stockett's debut novel. It took her five years to write and was rejected by forty-five literary agents before it finally reached the right hands. It was most favorably received by all three of my book clubs and was made into a movie in 2011 starring Viola Davis, who won the Academy Award for Best Actress in 2012. Octavia Spencer won Best Supporting Actress, Jessica Chastain Best Supporting Actress nominee, and Best Picture. I suppose the moral of this story is that you can please some of the people some of the time, etc. *The Help* reached the perfect hands when it reached the forty-sixth literary agent.

"He, (Ralph Truitt), placed a notice in a Chicago paper, an advertisement for a "reliable wife." She, (Catherine Land), responded, saying that she was a "simple, honest woman."

~ From Robert Goolrick Home Page

JUNE 2010: A Reliable Wife by Robert Goolrick

But what follows this advertisement, is a chilling scenario, set in 1907 and played out during one of Wisconsin's interminable snowbound winters. Love, murder, insanity, dishonesty, "such things happened."

Time Out New York described *A Reliable Wife* as "a weighty psychodrama laced with Hitchcockian suspense." The Palm Beach Post called *A Reliable Wife* "…. a book that would have made a great movie for Bette Davis and Claude Raines."

'The Literary Gallery' enjoyed the many twists and turns in the plot, and compared the bleak Wisconsin tundra, in A Reliable Wife, to the wilderness so beautifully evoked in David Wroblewski's, *The Story of Edgar Sawtelle.*

(Cross Reference: *The Story of Edgar Sawtelle*, by David Wroblewski, (June 2009).

"Good books don't give up all their secrets at once."

~ *Stephen King*

JULY 2010: Secrets of Eden by Chris Bohjalian

An apparent murder-suicide in a small Vermont town, domestic abuse, an affair between Pastor Steven Drew and a newly baptized member of his flock, Alice Hayward, an orphaned fifteen-year-old daughter, perhaps the only link to what happened the night of the murders. Was it an accidental death or a premeditated murder-suicide?

We had an insightful SKYPE chat with the ever-charming, book club loving author, Chris Bohjalian, on that Monday morning. As he has done for us numerous times in the past, Chris Bohjalian willingly responded to our questions and readily supplied insider information about his characters and his writing process. It was a most enjoyable book club experience.

Cross Reference: *Midwives*, (November 1999), *Before You Know Kindness*, (December 2004), *The Double Bind*, (March 2007), *The Sandcastle Girls*, (October 2012).

"We read to know we're not alone."

~ William Nicholson

AUGUST 2010: A Silent Ocean Away: Colette's Dominion – The Colette Trilogy (Book One) by DeVa Gantt

(Sisters - Debra Gantt Severs and Valerie Gantt Palmer * Guest Author)

Part love story, part family drama, set in the 19th century in Virginia and the fictional islands called "Les Charmantes" in the West Indies, *A Silent Ocean* Away is the first book in this sweeping blend of history, intrigue, adventure, romance, and deceit.

We were treated, at Barnes & Noble, to the personal story behind the creation and success of their 900-page novel that was 30 years in the making. Debra Gantt Severs, one half of the sister duo who wrote as DeVa Gantt, proudly told us of their journey through the world of publishing and self-promotion, of the way the sisters were forced to write in those stolen moments between Val's teaching job and Deb's studies at Montclair State College, and then as wives and mothers busy living their lives. Their story paralleled the life of the Duvoisins they had written about in length and in interest…both fascinating and rich.

"Charity begins at home, and justice begins next door."

~ Charles Dickens

SEPTEMBER 2010: Girl in a Blue Dress: A Novel Inspired by the Life and Marriage of Charles Dickens by Gaynor Arnold

Author Gaynor Arnold gives us a look into the Victorian Age, and the hapless marriage of Charles Dickens and the girl in the blue dress he fell in love with and grew to abhor.

Arnold, employing the literary device of a "roman à clef," (a novel in which real people are depicted under fictitious names), paints a bleak picture of the relationship between Charles Dickens, the man, it has been said, who created Christmas, and ultimately his estranged wife, Catherine, (aka Alfred and Dorothea (Dodo) Gibson). This historical novel gives the reader a critical view of the great author's character, boundless energy, and the depth of his distaste for the woman he would reject, and eject from his home, and forbid to see their children.

Although it doesn't necessarily portray the man we have come to know through his great literature in a complimentary light, *Girl in a Blue Dress* is a great choice for any lover of Charles Dickens and/or historical fiction.

*'I'm interested in people who find themselves in
places, either of their choosing or not, and who are
forced to decide how best to live there. That feeling
of both citizenship and exile, of always being an
expatriate – with all the attendant problems and
complications and delight."*

~ *Chang-Rae Lee*

OCTOBER 2010: The Surrendered by Chang-Rae Lee

A study of the horrors of war, (the Korean War) and the pain of survival. The characters in Chang-Rae Lee's fourth novel bear the permanent scars of warfare, the trauma of loss, and the cry for mercy. Death lurks on every page. *The Christian Science Monitor* noted that Lee "may have written the feel-bad novel of the year, but for many readers, that's a good thing."

The Surrendered was nominated as a finalist for the 2011 Pulitzer Prize. Decide for yourself before you take this almost five-hundred-page plunge. And, by all means, do remember 'Nancy Pearl's 'Rule of 50'!

Cross Reference: *A Gesture Life*, March 2000), *Aloft*, (June 2004), *Native Speaker*, (April 2008).

"It's time to write our own story."

~ *Misty Copeland*

NOVEMBER 2010: Half a Life by Darin Strauss (Guest Author)

Our November 2010 selection is a memoir in which the author painstakingly details how, while driving his father's car, he killed a classmate on a bicycle, who veered across two lanes of traffic.

'The Literary Gallery' was thrilled to invite author, Darin Strauss, back to speak with us and sign copies of his first work of non-fiction, *Half a Life*. The author of three previous novels: *Chang and Eng*, (2000), *The Real McCoy* (2002) and *More than It Hurts You*, (2008), Darin Strauss spoke honestly and diffidently about the moment he was driving his father's Oldsmobile and sixteen-year-old classmate, Celine Zilke, inexplicably swerved in front of him. He spoke of how his life changed irrevocably on that fateful day. He told us of the tragedy, his guilt, and the repercussions of that momentary action. He conveyed the reactions of family and friends, and he detailed the long, multi-million-dollar lawsuit that ensued. Half a life ago, Darin Strauss was an eighteen-year-old high school graduate looking forward to college. Half a life ago Celine Zilke's parents looked forward to a bright future with their sixteen-year-old daughter.

Strauss was eventually exonerated, but his life would remain altered by that split-second event. Because he was so forthcoming and generous with his time, (he took the LIRR from Penn Station (NYC), and I picked him up in Huntington and escorted him to Barnes & Noble), we invited Darin Strauss to join us again at other venues.

Cross Reference: *More Than it Hurts You*, (October and December 2008).

"Keep in mind that I'm crazy, won't you?"

~ Stieg Larsson

DECEMBER 2010: The Girl with the Dragon Tattoo by Stieg Larsson

This first book in the Millennium Series Trilogy centers on the search by a disgraced journalist, (Mikael Blomkvist), and a tattooed/body pierced computer hacker, (Lisbeth Salander), for a woman missing forty years.

The Girl with the Dragon Tatoo, by deceased Swedish writer, Stieg Larsson, is violent, unnerving and chilling with crude language, not the type of book I would ordinarily find appealing. But I loved it! And I loved Lisbeth Salander, a flawed underdog, a modern-day misfit, an outcast trying to rid the world of serious bad guys.

I couldn't wait to devour Book #2, *The Girl Who Played with Fire*, and Book #3, *The Girl Who Kicked the Hornet's Nest*. Perhaps, at another time in my life, I might have found this book and all of the characters repugnant; however, for me, Lisbeth Salander is a heroine for the ages. This protagonist will not be easily forgotten.

Do you know the song, ('And then) ......? 'Along Comes Mary' by The Association:

"And then along comes Mary,

And does she want to give me

Kicks, and be my steady chick,

And give me pick of memories...."

On December 8, 2010, along came a baby girl, Alice Elizabeth Westfall, to bless Dani & Greg's, PopPop and Mimi's lives, and join her two older sisters, Lily and Lauren. Alice was the best Christmas gift any of us could have imagined!

Chapter 15

Writing 'Questions for Discussion' for Simon & Schuster and Reading More Great Books (2011)

> *"How could I share with you how I felt when two towers that I loved, two pieces of steel and glass and concrete fell down when actually they took with them thousands of human lives? That is the actual tragedy. But those towers were almost human for me. I was in love with them, and that's why I married them with a tight rope."*
>
> ~ *Philippe Petit in an interview with Jessica Gross (The New York Times, May 11, 2014, 'Half-Man, Half-Bird,' pg.14.)*

JANUARY 2011: Let the Great World Spin by Colum McCann

I think sometimes a book can be more enjoyable after you have turned the final page, than while you are in the process of reading it. Such was the case for me with Colum McCann's, *Let the Great World Spin*. This brilliant author has created a story based on a single day in New York City and a singular action…. Philippe Petit's brazen high-wire dance between the World Trade Center Towers on August 7, 1974.

I needed to digest what I had just read, ponder over the ten narrators whose stories converged on that fateful afternoon. We meet Corrigan, an Irish monk intent on saving Tillie and Jazzlyn and the prostitutes and heroin addicts that dwell in a Bronx slum where he, himself, lives, the wealthy but devastated, Claire, who shares her toney Upper East Side apartment with husband, Judge Solomon Soderberg, as they try to deal with their grief over the death of their son. We are introduced to the women in Claire's support group, to a computer hacker, to Lara, the heiress and to Adelita from Guatemala.

Let the Great World Spin takes place in a cynical New York City in the 1970s, amidst the garbage strike and President Nixon's resignation. It is a dark novel that parallels the horrific events that took place on September 11th and, like Joseph O'Neill's, *Netherland* and Claire Messud's, *The Emperor's Children, Let the Great World Spin* is categorized with other 'Twin Towers' novels.

Colum McCann was the recipient of the National Book Award for Fiction in 2009 for this stunning, deeply thought-provoking work.

I had the pleasure of meeting this delightful man at the Book Revue in Huntington when he first signed my copy of *Let the Great World Spin*.

"A writer only begins a book. A reader finishes it."

~ *Samuel Johnson*

FEBRUARY 2011: Freedom by Jonathan Franzen

It took a combination of "literary events" to converge or, I should say, collide in 2010 before I would choose Jonathan Franzen's *Freedom* for our book club to read in February 2011. The author's face would adorn the cover of *TIME* Magazine on August 23, 2010, beside the caption, "Great American Novelist," with an extended article by Lev Grossman. Book Page, Sept. 2010, Interview by Alden Mudge, pg. 14, claimed "Franzen's Freedom Rings True." Borders announced their year-end 'Best Of' Lists and placed Jonathan Franzen alongside literary heavyweights like Junot Diaz, (*The Brief and Wondrous Life of Oscar Wao*), and David Mitchell, (*The Thousand Autumns of Jacob de Zoet*).

But it took Franzen's appearance (at last!) on the Oprah Winfrey Show on December 6, 2010, to convince me that this should be a title and an author that we should read in our book club. We were all well aware of Franzen's dismissal of some of Oprah's book selections as being "schmaltzy" and "one dimensional," (*The New York Times Book Review*, Sun., Dec. 19, 2010, Jennifer Schuessler, 'Take Two', pg. 18,) and Winfrey's subsequent *"disinvitation" to him for *The Corrections.*

Note: A similar *"disinvitation" occurred for us later in 2011 when 'The Literary Gallery' was forced to rescind an invitation to a popular author of women's novels, ("chick lit"), because her overly aggressive, "pushy" publicist sought to control the questions we could ask the author, and the

390

direction our book discussion could take. We refused to be programmed and pre-recorded.

How could we not be familiar with a book that received this kind of attention and notoriety? *Freedom* recants the long tale of the dysfunctional Berglund Family, (husband Walter and wife, Patty and their children, Jessica and Joey,) and Walter's college friend, rocker Richard Katz, who competes with Walter for Patty's attention. This novel received mixed reviews from the group. Once again, a highly praised work such as *Cold Mountain* by, Charles Frazier (Cross Reference Feb. 1998) and *The Story of Edgar Sawtelle*, by David Wroblewski (Cross Reference June 2009,) could create enormous "literary buzz" without delivering the reader satisfaction PUNCH of a book like *Cutting for Stone*, by Abraham Verghese. (Cross Reference July 2011).

*"Children are made readers on the laps of their
parents."*

~ Emilie Buchwald

*Our twins, Brielle and Brett, were born on Thursday, February
17, 2011, almost three weeks before their due date of March 11th
(Mom's 86th birthday).*

*I was getting a manicure when my cell phone rang. I rarely use my
cell or receive many calls on it. This, however, was a call from
Ted saying that Brett had phoned with an urgent message for us to
leave immediately for New Jersey. Rebecca was experiencing
complications with her pregnancy, and the twins would be delivered
by Caesarian Section within a few hours.*

*The word "fast" has never been a word that can be applied to me.
Although I have often imagined that I have the speed of Mercury,
the bottom line is that I more often have the slow determination of
the proverbial tortoise. But this time I surprised even myself when
I raced home, threw some clothes in a suitcase, grabbed my medicine
and cosmetics and, of course, my reading material, and flew out the
door with the new PopPop-to-be. The plan was that I would stay
with my son while his wife was in the hospital and then remain to
help with the babies once they were released. I needed to make sure
that I had the proper reading material for those times when our
babies would be asleep. So, I brought along my signed copy of
Suzanne Collins's Mockingjay, even though I wasn't a fan of this
very violent, young person's futuristic genre, The Warmth of Other
Suns, by, Isabel Wilkerson and The Night Circus, by Erin
Morgenstern.*

But who was I kidding to bring books?

*Brielle arrived first at 5:57PM weighing 5 lbs. 9 oz., her twin
brother, Brett, just one minute later at 4 lbs. 8 oz. Brielle would*

392

forever after have bragging rights that SHE was the oldest, and I would never find the time to read while our babies slept. Too tired after first feeding one twin, then the other twin needed to be fed, both Rebecca and I wisely chose to take advantage of their erratic nap times to catch some well-needed sleep ourselves.

During the twelve days that I spent with Brett and Rebecca; it was apparent that they would have their hands full with this double blessing. Ted and I, (PopPop and Mimi,) were now the very proud grandparents to four EXTRA special little girls, Lily, Lauren, Alice and Brielle, and our one UNIQUE and LOVABLE 'Little Prince', Brett.

✻✻✻

We left for Los Angeles on Wednesday, March 2, 2011. It was to be an overnight pit stop spent dining with our buddies, Jack, and Cindy Curphey, before heading to Maui the following morning. There we would reconnoiter with Frank and Libby Canova who, we knew, would meet us in the appropriate Hawaiian sartorial splendor, in this case, a coconut bra and grass skirt for Frank and floral muumuu for Libby and naturally, leis all around. They even sang their 'Hawaiian Wedding' song as a greeting in our honor. What a fabulous lifelong friendship we've had! From Bermuda to Tahiti, from California to Las Vegas and in between, from Florida, Hilton Head, Chicago, Cape Cod, and the Hamptons, to Aruba, to infinity and beyond! We did it, we saw it together.

And while Ted and Frank did their famous bobbing in the ocean, Libby and I would talk and talk and talk. We never ran out of things to talk about. This time our grandkids were the main topic of discussion. We were amazed to find that we four, best friends since college, each had five grandkids, a set of twins, four girls, and one "petit prince."

Books were always the subject of our conversations, too. Amidst the tropical breezes and the Pina Coladas, we talked about *Cutting for Stone*, by Abraham Verghese and *Unbroken: A WWII Story of Survival, Resilience & Redemption*, by Laura Hillenbrand. We spoke with other couples staying at Napili Kai, who also praised the aforementioned books. As 'The Ultimate Hard-core, High-handed, Card-carrying Bibliophilist,' it was my pleasure to spread the word about great books that I had read. I never got tired of the subject.

We went whale watching and had dinner in Lahaina at Kimo's, where they made the best drink, an Island Sunset, and served the most amazing Hula pie for dessert.

Then it was on to Kauai for my Theo and me. We had an early dinner the night we arrived at Duke's, at the Marriott, then returned to our room for what we thought would be some quiet time. As we mindlessly watched TV, the broadcast was interrupted by the news of a 9.0 earthquake and tsunami in Japan. THEN THE HOTEL ALARMS SOUNDED, and we were told to evacuate. Kauai was a bulls-eye target for the earthquake-generated tsunami that was heading across the Pacific to the Hawaiian Islands at speeds of 400 miles per hour. We were handed a map and instructed to go to a designated county shelter.... Kauai High School, Home of the Red Raiders. It was March 10th/11th, 2011. We were packed into a gymnasium along with other evacuees. If you were lucky enough, you managed to grab a seat on a bench or a small corner of a gym mat on which to lie down. We watched, and we waited. One man had a radio, which provided sporadic and intermittent information about the tsunami.

My husband didn't say much. He never does when confronted with a problem over which he has no control. His very analytical mind was thinking of ways to protect us. It was a long night that stretched from 8:00 PM on March 10th to 8:00 AM on March 11th.

394

Ted always gets a kick out of the fact that I swear we were taken to a shelter that extended 10,000 feet up a mountain, but that isn't true. We were safe and together. We knew our families would be worried sick. Despite much interference, we were able to contact them the next day, after we had slept for more than twelve hours.

Our Hawaiian adventure came to a close with the advent of daylight savings time on Sunday, March 13th. I would return to Seagirt, (New Jersey) and our twins with stories to tell nine days later.

"The hardest choices in life aren't between what's right and what's wrong, but between what's right and what's best."

~ Jamie Ford, Hotel on the Corner of Bitter and Sweet

MARCH 2011: Hotel on the Corner of Bitter and Sweet by Jamie Ford

One of my favorite authors once asked me to pick a title from a list of five possible titles for his new book. I read them all and studied the list before I made my selection. Then I asked him if he would think I was shallow if I was drawn to a particular book because I liked the sound and the name of said book, and the picture on the cover before I would pick it up and read the dust jacket synopsis.

He said, "NO!"

I loved and still love the title of Jamie Ford's debut novel, *Hotel on the Corner of Bitter and Sweet.* The setting is Seattle, WA. The time flicks back and forth between wartime 1940s and forty years hence. The protagonists are Henry Lee, a young Chinese boy, and his Japanese girlfriend, Keiko Okabe. The story deals with national pride, old-world prejudices, duty, American internment camps, innocent love, and promises to keep. *Hotel on the Corner of Bitter and Sweet* is historical fiction accurately researched and beautifully told. It was considered to be a "keeper" by all three of my book clubs.

"A life spent making mistakes is not only more honourable but more useful than a life spent doing nothing."

~ George Bernard Shaw

APRIL 2011: Sag Harbor by Colson Whitehead

*(Our Long Island Reads Selection 2011)

One of the criteria for consideration as a Long Island Reads book is that said book must be written either by an L.I. author OR the book, itself, must take place on Long Island. *Sag Harbor* by Colson Whitehead satisfies the latter requirement.

The story takes place during the summer of 1985 when brothers Benji and Reggie Cooper, two wealthy black teens who attend a majority white prep school in Manhattan, escape to their family's Sag Harbor beach house in the Hamptons. There they will meet up with their friends, the children of other African American professionals, where they play hard with relatively little or no supervision from their parents, who are only occasional weekend visitors.

Sag Harbor is a coming-of-age story of young boys experimenting and trying to fit in. It's funny and beautifully written by an author who wowed his audience at the culmination of our Long Island Reads event at the Plainview/Old Bethpage Library.

Sag Harbor reminded me of summers spent in Bolton Landing with my sisters and cousins under the watchful eyes of our Grandmother.

"Writing is nothing more than a guided dream."

~ Jorge Luis Borges

MAY 2011: The Distant Hours by Kate Morton

We received ARCs (Advance Reader's Copy) of Australian author, Kate Morton's, The Distant Hours from Hillary Tisman at Simon & Schuster. We were asked to write questions and a 'Reading Guide' in exchange for copies of the book. Filled with gothic enchantment, mystery, castles and family secrets, this five-part saga is, to me, reminiscent of Anya Seton's 1972 novel, *Green Darkness*, which became Libby Canova's and my favorite book at the time.

Infused with plot twists, good guys and bad, *The Distant Hours* is a good choice for a light summer or holiday read.

"A man is known by the books he reads."

~ Ralph Waldo Emerson

JUNE 2011: The Uncoupling by Meg Wolitzer

Meg Wolitzer took the LIRR to Huntington to join us in our discussion of her latest novel, *The Uncoupling*. Oh, what an incredibly outrageous premise to her story…. a modern-day telling of the comic play, Lysistrata, by Aristophanes, in which the women of Greece withhold sex from their men in an effort to convince them to end a war (the Peloponnesian War).

Our discussion of *The Uncoupling* was animated, and Meg freely responded to the many questions that were posed by the group, both during our meeting and continuing over lunch two hours later. She is a fabulous speaker as well as a writer. Her writing is smart and reflects her astute observations of American culture.

Meg Wolitzer loves book clubs. You would be wise to read her. You would be fortunate to hear her speak.

Cross Reference: *The Ten Year Nap*, (Sept. 2008)

"I will not cut for stone."

~ *Hippocratic Oath*

JULY 2011: Cutting for Stone by Abraham Verghese

Born in Ethiopia of Indian parents, medical doctor, Abraham
Verghese, tells the story of identical, conjoined twin brothers,
Marion and Shiva Stone, in his debut historical novel, *Cutting
for Stone.* Orphaned at birth by the death of their mother,
Carmelite nun Sister Mary Joseph Praise, and abandoned by
their father, Dr. Thomas Stone, the story is narrated by
Marion and details the lives of the twins as they are raised by
two loving physicians, Kalpana Hemlatha (Hema) and Abhi
Ghosh, in "Missing."

Cutting for Stone is set mainly in Addis Ababa, Ethiopia during
the turbulent reign of Haile Selassie, and later in the United
States (New York). The brothers Stone will come to choose
different paths in medicine and in love. There will be a
betrayal. There will be blood. There will be more medical
terminology than you will ever need to know, but you will be
unable to quit this epic love story. You will be dazzled by the
author's writing. You will be taken in by the brothers' story.
You will be touched, and you will be saddened. You will find
hope in Verghese's emphasis on the Physician-Patient
Relationship, something that he stresses in his own bedside
manner. And you will tell everyone that you know to hurry
out and read this thoroughly engrossing and informative
novel.

*"To persevere, I think, is important for everybody.
I'd made it this far and refused to give up because
all my life I had always finished the race. I think
the hardest thing in life is to forgive."*

~ *Louis Zamperini*

AUGUST 2011: Unbroken: A WWII Story of Survival, Resilience, and Redemption by Laura Hillenbrand

When a book is given a 5***** rating (out of five) by book clubs, it is wise to take heed. Laura Hillenbrand has done it a second time with the writing of Louis Zamperini's life story. As with her first book, *Seabiscuit: An American Legend*, (Cross Reference May 2003,) the author has captured the Olympic runner, the hotshot bombardier, the dehydrated skeleton floating in shark-infested waters, the imprisoned downtrodden war refugee, the returning war hero, the forgiving man, in her non-fiction work, which reads like an engrossing novel.

Louis Zamperini's unbroken spirit is the stuff of legends. He lived long enough to see his life story written in book form by Hillenbrand and in beginning production for the big screen by Angelina Jolie. Louis Zamperini is an inspiration. He died on July 2, 2014, at the age of 97.

SEPTEMBER 2011: Making Toast: A Family Story by Roger Rosenblatt and Room by Emma Donoghue

There were two very interesting books that I was anxious to discuss with my book group. They were both relatively short and, in their own way, but different, dealt with the subject of child-rearing. I wondered, "Could we discuss both books at one meeting?"

The first, *Making Toast: A Family Story,* by Roger Rosenblatt, concerns the sudden and tragic death of Amy, the author's daughter, a doctor, wife, and mother of three young children ages six, four and one, from an asymptomatic heart condition. Rosenblatt and his wife, Ginny, (Boppo and Mimi) elect to leave their home and move in with their grieving son-in-law and three very frightened grandkids. Being a "Mimi," myself, I was curious to know whether Ted (PopPop) and I could rise to the occasion, at our advanced age, and meet the challenge of raising a trio of extremely young, totally dependent children.

"Making Toast was the one household duty that (Roger) would perfectly master to each child's liking." He marveled as his wife and son-in-law, Harris, navigated the channels of loss and confusion. Ultimately, they would all come together as a family and move forward through their unspeakable heartache.

I had read the favorable reviews of *Room*, by Emma Donoghue, made a note of the prizes it had won, (the 2011 Commonwealth Writer's Prize regional prize (Caribbean and Canada,) longlisted for the 2011 Orange Prize, and shortlisted for the Man Booker Prize in 2010.) I saw that it appeared on multiple bestseller lists, but still, I was reluctant to read the book. As a mother and a grandmother, the thought of reading about a child, Jack, and his mother, who was being held captive in a tiny room by a child molester, was anathema to me. It was only when I heard praise from book friends whose taste and opinions I valued, that I made up my mind to meet five-year-old, Jack, first-hand.

He was amazing.

ROOM is the only world Jack has ever known. There is WARDROBE, where he sleeps, RUG, DOOR, and TV. And there is MA, who does everything within her very limited power, to keep her boy healthy and safe.

Like *Making Toast*, *Room* is a celebration of life, of the love between a parent/grandparent and child. And, as in *Unbroken*, both books illustrate resilience in the face of unimaginable loss and leave the reader with a feeling of hope rather than horror. I am so glad that I had the opportunity to read all three of these books that speak of survival at all costs.

<u>Note</u>: Between 2002- 2004 three young women, Michelle Knight, Amanda Berry, and Georgina "Gina" De Jesus, were kidnapped by Ariel Castro and imprisoned in his house on Seymour Ave., Tremont, Cleveland, Ohio. On May 6, 2013, Amanda Berry escaped with her six-year-old daughter. Police freed the others later that day. Castro was sentenced to life without parole. He committed suicide by hanging himself with bedsheets. (Wikipedia, the free encyclopedia.)

The women have written about their captivity:

Hope: A Memoir of Survival in Cleveland, by Amanda Berry and Gina De Jesus, with Mary Jordan and Kevin Sullivan.

Finding Me: A Memoir of the Cleveland Kidnappings, "A Decade of Darkness, a Life Reclaimed," by Michelle Knight, with Michelle Burford.

"I would carry my pillow from bed to bed in the apartment like a graying Goldilocks still trying to find a place that was just right."

~ *Hilma Wolitzer, The Doctor's Daughter*

OCTOBER 2011: Diamond Ruby by Joseph Wallace

*Guest Author

It was nearing the end of baseball season.... October, playoffs and the World Series. There was no better time to read a book about baseball or to host a true baseball aficionado. We found both in Joe Wallace and *Diamond Ruby*.

Inspired by a real girl named Jackie Mitchell, the sixteen-year-old pitching phenomenon from Chattanooga, TN, who struck out both Babe Ruth ("Jidge") and Lou Gehrig, *Diamond Ruby* is the story of Ruby Thomas, with the long arms and the powerhouse fastball, brought so vividly to life by author, Joe Wallace. The time ranges from 1918 through the 1920s. The place is Brooklyn and New York City. We meet colorful characters, both real, (Babe Ruth, Casey Stengel, Jack Dempsey) and imagined, (Ruby Thomas and her two nieces, Amanda and Allie). We live through the devastation of the Spanish Influenza of 1918-19 and the Triangle Shirtwaist Factory Fire. We have a thirst as we vicariously experience Prohibition and the 1919 World Series between the Chicago White Sox and the Cincinnati Reds. We meet Kenesaw Mountain Landis, the first Commissioner of Baseball, famous for the 'Black Sox Scandal' and his expulsion from organized baseball of "Shoeless" Joe Jackson and his teammates for conspiring to rig the 1919 World

406

Series. We find Rockefellers, W.K. Vanderbilt and Florenz Ziegfeld, Jr., President Harding and Rudolph Valentino, Honus Wagner and Ty Cobb.

My book clubs responded to and reminisced over the time period and the places that were mentioned in *Diamond Ruby*, highlights such as Coney Island and Ebbets Field. Joe Wallace brought the world of Ruby Thomas to life with his exuberance and knowledge. He is a pleasure to talk to and a joy to host.

> *"A revolution is not a dinner party or writing an essay, or painting a picture, or doing embroidery; it cannot be so refined, so leisurely and gentle, so temperate, kind, courteous, restrained and magnanimous. A revolution is an insurrection, an act of violence for which one class overthrows another."*
>
> ~ *Chairman Mao Tse-tung*

NOVEMBER 2011: Dreams of Joy by Lisa See

* Telechat with the author

Lisa See once again agreed to talk with us about her latest book and about her Chinese heritage. She joined us on November 14th, 2011 to share the background for *Dreams of Joy*, her sequel to *Shanghai Girls*, which recants the further exploits of May and Pearl Chen and Pearl's headstrong daughter, Joy.

Family secrets are revealed, Joy flees to Shanghai in pursuit of her biological father and becomes inexorably entwined in Mao's Great Leap Forward and Communism, poverty and the pursuant hardships. Determined to assuage her guilt over lying to her daughter, Pearl follows Joy to China and attempts to free her from the famine and poverty that surrounds her and cripples the country.

Dreams of Joy is a story about the Chen Sisters, Pearl and May, and their relationship to one another. It is a mother/daughter love story, and it is a tale about China during the late 1950s when Mao's (Zedong) misplaced idealism forced millions of people to cheat, steal, beg and ultimately die of famine. *Dreams of Joy* is a worthy sequel to *Shanghai Girls.*

"We are not makers of history. We are made by history."

~ *Martin Luther King, Jr.*

NOVEMBER 2011: The Time in Between by Maria Duenas

* Guest Author

'THE Literary Gallery' was pleasantly surprised at a second meeting in November when Spanish author, Maria Duenas, stopped by to pay us a 'Thank You' visit at the start of her U.S. Book Tour.

Hillary Tisman, our publishing friend from Simon & Schuster, had sent thirty ARCs (Advance Reader's Copy) of Maria Duenas's international bestseller, *The Time in Between*. In exchange for the books, we were asked to write the 'Reading Group Guide' and 'Questions For Discussion' that would be affixed to the paperback edition. What a thrill! What an honor for us to be invited to partake in this experiment. (I thought of Jim Fergus's premise in writing *One Thousand White Women: The Journals of May Dodd*, whereby 1,000 white women would be given to the Cheyenne Indians in exchange for 1,000 horses. Fortunately, we weren't required to whinny or snort. (Cross Reference August 2007).

Hillary Tisman and Wendy Sheanin from Simon & Schuster Publishing had joined our book discussion of, *The Distant Hours*, by Kate Morton. Apparently, they had never partaken in a book discussion before, and they were impressed by the dialogue and exchange of intelligent questions that were posed by the group.

Upon receipt of the ARCs, I assembled a "Brainstorming Group," a kind of "Think Tank" to gather and formulate the 'Reading Group Guide.' Fifteen of us met over coffee and pastries at the Elwood Library. We were so successful that we would be invited twice more to create a set of 'Questions For Discussion' for Joseph Kanon's, *Istanbul Passage*, (June 2012) and Daniel McCaig's, *Ruth's Journey: The Authorized Novel of Mammy from Margaret Mitchell's Gone with the Wind*, (2014.)

The Time in Between is the story of Spanish heroine/seamstress, Sira Quiroga, as she fights to save her life and form her own identity. From Madrid to Morocco, gutsy dressmaker cum spy, Sira will forge friendships with the wives of Nazis and the mistresses of the revolutionaries of the Spanish Civil War as she cuts fabric and seams together her haute couture designs.

The Time in Between has been described as part *Casablanca*, part *The Shadow of the Wind*, by Carlos Ruiz Zafon. It is a light read, more a romantic adventure than a historical document. If you are into fashion, soft espionage, daring heroines and handsome war heroes; if you enjoy reading about true freedom fighters and Spanish guerrillas who encounter fictional foes, then *The Time in Between* is the book for you.

The "only advice, indeed, that one person can give
another about reading is to take no advice, to
follow your own instincts, to use your own reason,
to come to your own conclusions."

~ Virginia Woolf

DECEMBER 2011: Onward Brave Readers

BOOKS, BOOKS, BOOKS – 15 YEAR RECAP
DISCUSSION & ANECDOTES

For our last book discussion at Barnes & Noble, Huntington, we would take a walk down Memory Lane and discuss the many books – the best and the worst – that we had read through the years. On our literary journey, we discussed authors we had met and read and authors that we looked forward to reading in the years to come. We talked about our beginnings as 'The Literary Gallery' Book Discussion Group back in May of 1996. We fondly remembered our original members (Elvira Lubrano, Ellen Davis, Connie Sabatino, and Rita Silver), those who still participate each month, and those who left us to pursue other interests, and those who have since passed away. We talked about new members who have joined us over the years and brought their family members and other friends. We discussed our shared love of reading.

It would be sad to leave our comfortable home at Barnes & Noble after five wonderful years working with Debra Gaynor in our private room, the area designated for visiting authors and the launch of a new book. The store would close, and we would move with Debra to the new location of B&N in East Northport.

But things would never be the same.

We concluded with our 16th Annual Holiday Luncheon and our hopes for good health and happiness and HAPPY READING in 2012!

Chapter 16

A Year of Highs and Lows: Reading Books, Taking a Walking Tour, Writing 'Questions for Discussion' for Simon & Schuster, Standing Up for Heroes, Reading Throughout Superstorm Sandy, (2012)

"A writer only begins a book. A reader finishes it."

~ Samuel Johnson

JANUARY 2012: Another Piece of My Heart by Jane Green

When we moved to our new home at Barnes & Noble, East Northport, NY, in January 2012, our comfort level was as unsettled as our discordant discussion of Jane Green's novel, *Another Piece of My Heart.*

Suffice it to say that the author was undermined by a very truculent and confrontational representative.

"A nation that forgets its past can function no better than an individual with amnesia."

~ David McCullough

FEBRUARY 2012: The Greater Journey: Americans in Paris by David McCullough

Master historian, David McCullough, brought to life the story of celebrated American pioneers, who went to Paris to study and create and be inspired, famous painters like John Singer Sargent and Mary Cassatt, architect Stanford White, writer James Fenimore Cooper, and Augustus Saint-Gaudens, who designed and sculpted the golden 13-foot high statue of General William Tecumseh Sherman on horseback that sits prominently in New York City's Central Park.

We were all moved by McCullough's telling of the adventurous men and women who sought enlightenment in 'The City of Light' during the period between 1830-1900.

The Greater Journey is an excellent choice for book clubs, history lovers, artists, and francophiles.

"I love sleep. My life has the tendency to fall apart when I'm awake, you know?"

~ Ernest Hemingway

MARCH 2012: The Paris Wife by Paula McLain

The unsophisticated, older woman, Hadley Richardson, married a young and energetic, Ernest Hemingway, in 1921. She was his first (of many) wife, his "starter wife," his sounding board, his outmoded Paris spouse. Book clubs were quick to order copies of this novel that features F. Scott Fitzgerald and Zelda, Ezra Pound and Gertrude Stein, along with an ambitious and heavy-drinking "Hem," as their careers flounder or take flight.

The Greater Journey: Americans in Paris, showed us the brighter side of a more inviting Paris where Americans came in search of knowledge. The Paris of the 1920s that we see in *The Paris Wife* is darker and more decadent. You may not be happy with what you find, but you will enjoy reading about the brash, swashbuckling, Hemingway, and his plain, unobtrusive "Paris Wife."

THE TIME: Late March 2012

THE PICK-UP: Upper Saddle River, NJ (Brett & Rebecca's Home, Babysitting our twins)

THE DESTINATION: The West Village, NYC

THE OCCASION: Adriana Trigiani's Walking Tour for the launch of her new book, *The Shoemaker's Wife*.

Acclaimed, best-selling author, Adriana Trigiani, called and invited me to join her and several friends in New York City's West Village for a tour of some of the sites mentioned in her books. I was to be interviewed by CBS MORNING SHOW contributor, essayist, author and media consultant, Lee Woodruff. Our talk was to be about my long, literary history with Adri. We hit it off immediately, Lee Woodruff and me, fellow bibliophiles and Lake George denizens. As we walked those charming cobblestone streets and later savored cannoli and cappuccinos, I wondered, "What could be better?" It was a glorious afternoon spent with Adri, Lee and other book-loving friends in the greatest city in the world! (The cannoli weren't too shabby either).

*Tip – Google Adriani Trigiani Walking Tour of New York City – re CBS Video, The Shoemaker's Wife. You may catch a glimpse of me with Adri and Lee.

"Let us read and let us dance—two amusements
that will never do any harm to the world."

~ Voltaire

APRIL 2012: The Lost Wife by Alyson Richman (Guest Author)

*(A Long Island Reads Selection 2012)

I was very happy when the Long Island Reads Committee unanimously chose Alyson Richman's novel, *The Lost Wife*, as our 2012 selection. Alyson is a Long Island girl and a prodigious writer. I was proud to have read her books and previously hosted her at my book clubs.

When she visited my three-book groups in April 2012, she told us how she became inspired while sitting under the dryer at her hair dresser's and listening to the unbelievable, but true, story of a husband and wife who met, fell in love and married in Prague prior to WWII, were separated when war broke out, married other people believing that their spouses were dead, then meeting again decades later in NYC at the marriage of their grandchildren.

"Truth is stranger than fiction," but this truth is retold in a novelistic narrative. Ms. Richman's deft hand at writing, after extensive research trips to Eastern Europe, exemplifies her ability to capture a story, particularly Lenka and Josef's, and make it come alive on the page. *The Lost Wife* spawned travel to Czechoslovakia and (the) Terezin (Theresienstadt) Concentration Camp. It was very highly received (and Alyson Richman was warmly welcomed,) by 'The Literary Gallery,' 'Page Turners,' and 'From Cover To Cover' Book Clubs.

*"Every Action done in Company, ought to be with
Some Sign of Respect, to those that are Present."*

*~ Rules of Civility and Decent Behaviour In
Company and Conversation, by George
Washington*

MAY 2012: Rules of Civility by Amor Towles

Rules of Civility, the first novel by Amor Towles, takes place in
Manhattan during the post Jazz Age years of the 1930s.
Katey Kontent, Eve Ross and Tinker Grey form the
triumvirate of stars in this drama of manners and behavior.
Mysterious Tinker Grey, handsome and elusive, has based his
life and comportment on 'George Washington's 110 Rules of
Civility and Decent Behavior in Company and Conversation.'

Circumstances will conspire to alienate Katey and Eve,
Tinker and Eve, and Tinker and Katey. Love and loss in high
society, betrayals, and choices made in a moment, will render
Katey haughty and alone, Eve restless and flighty and Tinker,
ever sophisticated but penniless, and then princely and
penniless once more. This is a good book for discussion.
The characters may or may not be to your liking, and that
may determine your rating. The music of the era will ring in
your ears, and the slang will be familiar to that time, not so
long ago, when jazz nightclubs were in vogue.

"If the earth were a single state, Istanbul would be its capital."

~ *Napoleon Bonaparte*

JUNE 2012: Istanbul Passage by Joseph Kanon *(Telephone Chat)

'Reading Group Guide' Written by 'The Literary Gallery.'

We had been invited to write the 'Reading Group Guide' for Joseph Kanon's latest thriller, a dark novel set in Istanbul in the years immediately following the Second World War. We were anxious to query the author on his characters, especially those who bore the names of chess pieces, one King, one Bishop, one Pawn (Bauer). There is intrigue in Istanbul. There is espionage and alliances made and broken in this neutral capital that straddled Europe and Asia.

There is a sense of weightiness as you read *Istanbul Passage*. As in *Snow Falling on Cedars*, by David Guterson, (May 1996) you can almost feel the mist as it settles over the city. You can sense deceit and double-dealing. The city of Istanbul is as much a player in this novel as Bainbridge Island is in the latter. It is clammy and wet, and it reeks of death. It is a great spy thriller and travelogue through Istanbul.

Tip #12 - Travel/Destination Book

Tip #21 - Food/Beverage Themed Books

      Serve Turkish coffee and Turkish Delights (Candy) or Halvah

Tip #22 - Create a Mood (a la CASABLANCA)

"The safety of the people shall be the highest law."

~ *Marcus Tullius Cicero*

JULY 2012: Defending Jacob by William Landay

I love it whenever I hear about a new (or old) "must-read." *Defending Jacob* is one of those psychological suspense novels that creeps under your skin, and has you questioning the actions and motives of its protagonists and the resultant consequences of those actions. It is the story of a family torn apart by a shocking murder, accusations, lost innocence (not just of children) and naiveté. Andy Barber is an Assistant District Attorney living in a close-knit suburban town in Massachusetts, where families take pride in their community spirit and low crime rate. Life is good for Andy and his wife, Laurie, until their fourteen-year-old son, Jacob, is questioned, and then suspected, of murdering a fellow student. What ensues are secrets and lies and revelations that threaten to undermine Andy's job, the parent/child relationship, and the husband/wife bond. How well do we really know our spouse? (Cross Reference: *The Pilot's Wife*, by Anita Shreve (Sept. 1999) and *The Memory Keeper's Daughter*, by Kim Edwards, (Feb. 2007,) and *The Light Between Oceans*, by M. L. Stedman, (Feb. 2013.) And how well do we know our own child? (Refer to *Empire Falls*, by Richard Russo, (Nov. 2002) and *Nineteen Minutes*, by Jodi Picoult (Oct. 2007). *Defending Jacob* speaks of the possibility of a "murder gene," a variant of the monoamine oxidase A (MAOA,) which predisposes an individual to violent and impulsive behavior.

Read this compelling thriller and decide for yourself.

"Women can do anything men can do and do it in 5-inch heels."

~ Brian Atwood

AUGUST 2012: The Shoemaker's Wife by Adriana Trigiani

*(Telephone Chat)

We had a telephone chat with the ebullient author, Adriana Trigiani, on August 6th, 2012. Our book club loving friend had previously sent signed bookplates to our members and was prepared to chat with us about her grandparents', (here known as Enza Ravanelli and Ciro Lazzari), love story. Set both in Italy and the United States, and book-ended by two World Wars, *The Shoemaker's Wife* is a colorful historical novel in which we meet the great tenor, Enrico Caruso, and learn a few things about the shoemaking trade, and the world of a seamstress. As with all of Trigiani's novels, the reader is treated to a feast of home-cooked meals, made from scratch, and to the joys and struggles of families and family life. The novel is replete with details: a perilous ocean journey in the early 1900s, surviving the immigration process at Ellis Island, sewing costumes for the Metropolitan Opera, and digging deep in Minnesota's Iron Range.

There is sadness and tension and page-turning adventures, but most of all, *The Shoemaker's Wife* is a paean to friendship and familial love and pride in one's work done well.

"Eating and reading are two pleasures that combine admirably."

~ *C. S. Lewis*

~ *(Note* I know, because my M&M peanuts are always nearby)*

~ *Donna Diamond*

SEPTEMBER 2012: Ten Girls to Watch by Charity Shumway

We were invited, Ted, Dani, Greg and I, to attend the book launch of a debut novel written by Charity Shumway, the wife of one of my son-in-law, Greg's William & Mary College (and soccer) buddies. Charity was such a wonderful speaker that I promptly invited her to join us at Barnes & Noble a few months later.

During her time working at *Glamour* in 2007, Charity reported on the 50th Anniversary of the magazine's "Top Ten College Women" contest. This became the inspiration for her book, a story about recent Harvard graduate, Dawn West, struggling to make a name for herself as a writer. When she lands a job at *Charm* magazine and is paid to track down past winners of *Charm's* "Ten Girls To Watch" contest, Dawn is on her way to meeting friends, both of the male and female gender, and potential role models of her own. She will come into contact with the Robert Rolland Pretzel Baron Family and take lessons from the successful women who preceded her, while ultimately learning to forge a path of her own.

Charity Shumway is an author to watch. You won't be disappointed.

"The two most powerful warriors are patience and time."

~ Leo Tolstoy

OCTOBER 2012: The Sandcastle Girls by Chris Bohjalian

Chris Bohjalian has stated that *The Sandcastle Girls* is the most important book he has ever written. The author's 15th work, based in part on his Armenian heritage, inspired by his father, Aram Bohjalian, and his mother-in-law, the late Sondra Blewer, who encouraged him to write it, takes us to Aleppo, Syria in 1915 during the Armenian genocide, "The Slaughter You Know Next To Nothing About", then forward to Bronxville, New York in 2012.

The Sandcastle Girls s a love story between American born "nurse in training," Elizabeth Endicott, who has volunteered to deliver food and medicine to the refugees in Aleppo, and Armen Petrosian, an Armenian engineer. Although married but believing that his wife and daughter have been slaughtered, Armen falls in love with Elizabeth through their exchange of letters, as he travels to Egypt to join the British Army. Decades later, Elizabeth and Armen's granddaughter, Laura, will uncover secrets, as she seeks to trace her family's history.

Part love story, part history lesson, *The Sandcastle Girls* is a timely read, a political current events read, and a heartbreaking story of love and loss. While researching the Armenian genocide, I was simultaneously taking part in a French conversation course to brush up on my language skills. (The old saying, "Use it OR lose it," applied to me and I was anxious to resurrect my fluency and thinking "in

French.."). When we were asked by our native Professeur to select un auteur ou un chanteur favori, I chose Charles Aznavour, "France's Frank Sinatra.". For years I have listened to his melodious tunes and lamented over the romantic lyrics. Many a night as a young teen, I cried myself to sleep, vicariously imagining Aznavour's sadness as he sang, "Que C'est Triste Venise," "Hier Encore," et "Il te suffisait que je t'aime, » It was only recently that I became aware of the fact that Charles Aznavour, the French singer, was actually born Shahnour Varinag Aznavourian, and is a French and Armenian singer, arguably the most famous Armenian of his time. Along with his longtime friend, Levon Sayan, he founded the charitable organization, 'Aznavour for Armenia,' in response to the 1988 earthquake in Armenia and was appointed Armenia's permanent delegate to the United Nations at Geneva.

Add *The Sandcastle Girls* to your list of "must-reads" and listen to the crooning of my favorite French and Armenian chanteur, Charles Aznavourian.

We were celebrating Bekah and Joe Balsamo's nuptials (my cousin/sister, Karyn's daughter), in St. Thomas, U.S. Virgin Islands, when news of Hurricane Sandy, also known as "Superstorm Sandy," or "Frankenstorm Sandy," struck Long Island, New York City, and New Jersey with a vengeance, an unwanted CRASH!, BOOM!, BANG!, the end of October, 2012. Torrential rains and unprecedented howling wind gusts ravaged homes, knocked out electricity and caused bounteous flooding. There were hundreds of fatalities and hospitalizations. Heat and water, necessary for survival, were impacted by this post-tropical storm/cyclone that originated in the Caribbean Sea. Schools and businesses were closed. Families, at least the lucky ones, lived as campers, surviving on canned goods and bottled water, candles and flashlights. Trees were toppled. Cars were trapped. Homes were evacuated.

From October 22nd, when it first gained strength, to November 5th, 2012 (and to Tuesday, November 6th when Barack Obama was re-elected to serve a second term as President of the United States), Hurricane Sandy left a path of destruction from Cuba to the United States and Canada.

Ted and I were among the lucky ones. We only lost two trees, (one broke through the fence and fell into our neighbor's backyard, narrowly missing the roof of their house), and power for two weeks.

Dani and Greg and our girls in Manhasset, in an older but apparently better-built home with a chugging boiler, were able to keep the house, and several neighbors, warm during the worst of Sandy's wrath.

Brett and Rebecca and our year and ½ old twins, plus the family pet, a Cavalier King Charles Spaniel named Floyd, (short for Pink Floyd, Brett's favorite rock band), in New Jersey, didn't fare as well. Their water supply, coming from wells in the ground, was

426

interrupted. With no heat or running water or flushing of toilets and two little babies, the Junior Diamonds sought shelter wherever they could.

We returned home and heard the horror stories of those who weren't as fortunate as we. Superstorm Sandy would, henceforth, become the benchmark against which other storms would be compared. We would add a new "Event" to the already growing list of "Where Were You When?" stories.

<u>NOTE</u>: In October 2012, I also read, *The Lace Reader* by Brunonia Barry and *Brooklyn*, by Colm Toibin, two books that we would later discuss in my Harborfields Library "Morning Book Discussion Group" .... a testament to the power of reading through hail and rain and reliance on daylight and flashlight.

*"Ever has it been that love knows not its own
depth until the hour of separation."*

~Kahlil Gibran

NOVEMBER 2012: Those We Love Most by Lee Woodruff *(Author Visit)

The very lovely author, essayist and media consultant, Lee Woodruff, visited our book club at Barnes & Noble, East Northport, immediately after her appearance on the 'TODAY' Show with Kathie Lee (Gifford) and Hoda (Kotb). Intelligent and upbeat, with easy grace, Lee spoke of the ways in which a person's or a family's life can be irrevocably changed. *In an Instant* is the title of the book she co-wrote with husband, ABC television journalist, Bob Woodruff, who was severely injured by a roadside bomb while reporting on the war in Iraq in 2006.

 Lee spoke of how a woman in today's world trying to "micro" or "macro" manage life in the fast lane, is a "myth." She describes this falsity in her book, *Perfectly Imperfect: A Life in Progress*.

We spoke of her fiction debut, *Those We Love Most*, about a family torn apart by tragedy trying to heal itself, just as her family had struggled when her husband was gravely injured.

Invite Lee Woodruff to join your book club or address your organization, as I did when she spoke to my "Page Turners" book club in Northport or addressed a crowd at the 10th Annual VIBS (Victims Information Bureau of Suffolk - Family Violence and Rape Crisis Center) Luncheon in Woodbury. She is an inspirational speaker/writer who will leave you feeling renewed and better able to cope with whatever obstacles may befall you.

IGNORE Tip #7 Regarding NO PERSONAL DISCUSSIONS OF FAMILY OR HEALTH!

His Preference: "Chivas on the rocks, Club Soda on the side, I'LL MIX IT!"

And Mine: "Decaf Venti, 4 Pump, Skinny Vanilla Latte."

My Theo was my hero to the end, literally TO THE END of the wind tunnel we got caught in en route to the 7th Annual Bob and Lee Woodruff – STAND UP FOR HEROES Concert in New York City. It was a balmy evening, Wednesday, November 6, 2013. As we parked the car and started our walk to the Theatre at Madison Square Garden, a huge gust of wind snatched the hairpiece from the back of my head. Before I even knew it was gone, I saw the man I married chasing this puffy, blonde, hairball down the alley. What an auspicious way to begin our enchanted evening of laughter, music, and love!

Jon Stewart, Bill Cosby, Jim Gaffigan, and Jerry Seinfeld, elicited chuckles and guffaws from the crowd. Roger Waters and Bruce Springsteen had us tapping our feet and singing along to 'Halleluiah!' and 'Dancing in the Dark,' and the house rocked to 'Comfortably Numb' as Roger Waters called out the names of the Vets who were onstage to accompany him.

Seated in the front, in uniform and smiling, our Vets, our women, and men, our 'Wounded Warriors,' were feted.

Our thanks to all of our Vets for their service and to Bob and Lee Woodruff for a very special evening.

"Associate yourself with men of good quality if you esteem your own reputation; for 'tis better to be alone than in bad company."

~ George Washington

DECEMBER 2012: The President's Club: Inside the World's Most Exclusive Fraternity by Nancy Gibbs and Michael Duffy

I chose a work of non-fiction for our final meeting of 2012. Debra Gaynor, formerly my coordinator at Barnes & Noble, had moved to the John W. Engeman Theater in Northport, which presents Broadway-caliber productions in a sophisticated cabaret-like setting at off-off-Broadway prices.

After Debra conducted a tour of the facility and offered a light repast, I gave a brief biographical sketch of the authors, Nancy Gibbs and Michael Duffy, editors at TIME magazine.

The President's Club is the story of a "closed society" of men, Democrats, and Republicans, who held the highest office in the United States.   When describing the book, I didn't talk so much of petty jealousies, "two scorpions in a bottle," (quote taken from *The President's Club*, and referring to Lyndon B. Johnson and Richard M. Nixon,) or "the rascal and the rebel",(referring to Bill Clinton and George W. Bush), and rivalries, as much as I did about the guidance and helpfulness of former leaders to those who succeeded them. We spoke of unlikely alliances.

Our discussion wasn't tainted by political agendas or Republican vs. Democratic affiliation.

Book clubs and history buffs and politically savvy readers will enjoy Nancy Gibbs's and Michael Duffy's *The President's Club: Inside the World's Most Exclusive Fraternity.*

And all thirty of us, who gathered for our year-end discussion, are still speaking to one another.

IGNORE MY TIP # 6 – Re: NO POLITICS OR RELIGION

Chapter 17

A New Home for 'The Literary Gallery,' Year-End Recap 2013

We found a warm and welcoming home at the Elwood Public Library after we left Barnes & Noble in June 2013. We were all saddened to leave the book store where we first began our book discussions seventeen years prior, but we were eager to start again in a private venue, where we could hold SKYPE chats with authors and have the internet available to augment our gatherings. Susan Goldberg, Library Director, and her staff were most accommodating.

Just as it is difficult for me to name a favorite book, it is equally exacting to choose a favorite year of reading. The year 2013 offered us unlimited possibilities; therefore, our selections tended to mirror what was currently being read by other book clubs and reflected the bestsellers that were being highlighted in *The New York Times* and *USA Today*.

"The highest happiness on earth is the happiness of marriage."

~ William Lyon Phelps

JANUARY 2013: A Wedding in Great Neck by Yona Zeldis McDonough

What fun we had when the very stylish Yona Zeldis McDonough paid us another visit to talk about the Silverstein family and the nuptials of "the favorite child," Angelica. The book jacket is magnificent! We see the back of a gorgeous wedding gown, and the hands of four women tying the bow on Angelica's dress, each seeking to interfere and impose her will on the bride.

New York Times Bestselling author Caroline Leavitt has called Yona's novel, "A funny, moving look at the bonds of love, the ties of family, and the yearning for happily ever after." *A Wedding in Great Neck* takes place on Long Island and is a great beach read. Open this book and find out what happens to Angelica and her former fighter pilot fiancé.

"Don't forget that maybe you are the lighthouse in someone's storm."

~ Unknown

FEBRUARY 2013: The Light Between Oceans by M. L. Stedman

Tom and Isabel Sherbourne live together, isolated at the lighthouse on Janus Rock, Australia. Their world is happy and exclusive, but they yearn to have a child to share their joy. Dejected after several miscarriages and a stillbirth, Isabel is overjoyed when a boat washes up with a dead man and a crying baby. Isabel views this as a sign and pleads with her husband, a war veteran who keeps precise records and believes it is his job to report the incident. Against his better judgment, Tom succumbs to his wife's entreaties and easily falls into the role of father to baby Lucy. Their world is complete until they return to the mainland and hear stories of a missing man and his baby daughter.

The Light Between Oceans is one of my favorite books. The moral dilemma that is at the heart of the story intrigued me and kept me quickly turning the pages. Tom is an ethical man, a leader during the war, a man who always tries to do "the right thing." His love for his wife, Isabel, and baby daughter is his number # 1 priority; yet his conscience eats at him, tormenting him to find out who these missing people are. This is a book for any mother or father, sister or brother, aunt or uncle, grandfather or grandmother, or any person who has suffered a loss, or who has felt guilty about something they have done (or neglected to do). I cried, and I agonized over Tom and Isabel's plight. I won't tell you about the ending, only that I wish it had been different.

"All this time I'd thought we were strangers, and it turned out we knew each other intuitively, in our bones, in our blood. It was kind of romantic, catastrophically romantic."

~ *Gillian Flynn, Gone Girl*

MARCH 2013: Gone Girl by Gillian Flynn

Sociopath, psychopath, conniver, manipulator, liar, temptress, murderer, enabler, are words used to describe the beautiful "Amazing Amy" (Dunne) in this fast-paced, bestselling thriller about Nick Dunne and his wife. Reviewers praised this book for its plot and its well-written prose. *Library Journal* starred review has said of Gillian Flynn's novel: "Flynn cements her place among that group of mystery/thriller writers who unfailingly deliver the goods….Once again Flynn has written an intelligent, gripping tour de force, mixing a riveting plot and psychological intrigue with a compelling prose style that unobtrusively yet forcefully carries the reader from page to page."

Flynn was a former TV critic for *Entertainment Weekly*. Her first novel, *Sharp Objects* was the winner of two CWA Daggers. *Dark Places* followed, but it was her third novel, *Gone Girl*, that rocked the bestseller list for weeks.

Gone Girl, the movie, starred Ben Affleck as Nick Dunne and Rosamund Pike as Amy. Although Gillian Flynn worked on the movie, there are many differences between the book and the film.

"I rob banks because that's where the money is."

~ *Willie Sutton*

APRIL 2013: Sutton by J. R. Moehringer

Who hasn't heard of the (in)famous Willie "the actor" Sutton? J.R. Moehringer brought the man and his times to life in his historical novel, *Sutton* (our L.I. Reads Selection 2013), named after this very complicated bank robber, who grew up in the tough neighborhood of Irishtown, near the Brooklyn Navy Yard. Moehringer opens the story with an old man, Willie, leaving prison accompanied by 'Reporter' and Photographer', most likely based on Ed Kirkman and Gordon Rynders of *The Daily News* (*New York Times Sunday Book Review*, *Gentleman Outlaw*, 'Sutton' by J. R. Moehringer, by Robert Polito, Nov. 2, 2012). Willie was nicknamed "the actor" because he would dress in various disguises, in the uniform of a policeman, postal worker or messenger, sporting different mustaches, as he robbed banks and jewelry stores.

This fictional account is narrated by Willie himself, as he talks of half his life spent in jail (Sing Sing, Holmesburg, Eastern State Penitentiary in Philadelphia). He speaks of his thwarted rich girl/poor man love affair with the lovely Bess Endner, daughter of a wealthy shipbuilding magnate.

Willie Sutton was a "Top 10 Most Wanted Fugitives" celebrity sought after as talk show guest by Dick Cavett and Merv Griffin. My book clubs thoroughly enjoyed reading of Willie Sutton's exploits. His adventures and the very charming J. R. Moehringer, (ref: *The Tender Bar*, August 2006) made for a very successful Long Island Reads program at the Plainview/Old Bethpage Library in 2013.

437

"Three may keep a secret if two of them are dead."

~ Benjamin Franklin

MAY 2013: The Secret Keeper by Kate Morton

Kate Morton filled her novel with twists and turns as we read ARCs (Advanced Reader's Copy) of *The Secret Keeper*, supplied by our good friend, Hillary Tisman, at Atria (Division of Simon & Schuster). In her note, Hillary writes: "Beginning in 1959 England with a shocking crime, the spellbinding narrative moves through time from pre-World War II England to the fifties and beyond, examining the secret history of three strangers who meet by chance during the blitz and whose lives become forever entwined. It's a fascinating exploration of longings and dreams, and the lengths that people will go through to fulfill them, regardless of the costs."

The eldest of three sisters, Kate was born in South Australia and moved with her family many times before finally settling on Tamborine Mountain. An avid reader from a young age, she and her siblings would act out plays and games of make-believe. It isn't any wonder that Kate Morton would become a writer, penning stories about secrets, tricks, and puzzles. Allen and Unwin Reading Group Notes asked the author about how her novels draw from the Victorian gothic novels. Morton replied: "My books have similarities to Victorian novels: they are multi-layered with numerous characters and time periods and settings, and I put a lot of time into creating a very detailed fictional world. I always include a contemporary storyline, though, because I'm far more interested in the relationship between the present and the past – the idea that the past and its secrets are always with us – than I am by the historical aspect on its own."

Kate Morton holds degrees in dramatic art and English literature, specializing in 19th-century tragedy and contemporary gothic novels. She lives with her husband and sons in Brisbane, Australia.

*"In the depth of winter, I finally learned that there
was in me an invincible summer."*

~ *Albert Camus*

JUNE 2013: A Week in Winter by Maeve Binchy

This gentle balm by Irish author, Maeve Binchy, was published posthumously in 2012 and set a record for the most pre-orders ever for a book on Amazon.com. We had read other works by this beloved author, (*Scarlet Feather*, July 2001, *Heart and Soul*, August 2009), enjoying each story Binchy so lovingly told.   This one takes protagonist Chicky Starr to the windswept Atlantic and the small town of Stoneybridge, where she is determined to renovate a decrepit mansion and turn it into an idyll for a seaside vacation.

A Week in Winter is a cozy read most savored by the fire, with a cup of hot coffee (flavored with strong Irish whiskey, Jameson, of course!)

*"And it was too late. No one wants to believe
something is too late, but it is always becoming too
late, and then it is."*

~ *Elizabeth Strout, The Burgess Boys*

JULY 2013: The Burgess Boys by Elizabeth Strout

'The Literary Gallery' was on the move still again. The ditsy
manager at Barnes and Noble told us that we weren't
bringing enough revenue to the store during our once- a-
month Monday morning book discussions. Seriously? We
were told back in May of 1996 that it would be best to hold
our meetings on Mondays because that was the quietest day
at the store. And now you're telling us we have to leave?
Really? A bookstore removing an established book discussion
group, especially a large group such as ours? (Note: Thirty-
two 'regulars' attended our discussion in July 2013, including
Jackie Metzger, Barbara Golden, Jane Cavuoto, Mary Wood,
Pat DeSilva, Judy Phillips, Judy Gleicher (one of our
snowbirds), Jill Mancini, Ellen Main, Pat Craig, Gina Henry,
Kathy Dreschler, Kathy Kreytak, Elaine Campanella, Fran
Jacklets, Carolyn Sciortino, Mary O'Donnell, Marie
Mastellon, Diane McCarthy, Michele Bisom, Maureen Spisak,
Lois Hass, Melanie Lugar, Helaine Bank) .

My home library is the Elwood Public Library in Elwood,
NY. I approached Belle Baxter, then Head Reference
Librarian and a friend, who willingly joined our escapades
into the city and who was part of the 'Brainstorming
Sessions' we would hold to create 'Questions for Discussion'
in exchange for ARCs. I asked her if she thought it might be
possible for us to hold our monthly meetings at the library on
the second Monday of each month between 11:00- 12:30PM.
She told me to speak with the Director of the library, Susan

441

Goldberg, who graciously opened up its doors to us immediately.

Elwood is a small library that only came into existence a few years prior, occupying the space formerly held by Blockbuster Video on the corner of Elwood Road and Jericho Turnpike. We were given a very large room, access to the computer, videos, and accessibility for SKYPE chats and telephone chats. We could bring in food and beverages if we so desired.

So, in July 2013 'The Literary Gallery' walked into the Elwood Library for their first book discussion. Elizabeth Strout, the author of the highly regarded, *Olive Kitteridge*, for which she was awarded the Pulitzer Prize for Fiction, a tough act to follow, had written her sophomore novel, *The Burgess Boys*, the subject of our discussion that morning. Strout tackles themes of family, identity, race, immigration, class, and politics here. *The Washington Post* has praised her "tender understanding" of family and individual turmoil. Robin Vidimos, writing for the www.denverpost.com, Book Review: In Elizabeth Strout's new novel, "The Burgess Boys," Trouble Reunites Reluctant Siblings, has written, "The siblings in The Burgess Boys aren't dysfunctional as much as they are family members who don't much like each other."

There is plenty of dysfunction in the Burgess Family, but after all, isn't "dysfunction" just another word for "family?"

"We are each our own devil, and we make this world our hell."

~ *Oscar Wilde*

AUGUST 2013: Fever by Mary Beth Keane

(*Skype Chat with author)

Twenty-seven of us gathered around the table at our new home in Elwood to discuss "Typhoid Mary" with the author of *Fever*, Mary Beth Keane. Mary Mallon was a feisty and robust Irish immigrant, who came to America alone and fought to raise herself up from the lowest ranks of domestic service. She discovered she had a talent for cooking. From 1899-1915, she found lucrative employment working in the kitchens of some of the wealthy families of New York, leaving a path of disease behind her.

Enter one ingenious "medical engineer," George Soper, who determined that Mary Mallon was the first known healthy carrier, ("asymptomatic") of typhoid fever. Soper had Mary quarantined on North Brother Island in the East River in 1907. She was released after three years by a kindly warden and set free with the warning that she must never work as a cook again. But Mary Mallon was not satisfied to work as a laundress, so, once again she sought employment in a pastry shop. "George (Soper) to the rescue, once again!" He confronted a "blameless" Mary Mallon and returned her to North Brother Island, where she spent the last twenty-three years of her life.

Mary Beth Keane's first novel, *The Walking People*, embraced the same themes of social exclusion and exile as she did in *Fever*. The author didn't glamorize "Typhoid Mary" or pardon her for her most grievous offenses. Mary was given many

443

opportunities to live her life freely, yet time and again, she played the martyr, blaming fate for her bad luck. In a *New York Times* article, 'The Things She Carried,' March 22, 2013, Patrick McGrath referred to Mary's "moral blindness and lack of remorse."

Our Skype chat with Mary Beth Keane was most pleasant and informative. We all left the meeting and went straight to the doctor for an 'anti-typhoid' injection.

"If life were predictable, it would cease to be life,
and be without flavor."

~ Eleanor Roosevelt

SEPTEMBER 2013: Life After Life by Kate Atkinson

Kate Atkinson is a prolific English author of short stories and plays, but best known for creating the Jackson Brodie series of detective novels. In *Life After Life*, she has written a story that changes in circumstance and time with each reading, a kind of "write your own ending" story. *Book Page*, Jan. 2014 raved about "the captivating Life After Life." *The New York Times Book Review*, Sunday, Dec. 15, 2013, called *Life After Life*, one of 'The 10 Best Books of 2013'. Ursula Todd is the star of this novel, born into a privileged family. When she dies, she is reborn again and again, and again and again and again, ad nauseam. We, in 'The Literary Gallery,' did not agree with the reviewers. The majority felt that the story was tiresome and repetitive and repetitive and repetitive.

USA Today ('Life After Life' pulls literary double duty, Deirdre Donahue, 3/28/2013), tells of the publishing nightmare that turned into a publicity bonanza after two prominent novelists, Kate Atkinson and Jill McCorkle, chose the same title for their books, to be published six days apart. "The first, by Jill McCorkle (from Algonquin Books), is set in a North Carolina retirement center and explores community and family bonds…. The second, by Kate Atkinson (from Reagan Arthur/Little, Brown), revolves around Ursula Todd, born in England in 1910 only to die and be born and die again repeatedly." As publication day dawned, there was" a silver lining in media attention. Adding to the sense of a jinx turned lucky. For the first time, independent booksellers

445

have declared a tie for their No. 1 Indie Next Pick, selecting both *Life After Life* novels for April."

What might be interesting would be to watch 'Ground Hog Day' with Bill Murray at the same time you read Kate Atkinson's *Life After Life*. You be the judge of that.

> *"Slowly, a family began to take shape in my mind*
> *– not unlike the many I had visited – one living in*
> *a remote village, forced to make a painful choice*
> *that most of us would find unbearable. At the*
> *heart of this family, I pictured a young brother and*
> *sister, who become the unwitting victims of their*
> *family's despair. The novel begins, then, with this*
> *single act of desperation, of sacrifice, an act that*
> *ruptures the family and ultimately becomes the tree*
> *trunk from which the novel's many branches*
> *spread out."*
>
> ~ *Khaled Hosseini, And the Mountains*
> *Echoed*

OCTOBER 2013: And the Mountains Echoed by Khaled Hosseini

Khaled Hosseini was born in Afghanistan but left the country in 1976 at the age of eleven. He moved with his family to the United States and became a doctor. This is the third book by this author that we would read. (Cross Reference: *The Kite Runner*, Jan. 2005 and *A Thousand Splendid Suns*, Nov. 2007).

"Hosseini first began to consider the plot of *And the Mountains Echoed* during a 2007 trip to Afghanistan with the UN Refugee Agency. While there, he heard stories from several village elders about the deaths of young, impoverished children during the winters, which gave the foundation for the fundamental event of the novel: a parent's choice to sell a child to prevent this from occurring." (Wikipedia, *And the Mountains Echoed*).

The general consensus was that this author writes beautifully about his homeland, always tells a very sad and poignant tale and leaves us forever with tear-smudged pages in our books.

"In the middle of the journey of our life I found myself within a dark woods where the straight way was lost."

~ *Dante Alighieri, Inferno*

NOVEMBER 2013: Inferno by Dan Brown

While there were no Knights Templar for symbologist, Robert Langdon, to fight in this 4th book by Dan Brown, following *Angels and Demons*, the *Da Vinci Code* and *The Lost Symbol*, the Harvard professor finds himself, nonetheless, confronting a 'Transhumanist', (Bertrand Zobrist), obsessed with the end of the world. Seeking clues in Dante Alighieri's 14th-century epic poem, *The Divine Comedy*, this brilliant (mad?) scientist attempts to curb overpopulation. Once again, Dan Brown combines classical Italian art, history, and literature in this modern-day, scientific thriller. (Cross-reference *The Da Vinci Code*, Oct. 2003, *The Lost Symbol*, Dec. 2009). My folder was overflowing with articles from *The New York Times* (*Climate Change Seen Posing Risk to Food Supplies*, by, Justin Gillis, Saturday. Nov. 2, 2013), *USA Today, People Magazine*, biographical information on both the author, Dan Brown, and the mononymous Dante.

Inferno was # 1 on the *New York Times Bestseller List* for Hardcover Fiction and Combined Print and ebook Fiction for the first eleven weeks of its release and remained on the list of ebook Fiction for the first seventeen weeks of its release. The film adaptation, starring Tom Hanks as Robert Langdon, was released on October 28, 2016.

"I am Vishnu, destroyer of worlds."

~ Robert Oppenheimer, (at the moment he tested the first atomic bomb).

DECEMBER 2013: The Girls of Atomic City: The Untold Story of the Women Who Helped Win World War II by Denise Kiernan

(* Skype Chat with the author)

Thirty of us met at the Elwood Library on Monday, December 9, 2013, for our skype chat with the author, Denise Kiernan. We were to follow with our 18th Annual Holiday Luncheon at Ruvo's in Greenlawn, NY. Carol Purdy, a contributing member to our discussions, adventurer and experience-seeker par excellence was there, as well as my good friends, Kathy Kreytak and Elaine Campanella, who would ultimately become my weekly Tuesday Mah Jongg rivals/pals. Kathy and Elaine would introduce me to Chris Gadinis and Dot Schroeder, two more beautiful people, like Kathy and Elaine, intelligent and funny, compassionate and generous of spirit, yet competitive in their quest for Jokers, that I was proud to join in their weekly game. Fellow writer and Poet, Maureen Spisak, Sisters Mary Ellen Hofmann and Carolyn Sciortino were longtime members, Pat Craig, who always showed up at both Elwood Library and Harborfields Library despite having her vision compromised, Jane Cavuoto, who became a book friend through our mutual friend, Carol Mueller, Kathy Dreschler, my quiet bookworm, who rarely missed a meeting, gentle Mary Wood, Susan Hirschmann, my AAUW pal, Gerry Hardy, Helaine Bank brought her fellow teachers, girlfriends, Melanie Lugar, Lois Hass, Judy Dreyfus and Ellen Lambert, my five beloved

449

Plainview contingent, the ever-present and knowledgeable, Jill Mancini, who faithfully attended two of my three monthly book clubs right from the start, Elvira Lubrano, an original member since May of 1996, Marylin Biblow, Mary Ellen McCarthy, who, along with Kathy Dreschler, was always ready for a road trip, Michele Bisom, who comes all the way from Queens to attend our monthly discussions, Ruth Ann Trimarco, who first joined the group when we met at Barnes & Noble in Huntington, Barbara Golden, a steadfast bibliophile who never failed to join our outings, traveler and movie buddy, especially Bradley Cooper movies, Judy Phillips, Irish lass, Mary O'Donnell, Pat DeSilva, Ellen Main and Fran Jacklets, all joined the party, and the most informative and satisfying chat we had with this very talented author.

"The Tennessee town of Oak Ridge was created from scratch in 1942. One of the Manhattan Project's secret cities, it didn't appear on any maps until 1949, and yet at the height of WWII, it was using more electricity than New York City." (www.goodreads.com-the-girls-of-atomic-city).

Seventy-five thousand residents were recruited from small towns to this secret city, enticed by the promise of solid wages and war-ending work; very few actually knew what they were doing, unknowingly helping to build the atomic bomb.

The Washington Post has said of this true story, this New York Times Bestseller, "Kiernan has amassed a deep reservoir of intimate details of what life was like for women living in the secret city…Rosie, it turns out, did much more than drive rivets."

And thus, we ended the year 2013 with our annual Holiday Luncheon and 'Recap,' which had become quite popular, a staple with each of my book clubs. Since 1996, it has been such fun for me to compose and distribute a synopsis of the many books that we read during the year. We would talk about the story and the author, and the characters once again, and give either a thumbs up or a thumbs down accordingly. This, too, would later translate to our Rating System *****

To all of my friends in the
"Literary Gallery"

from

Donna Diamond

Wishing you all a very Happy, Healthy,
Holiday Season !

'THE LITERARY GALLERY' – YEAR END RECAP AND ANALYSIS 2013

2013 was an interesting year for us in "The Literary Gallery". We continued to meet at Barnes & Noble, East Northport through the month of June. Then, because of an abrupt and disturbing email from one "DC", we were advised that our book discussion group did not bring enough revenue to the store and as a result B&N could no longer host our meetings. WHAT?????? A mega-bookstore no longer welcoming reading groups?????? Being the quiet and demure ladies that we are, we did not accept this rejection lightly. We wrote a letter to the President of Barnes & Noble and cc'd the CEO, the District Manager and the Store Manager. Their "mea culpa" letter of apology was well received but "too little too late". They invited us to return and share some coffee and cheesecake. We thanked them for their letter and the almost 20 years our book discussion group met at their store but promptly told them that we would be taking our book club elsewhere.

The Elwood Public Library, specifically Susan Goldberg, Library Director and Belle Baxter, Head of Adult Services, opened its doors to us and welcomed our monthly Monday morning book discussion group. We had found a very comfortable and accommodating new home in which to hold our very lively discussions and host both SKYPE and telephone chats.

We added some new members to our growing number and we celebrated our good fortune. And, as always, we continued to read......
"So many books, so little time"

Let's take a look back at the year 2013, our 18th year of reading as " The Literary Gallery".

. . . .

We began the month of January as our guest author, Yona Zeldis McDonough, took us to **A WEDDING IN GREAT NECK.** In February we were caught in a moral dilemma as we read M.L. Stedman's **THE LIGHT BETWEEN OCEANS.** We were quickly brought back to reality when Gillian Flynn introduced us in March to her psychopathic "Amazing Amy" in **GONE GIRL.** And who hasn't heard of the (in)famous Willie "the actor" **SUTTON ?** J.R. Moehringer brought the man and his times to life in his historical novel (our L.I. Reads Selection 2013) named after this very complicated bank robber. Kate Morton filled her novel with twists and turns as we read ARCs of **THE SECRET KEEPER** supplied by our good friend Hillary Tisman at Simon & Schuster. Then in June we spent a final **WEEK IN WINTER** with one of our and Ireland's favorite authors, recently deceased Maeve Binchy. **THE BURGESS BOYS** by Elizabeth Strout was our selection for July, our first book discussion at our new venue, the Elwood Public Library. We didn't have a **FEVER** like "Typhoid Mary" (Mallon) caused many to experience but our SKYPE chat with author Mary Beth Keane was fascinating in August. Kate Atkinson's **LIFE AFTER LIFE** had most of us feeling like it was a very dull story repeated again and again and again and again and yet again ad nauseum. Khaled Hosseini's **AND THE MOUNTAINS ECHOED** was an enjoyable read in October but, at least for us it didn't quite attain the success of his debut novel, **THE KITE RUNNER.** Then we traveled to Florence and Istanbul and the dark recesses of Dante's **INFERNO**, the new spectacularly researched thriller by Dan Brown. And from Dante's Hell to the mud-splattered huts of Oak Ridge, Tennessee we walked with the great ladies and men of "The Greatest Generation" and we SKYPED with Denise Kiernan, **THE GIRLS of ATOMIC CITY:** The Untold Story of the Women Who Helped Win WWII.

Let's raise a glass "TO US" in "The Literary Gallery" as we celebrate 18 years together sharing our lives and our mutual passion for books. Let's give a heartfelt thanks to our friends here at the Elwood Public Library who have so graciously opened their doors to us.

Once again, we'd like to welcome the many newcomers to our group and bid a fond farewell to those whose lives and careers have taken them down a different path. I hope that everyone who joins us in "The Literary Gallery" each month will find joy in our mutual passion for reading and camaraderie from the group.

And in conclusion I'd like to share a few of my favorite quotes on reading that I think capture the essence of our book club.

"I declare after all there is no enjoyment like reading"
~ Jane Austen

"Reading is everything. Reading is bliss".
~ Nora Ephron

"She is too fond of books, and it has addled her brain".
~ Louisa May Alcott

I wish you all GOOD HEALTH !! MUCH LOVE AND HAPPINESS !! And many more years of "HAPPY READING" !! Thank you for sharing this great adventure with me.

With my best regards,

Donna~

MEMORABLE OR EASILY FORGOTTEN LITERARY HEROES AND HEROINES THAT WE HAVE
ENCOUNTERED DURING OUR BOOK DISCUSSIONS

From January 14, 2013 through December 9, 2013

We have read many novels, a few works of non-fiction and numerous bestsellers over the past
year. Some of the books, authors or literary figures that we have met may have touched us deeply while
others may have left us as quickly as we turned the final page. Some we might refer to over and over
again while others might cause us to say, "What was I thinking?" Let's each be the judge of who or what
affected us most (in either a positive or a negative way):

Book & Author	Character(s)	Memorable?	Forgotten?
A WEDDING IN GREAT NECK by, Yona Zeldis McDonough January 14, 2013 • Guest Author	Angelica (the bride- to- be) Gretchen, Betsy, Don, Teddy, Caleb, Ennis, Grandmother Lenora, Portia & Justine, Lincoln Silverstein		
THE LIGHT BETWEEN OCEANS by, M.L. Stedman February 11, 2013	Isabel (Izzy), Tom, Lucy, Ralph, Bluey, Hannah Roenfeldt		
GONE GIRL by, Gillian Flynn March 18, 2013	"Amazing Amy", Nick (Lance Nicholas Dunne), Hilary Handy, Desi Collings Rand & Mary Beth		
SUTTON by, J.R.Moehringer April 8, 2013 ** L.I.Reads Selection 2013	Willie "The Actor" Sutton, "Reporter", "Photographer", William (Happy) Johnston, Edward (Eddie) Buster Wilson, Bess Endner, Arnie Schuster		
THE SECRET KEEPER by, Kate Morton May 13, 2013 Note: ARCs given by Hilary Tisman @ Simon & Schuster	Dorothy, Dolly, Vivien, Laurel, Lady Gwendolyn, Jimmy, Rose, Iris, Gerry, Henry Jenkins		
A WEEK IN WINTER by, Maeve Binchy June 10, 2013	Chicky Starr, Rigger, Nuala, Carmel, Orla, Winnie & Teddy, Lillian, John (Cory Salinas), Henry & Nicola, Anders, The Walls, Freda, Miss Nell Howe		

NOTE: LAST BOOK DISCUSSION @
BARNES & NOBLE - June 10, 2013

THE BURGESS BOYS
by, Elizabeth Strout
July 8, 2013
NOTE: 1st BOOK DISCUSSION @
ELWOOD LIBRARY - July 8, 2013

Jim, Bob (& Susan) Burgess,
The Wally Packer Trial, Helen, Zach
The Somalis

FEVER
by, Mary Beth Keane
August 12, 2013
*SKYPE CHAT w/author

Mary Mallon (aka "Typhoid Mary"),
Alfred Briehof, Dr George Soper (Sanitary
Engr.), John Cane,
North Brother Island

LIFE AFTER LIFE
by, Kate Atkinson
September 9, 2013

Ursula Todd, Sylvie & Hugh Todd,
Teddy, (Aunt) Izzie, Maurice, Pamela

AND THE MOUNTAINS ECHOED
by, Khaled Hosseini
October 7, 2013

Abdullah & Pari, Nila & Suleiman Wahdati,
Uncle Nabi, Parwana & Masooma,
Dr. Markos & Thalia, Amra, Roshi, Idris,
Timur

INFERNO
by, Dan Brown
November 4, 2013

Robert Langdon (noted Symbologist &
Harvard Professor), Dr. Sienna Brooks,
"The Provost", Zobrist, DANTE ALIGHIERI

THE GIRLS OF ATOMIC CITY:
The Untold Story of the Women
Who Helped Win WWII
by, Denise Kiernan
December 9, 2013
* SKYPE CHAT w/author

"The Gadget" (atomic bomb), "The Project
Robert Oppenheimer, Enrico Fermi,
Celia Szapka, Kattie Strickland, Virginia
Spivey, Colleen Rowan, Jane Greer et al.

18th Annual Holiday Luncheon @ RUVO'S,
Greenlawn, NY

Female Authors – 9
Male Authors   - 3

Fiction   - 7
Non – Fiction   - 1
Historical Fiction – 4

Chapter 18

Our Year of Reading Women Authors (2014)

2014 was the year of women authors in 'The Literary Gallery'….powerful women, strong women, intelligent women, ambitious women, clever women, loving women, caring women.

> *"What you're supposed to do when you don't like*
> *a thing is change it. If you can't change it, change*
> *the way you think about it. Don't complain."*
>
> ~ *Maya Angelou, Wouldn't Take*
> *Nothing for My Journey Now*

JANUARY 2014: The Supreme Macaroni Company by Adriana Trigiani

January found us reading the final novel of the Valentine Trilogy, by Adriana Trigiani, *The Supreme Macaroni Company*. We shared a hearty laugh over the Roncalli Family's Christmas Eve dinner (Classic Trigiani!) …. the curmudgeonly Aunt Feen, with her sharp tongue and suffering intolerance, Dutch's mal à propisms, Mike's "George Clooney ready" look, and Gianluca and Bret's rivalry for Valentine's affection. But why did the author change the title, eliminating the word VALENTINE altogether from the front cover? You'll have to find out for yourself the reason why.

…. a funny woman, a caring woman, author Adriana Trigiani.

Cross Reference: *Lucia, Lucia* (June 2006), Very *Valentine*, (March 2009), *Brava Valentine*, (March 2010), The *Shoemaker's Wife*, (August 2012).

> *"We must have ideals and try to live up to them,*
> *even if we never quite succeed. Life would be a*
> *sorry business without them. With them it's grand*
> *and great."*

~ *Lucy Maude Montgomery, Ann of Avonlea*

FEBRUARY 2014: Jacob's Folly by Rebecca Miller

Miller's multi-layered romp through 18th century Paris by Jacob Cerf, a Jewish peddler who dies and is reincarnated as a fly in Patchogue, Long Island, might have been a perfect title for consideration by Long Island Reads. Perhaps.

Author and screenwriter, Rebecca Miller, is the multi-talented daughter of the famously brilliant, Arthur Miller, and the wife of the inimitable (Abe) 'Lincoln,' 'Gangs of New York' actor, Daniel Day-Lewis. Writing with wit and precision, this raucously funny historical novel captures the essence of the past, and being Jewish, in Paris, at a time when many restrictions were imposed on them, and the present in the affluent Hamptons on Long Island. The reader will meet a gluttonous Marquis de Sade-like character, a secretive aspiring Jewess actress, and a Mensch of a man with the name 'Senzatimore' (without fear.) But a fly on the wall as the protagonist? Why not? Marcus Zusak cleverly chose 'Death' as his narrator in *The Book Thief,* an all-time favorite book of mine, which still bears the markings of my smudged tears. How many times have I wished I could be said fly watching and hearing behind the scenes? Certainly, not a voyeur, just a silent observer.

The clever premise, captured by Rebecca Miller, can be compared to Jim Fergus's *One Thousand White Women*, in the sense of "imagine if?" This selection was well-received by two of my three book clubs. Remember: "You can please some of the people some of the time......"

Tip #10 - Re: Timing! (When you read a book)

> *"There is a stubbornness about me that never can bear to be frightened at the will of others. My courage always rises at every attempt to intimidate me."*
>
> *~ Jane Austen, Pride and Prejudice*

MARCH 2014: The Art Forger by B. A. Shapiro

Helaine Bank, who brought several friends and fellow teachers, (Lois Haas, Melanie Lugar, Judy Dreyfus, Ellen Lambert), to our monthly book sessions, invited me and my sister-in-law, Diane (DeDe) Barrett, to join her for an author breakfast at the Sid Jacobsen YJCC on Long Island. As funny as Saralee Rosenberg, my psychic author friend, a Jewish version of stand-up comedienne and author Adriana Trigiani, Barbara Shapiro regaled us with her stories over bagels and lox.

A huge success, but not without its many rewrites, edits, and revisions, according to its author, *The Art Forger* opens up the realm of the art world, exposing forgeries and duplicitousness in its galleries and museums. Using the art heist of thirteen stolen works from the Isabella Stewart Gardner Museum in Boston, MA on March 18, 1990, as a backdrop to her historical novel, B.A. Shapiro intersperses actual people (Edgar Degas, Isabella Stewart Gardner), with her colorful, imaginary characters, Claire Roth and Aidan Markel.

Like Mia Saul in Yona Zeldis McDonough's *Breaking the Bank*, Claire makes a Faustian bargain (not with an ATM machine), that will change the course of her life and her reputation. *The Art Forger* appealed to the many artists and art lovers in my book clubs and received a rating of + 4**** (out of 5).

…. another funny, clever woman, author B.A. Shapiro

"It's where we go, and what we do when we get there, that tells us who we really are."

~ *Joyce Carol Oates*

APRIL 2014: The Manor: Three Centuries at a Slave Plantation on Long Island by Mac Griswold

*A Long Island Reads Selection 2014

Sylvester Manor is a gem, an oasis that sits between the North and South Forks of Long Island. Landscape historian, Mac Griswold, spied a yellow house while rowing one afternoon, partially hidden by the towering boxwoods that surrounded it. Immediately taken by the grandeur and mystery of this unknown treasure, the author began her research. The result is her 480-page tome that tells the story of a family that held the house for eleven generations. There is a 'slave staircase,' the 1666 Charter for the land and correspondence from Thomas Jefferson.

This non-fiction work was well researched, (ten years in the making,) and serves as a textbook guide to the checkered history of the Indians, Quakers, Barbadians (Bajans) and Dutch who inhabited the land. As a supplement to the book, I introduced a film of the sugar plantations in Barbados, where the Sylvesters employed African slaves.

Mac Griswold visited several libraries while her book was being discussed. In addition to book discussions and movie viewing, the L.I Reads Committee escorted several busloads of people, who were eager to spend the day on Shelter Island, observing this untouched relic.

Tip #12 - Book a trip!

....an intelligent, ambitious woman, author Mac Griswold.

"All we have is the story we tell. Everything we do, every decision we make, our strength, weakness, motivation, history, and character—what we believe—none of it is real; it's all part of the story we tell. But here's the thing: it's our goddamned story!"

~ *Jess Walter, Beautiful Ruins*

MAY 2014: Beautiful Ruins by Jess Walter

It's hard to define *Beautiful Ruins*, categorize it, put it neatly into a classification, a story within a story, within a story. Is it a love story between Elizabeth Taylor and Richard Burton, who were thrown together while they were filming CLEOPATRA in Italy in the 1960s? Is it Pasquale's paean to his parents? To his feelings towards Dee? What about the Donner Party? Who is Michael Deane, "the fixer?" Who or what are the 'Beautiful Ruins' of the title? Does it describe the surroundings? The broken lives? And who is Alvis Bender, the 'One Chapter Wonder?'

Jess Walter has written a fascinating, often confusing, novel. He introduces his characters then jumps from Italy in the 1960s to Hollywood at the present time. His prose is beautiful, quotable, as Pasquale's mother said to him when he was a boy, "Sometimes what we want to do and what we must do are not the same….the smaller the space between your desire and what is right, the happier you will be." (Page 304, *Beautiful Ruins*).

Book Clubs will have an animated conversation discussing *Beautiful Ruins*.

Tip #28 - Choose a favorite sentence, quote or passage.

<u>Tip #29</u> - Ask what the book was about.

"The risk of love is loss, and the price of loss is grief—but the pain of grief is only a shadow when compared with the pain of never risking love."

~ Hilary Stanton Zunin

JUNE 2014: Me Before You by JoJo Moyes

Will Traynor and Louisa Clark. Every year, as I write my final recap, I ask my book groups to think about the characters we have encountered. Are they memorable? Will they stay with you for a long time, or will you forget about them as quickly as you turn the final page?

Will Traynor and Louisa Clark are embedded into my memory, leaving their mark upon my heart. Their love story is not unique. The decisions they have to make are not new. They are the questions we all face as we near the end of our life.

Will Traynor is a quadriplegic who, in his former life, was an athlete, an adventurer, a daredevil. Louisa Clark is his caregiver. *Me Before You* deals with the question of assisted suicide. Does a person have the right to choose for him or herself whether to live or die?

Twenty-nine-year-old, Brittany Maynard's, life and legacy came under scrutiny when she chose to end her own life, after being diagnosed with a malignant brain tumor, then with Grade 4 Brain Cancer, an even harsher diagnosis, with only a short time to live. Maynard, a newlywed, made the decision to move to Portland, Oregon so she could have access to Oregon's Death With Dignity Act.

Brittany Maynard died in her bedroom, surrounded by family and friends on Saturday, November 1, 2014.

Jodi Picoult wrote a novel, *Lone Wolf*, supporting assisted suicide. (*USA Today*, dated April 8, 2014, News Pg. 1A printed an article entitled, 'There Is Hope' Reversing Paralysis.) The debate over assisted suicide will go on. There will be religious and political dialogue implications. Dr. Jack Kevorkian's name will be invoked.

Can your book club withstand the potential pressure of voices being raised in anger? Can a civil tone set the mood for possible debate? Then *Me Before You*, by JoJo Moyes, will be an excellent choice of titles. It was for ours.

….. a clever woman, a caring woman, author JoJo Moyes.

"Three may keep a secret if two of them are dead."

~ Benjamin Franklin

JULY 2014: The Husband's Secret by Liane Moriarty

If you found a letter from your husband (or significant other), addressed to you which said, "To Be Read After My Death," and your husband is still alive, would you open it? Would you tell him that you read it?

Such is the premise of Liane Moriarty's novel, *The Husband's Secret*, a blockbuster MUST READ for many book clubs, including mine.

Three women, Cecilia, Tess and Rachel, and their families, become ensnared in a secret, not of their making. In this novel, we see that good people can do bad things, and innocent people can be forced to take responsibility for another's grievous crime.

The Husband's Secret poses the question of responsibility for one's actions, for one's knowledge of a secret revealed.

"You could try as hard as you could to imagine someone else's tragedy—

drowning in icy waters, living in a city split by a wall---but nothing truly

hurts until it happens to you. Most of all, to your child."

~ Liane Moriarity, The Husband's Secret

There are several people in my book clubs who like to read the ending first, so there are no surprises. I strongly caution them NOT to do so when reading *The Husband's Secret*........

The novel's strong women, caring women, loving women, author Liane Moriarty.

"I believe a strong woman may be stronger than a man, particularly if she happens to have love in her heart. I guess a loving woman is indestructible."

~ *John Steinbeck, East of Eden*

AUGUST 2014: Songs of Willow Frost by Jamie Ford

Jamie Ford captured the bittersweet wartime romance between a young Chinese boy and his Japanese girlfriend in *Hotel on the Corner of Bitter and Sweet* (Ref: March 2011).

Born in Eureka, CA in 1968, Ford's Father, a Seattle native, was of Chinese ancestry, his mother was of European descent. The Western name, Ford, comes from his great grandfather, Min Chung, who immigrated to Nevada in 1865 and later changed his name to William Ford. Ford's great grandmother, Loy Lee Ford, was the first Chinese woman to own property in Nevada. (From Jamie Ford, June 28, 2014, Wikipedia, The Free Encyclopedia).

Songs of Willow Frost, his second novel, also takes place in Seattle from 1921-1934. It is the story of young William Eng, a "supposed" orphan, (not truly an orphan since his mother is alive), who lives at the Sacred Heart Orphanage, and of William's mother, Liu Song/Willow Frost, a singer, and actress. It is a heartbreaking morality tale of old-fashioned traditions and prejudices, set during the Depression. Ford wove his plotline into Seattle's Chinatown history, the Wah Mee Club (the Wah Mee Massacre, thirteen homicides occurred on February 18, 1983), and discrimination against Asians, (the Chinese Exclusion Act). William Eng, the Chinese boy in the novel, sees a theatre entrance for "Colored" and wonders, "Am I colored?" And if so, what color am I?" (*USA Today*, Thurs., Sept. 12, 2013. (Novelist Jamie Ford likes to "excavate the past" by Bob Minzesheimer (D, Life Section).

Longtime book club member, Mary Ellen Hofmann's son and his family live in Seattle, WA. Once again, she was able to share some photos and personal accounts of life during those unsettled years of the Great Depression. Our book discussion was enhanced by her firsthand knowledge.

"Never look back unless you are planning to go that way."

~ Henry David Thoreau

SEPTEMBER 2014: The Goldfinch by Donna Tartt

*(Pulitzer Prize Winner for Fiction 2014)

It is difficult to have a life AND read a seven hundred seventy-one-page book, even a seven hundred seventy-one page Pulitzer Prize Winner, in one month. I had read all of the reviews, seen all of the accolades being awarded to Donna Tartt, and I'm not referring to Vanity Fair's Best Dressed List, which reflected the author's famous "menswear-influenced pieces long before androgyny became the hottest trend on the catwalk." (Vanity Fair's Best Dressed List: Donna Tartt's Life-long style/Fashion/THE Guardian.com, September 6, 2014.)

When I knew that readers would be talking about *The Goldfinch*, I gave the group notice that we would be discussing it five months in advance. That way everyone would know our book selection and have ample time to read it.

Donna Tartt, petite and private, was raised in Mississippi and brought up in a bookish family. Her third novel, (*The Secret History*, 1992 and *The Little Friend*, 2002), *The Goldfinch*, tells the story of thirteen-year-old, Theo Decker, and his mother, who dies in a terrorist attack at New York City's Metropolitan Museum of Art. Buried amongst the rubble of masterpieces, Theo finds the painting of 'The Goldfinch,' a 17th-century Dutch oil by Carel Fabritius, his mother's favorite work of art. Similarly, Fabritius died young, caught in the explosion of the Delft gunpowder magazine on October 12, 1654. Throughout the story, Theo finds himself tethered to the painting and to the memory of his mother. During Theo's Dickensian journey from New York to Las Vegas and Amsterdam, we meet many of his friends, including the Russian, Boris, who introduces him to the stupor of drugs and alcohol, and Hobie, the gentle antique dealer, who guides him and provides a safe haven.

In her novels, all of which took ten years to write, Tartt presents a number of recurring literary themes, such as "the themes of social class and social stratification, guilt and aesthetic beauty." (Donna Tartt/Wikipedia, *The Free Encyclopedia*, September 6, 2014.) Kirkus Review stated that (*The Goldfinch* "is an altogether lovely addition to what might be called the literature of disaster and redemption." (September 6, 2014.)

Our book club, like the literary critics, had mixed opinions regarding *The Goldfinch*. Vanity Fair, July 2014, published an article by Eugenia Peretz, "It's Tartt—But Is It Art?" And Lorin Stein, editor of The Paris Review states, "A book like *The Goldfinch* doesn't undo any clichés—it deals in them. It coats everything in a cozy patina of 'literary' gentility."

The Goldfinch is an example of a "Bildungsroman," a coming-of-age novel like *Oliver Twist*. The question is, "Will Theo Decker find a permanent place in your heart and on your bookshelf, or will both he and his friend, Boris, be banished like censored books?

…. a smart woman, author Donna Tartt

OCTOBER 2014: Dancing on Broken Glass by Ka Hancock

*(SKYPE chat with the author)

We had a SKYPE chat with this ebullient author, (and her husband, Mark, who made it all happen), who wrote a story about sisters, and a romance between a man who suffers from Bipolar Disease, and the woman who loves him, despite his mood swings and above all else. Before I knew what the book was about, I was drawn to this unusual title. My Goddaughter, Kirsten, had read it in her book club and first turned me on to this fascinating novel. I fell in love with the Houston girls, Lily, Lucy, and Priscilla and with Mickey, Lucy's "damaged" husband. I wanted to be cared for by Jan and Harrison Bates, and I wanted to move to the fictional town of Brinley, a kind of Norman Rockwellesque, Jan Karon- Mitford-kind of town, where everyone knew everyone else's business and looked out for one another.

Having always been interested in birth order, I passed around a sheet which lists the characteristics of the first, middle, last, and only child. According to somebody, a First Born Child is a natural leader, a high achiever, organized, on-time, know-it-all, bossy, and responsible. A Middle Child (like me, Ted and granddaughter, Lauren), is flexible, easy-going, social, peacemakers, independent, secretive, may feel life is unfair. The Last Born, the Baby of the Family, is a risk-taker, outgoing, creative, self-centered, financially irresponsible, competitive, and bored easily. And the 'Lonely-Only Child' is close to parents, self-control, a leader, mature, dependable, demanding, and unforgiving. We compared the above traits to those of the Houston sisters in the story. We talked about our own family dynamics. After almost twenty years together as a reading group, we were comfortable enough with each other to talk about personal family matters.

From the author's website, we knew that Ka Hancock was born and raised in Utah, had two degrees in Nursing, was married forever to the stud she met in High School, had four fabulous kids who married four fabulous kids who are reproducing at an alarming rate.

She was funny, Ka (pronounced KAY,) I think she said her mother forgot to put the "Y" on the birth certificate, as she joked with us and described her writing life and answered questions about her book. She thanked us for reading and enjoying her story.

Tip #17 - Invite an author

Tip #25 - Try to decipher the title

…. the Houston women, caring, loving, smart, ambitious, author Ka Hancock

*"Reading made Don Quixote a gentleman but
believing what he read made him mad."*

~ George Bernard Shaw (1856-1950)

*Let me tell you a little something about Diane, Renee and me and
the day we each came into this world. Diane was born on a
Saturday; "Saturday's child has to work for a living."*

*This tenet has sadly rung true for my older sister. Dad always
called her "Smokey." Mom still calls her "My Warrior." Diane is
very attractive, with a smile that lights her face if she gives it a
chance. She is also extremely intelligent and funny, with a caustic
wit. My sister is outwardly strong and full of bluster, but for
those of us who truly know and love her, Diane is our Don
Quixote battling her own handmade windmills. She values
"Family" above everything else. With her "smokey" brown eyes,
full face and well-positioned nose, like our brother, Chris, she
favors the Perlman side of the family. She is my history, my
"sharer of the memories," my laugh-out-loud go-to person to
exchange famous movie and SNL lines.*

*Renee (Doreen), on the other hand, was born on a Monday;
"Monday's child is fair of face."*

*A born blonde with blue eyes and a spitfire personality, Renee is
the polar opposite of Diane and, like me, most resembles our
Mother's "Irish" (Irish being Mom's maiden name. Ha!) side.
Sassy and flirtatious, "street smart" and lovable, Big Ed nicknamed
her "Skinny." Our Mother still calls her "My Rebel." Renee has
no tough veneer to pierce. She'll hold it all together for as long as
is needed, then fall apart quietly and privately when the work has
been done. She is the life of the party and greets every day with a
smile. She doesn't have to "stop and smell the roses." She'll make
you a daily bouquet from her garden. Renee is my childhood, my*

473

long-distance heartstring. And, although we've been separated by distance since we were both married, she has always been just a phone call away whenever I have joyful news to share or a sad tale to tell.

I was born on a Friday; "Friday's child is loving and giving."

(Certainly NOT 'The Ultimate Hard-core, High-handed, Card-carrying Bibliophilist' material.) It's not for me to say what all of this means. We are three girls, three sisters, three daughters born on different days of the week. We have each suffered our tragedies; Diane lost a daughter, just one-month-old, a never-ending heartbreak, and endured husbands that were ill-suited to her. Renee was afflicted with Scarlet Fever and Rheumatic Fever when she was just eight years old. Unable to walk because of a weak heart, our Dad would carry her to the garage and place her in a chaise longue. Friends would stop by and chat with her, tell her stories, and play simple games.

We three still carry the scars of the past.

My brother, Chris, was born on a Friday, too, February 14, 1964. He was our very special Valentine's Day gift.

The dynamics of birth order and the actual day of the week a person is born have always fascinated me. My Dani has three daughters. Lily was born in April on a Sunday.

"But the child who is born on the Sabbath Day is bonny and blithe and good and gay."

Lauren, in the middle, was a Thursday, January, Aquarius like her Mom. Her twin cousins, Brielle and Brett, were also born on a Thursday (in February).

"Thursday's child has far to go."

Alice came into the world on a Wednesday, like her great grandmother, Delores, Grandma Dee, on a cold December day.

"Wednesday's child is full of woe."

I see my childhood in each of my granddaughters and marvel at the way they interact with one another.

My Brett has twins, Brielle and Brett, born on a Thursday, one minute apart. I see in their togetherness my own twin, the baby boy my Mother lost, we lost. I see in their closeness that invisible and indivisible bond and I rejoice.

*"Bread and books: food for the body and food for
the soul—what could be more worthy of our
respect, and even love?"*

~ *Salman Rushdie – Imaginary
Homelands (1992)*

NOVEMBER 2014: Still Life with Breadcrumbs by Anna Quindlen

This is a wonderful light read, a romantic comedy of manners, whose central character, Rebecca Winter, is a sixty-year-old photographer, who leaves her old life and her New York apartment, and moves to a well-worn cottage in the country, and finds love.

The title, (once again the title alone piqued my interest), *Still Life With Breadcrumbs*, refers to "a photo of the detritus of a party, (her narcissistic ex-husband) refused to help clean up," "the photo she called 'Still Life With Breadcrumbs'—dirty wine glasses, stacked plates, the torn ends of two baguettes and a dishtowel singed at one corner by the gas stove."(*USA Today*, Tues., Feb. 4, 2014, 'Crumbs is more than a morsel of a love story,' by Patty Rhule (Special for *USA Today*.)

NPR wrote, "Quindlen has her finger firmly planted on the PULSE OF HER GENERATION."

The Daily Beast— "Personal, Intimate, And Honest."

The Chicago Tribune – "Astute observations…the sorts of details every writer and reader lives for."

We unthinkingly followed a pattern of reading books about art and artists in the recent books that we read in 'The Literary Gallery' in 2014, with our selection of *The Art Forger* in March, and *The Goldfinch* in September. In her book, *Still Life with Breadcrumbs*, Quindlen asks, "Is photography considered art?"

Quindlen's gently aging, but very vital heroine, Rebecca Winter, moves to a small town to escape the noise, the monetary obligations and the faux lifestyles of New York City. Just as the residents of Brinley in Ka Hancock's, *Dancing on Broken Glass* were accepting of Mickey's bipolar disease, Rebecca Winter discovered that "there's a kind of casual cruelty in a small town, but there's casual kindness, too." (*Still Life with Breadcrumbs, pg.* 163).

The symbolism of the white flag and the O. Henry Poem, and the chapters on the dog who arrives and departs, and safe houses, and how houses had personalities, are brilliantly written and flow as easily as the waters of my beloved Lake George, (where I first discovered books, especially Nancy Drew Mysteries, at the Bolton Public Library. Diane, Renee, Karyn and I made our weekly trek to pick out and return cherished books).

Quindlen's opinions and writings have been praised, and they have been criticized. In 2000 she was invited to give the Commencement Address at Villanova University (a school that is dear to my heart, since it is my Dani's Alma Mater). A group of conservative students, hearing of her invitation, protested against Quindlen's strong liberal views. Commencement was canceled. The author, refusing to bow to dissent, emailed her planned commencement address to a disappointed student. Her speech rapidly spread across the internet and Quindlen later expanded it into her book, *A Short Guide to a Happy Life* and presented it to her in 2014. The effect was certainly different from the angry protesters of 2000.

…...an intelligent, ambitious, strong woman, author Anna Quindlen.

"When the world is silent, even one voice becomes powerful."

~ Malala Yousafzai

DECEMBER 2014: I Am Malala: The Girl Who Stood Up for Education And Was Shot By The Taliban by Malala Yousafzai and Christina Lamb

In 2012, a fearless crusader was born in Pakistan. Malala Yousafzai was shot in the face by the Taliban for standing up for education for girls, and despite multiple surgeries and seemingly endless rehab, she became an activist for every child to go to school. Malala spoke up and spoke out, and her voice resonated around the world.

Malala Yousafzai received the Nobel Peace Prize in 2014, the youngest person ever to receive this honor. "This award is for all of those children who are voiceless…" (Yousafzai at a press conference in Birmingham, England, on October 10, said, "I speak for them."

…. a powerful, strong, intelligent woman, author, and activist, Malala Yousafzai.

In January 2015, we, in 'The Literary Gallery,' read Jane Smiley's, *Some Luck*, the first book in her 'Hundred Years Trilogy.' Lucky us to have had the opportunity to enter into the lives of the Langdon Family who lived, worked, married, had babies, died on, or left their Iowa farm, as the world moved on from the 1920s through the 1950s.

We returned to Jodi Picoult in February, *Leaving Time*, another of this author's highly researched (all about elephants), novels. This book will leave you wanting more than just peanuts the next time the circus comes to town. *(Note: The final performance of the Ringling Brothers Barnum & Baily Circus was on Sunday, May 21, 2017). In 2016 our Long Island Reads Committee chose Nesconset native, Jodi Picoult's *Leaving Time*, as our Island-wide selection.

Alyson Richman graciously held a SKYPE chat with us from her home (March 2015), as we discussed her collaboration with nine other authors on, *Grand Central: Original Stories of Postwar Love and Reunion*: Alyson had joined Melanie Benjamin, Jenna Blum, Amanda Hodgkinson, Pam Jenoff, Sarah Jio, Sarah McCoy, Karen White, Kristina McMorris and Erika Robuck in this enchanting endeavor.

Each April brings us to our 'Long Island Reads' Selection. For 2015 our Committee chose Alice Hoffman's, *The Museum of Extraordinary Things*. And, oh, what an extraordinary read it was, taking us to Coney Island and Dreamland, to the brutal hardships of the immigrant in search of a better life in the great melting pot of New York City in 1910. We met very human people being displayed as "freaks" in the sideshow, where spectators gawked or turned away in fear or disgust. Alice Hoffman painted a vivid picture of the seedy side of New York City in those early years of the 20th century.

*Monday, May 11, 2015 – The 19th Anniversary of 'The Literary Gallery' Book Discussion Group ~

It was fitting for us to celebrate our nineteen years of memorable reading together with the selection of a title that won the Pulitzer Prize in 2015, *All the Light We Cannot See*, by Anthony Doer. A work of historical fiction that took ten years to write, *All the Light We Cannot See* takes place during

WWII in France and in Germany, and introduces the reader to unforgettable characters, (Marie-Laure and Werner), who make difficult choices at a time when the world was going mad. You won't easily forget this book or the many lessons learned from it, not the least of which is about mollusks and electricity. BRAVO! Anthony Doer.

2015 AND TO INFINITY AND BEYOND

2015 AND TO INFINITY AND
BEYOND

~ Buzz Lightyear

May of 2015 marked my 19th year leading monthly book discussions, facilitating book summits or kicking off or closing a Summer or Winter Reading Club. I have made many "new" friends, (which I now proudly call "old" friends,) intelligent, well-read women and men, all bibliophiles like me. And what a joy it has been, to do something that I absolutely love to do, (read and talk!), and hopefully bring others, devoted readers or just occasional readers, along with me for this ongoing roller coaster ride called life, filled with books, books and more books, still waiting for me, and for us, to read and to discuss.

I have had the pleasure of meeting authors, who have written the books that we have savored, who have provided fodder for our animated discussions. We have read fiction, non-fiction, memoirs, and biographies. We have invited authors to personally join our discussions and held SKYPE chats to enhance our enjoyment of a book, taken road trips on Long Island, to New York City and New Jersey to celebrate the launch of an author's new book, and dined with writers and chatted about their work, their writing life, research and publishing today. We have seen plays as a group and viewed films that were based on one of the books we had discussed. We have laughed together, commiserated with one another, reminisced and cried, shared the birth of our children and

481

grandchildren, weddings, graduations, job offers, relocations and transfers of loved ones, and the death of one of our own, a spouse or a child.

Nineteen years can be a long time in a life, or it can fly quickly by. For me, reading has been a continuing love affair, and these last nineteen years have been especially glorious. Where did the time go? The French novelist, essayist, and critic, (Valentin Louis Georges Eugène) Marcel Proust, spent fourteen years (1913-1927) writing his monumental seven-part novel *A la Recherche du Temps Perdu*, 'Remembrance of Things Past,' also translated as 'In Search of Lost Time'). I'm not sure those fourteen years passed as quickly for him.

To paraphrase Jodi Picoult's *Nineteen Minutes*: "In nineteen years, I can read a novel by Chris Bohjalian, Ken Follett, Alyson Richman, Meg Wolitzer, or Lisa See. In nineteen years, I can read a biography by David McCullough, Doris Kearns Goodwin or Walter Isaacson, or an Adam Dalgliesh "Who Dunnit" by P.D. James, or a legal thriller by John Grisham. In nineteen years, I can read about China with Gail Tsukiyama or laugh out loud with Saralee Rosenberg and Adriana Trigiani, or hop on a barstool with J.R. Moehringer. In nineteen years, I can choose a favorite author and read all of his/her books. I can see a movie, take a literary road trip, or have a SKYPE chat. In nineteen years, I can read hundreds or thousands of books, and vicariously travel to India, Japan, Italy, France, Russia, Korea or Sweden and journey forward to a future dystopia or back in time to WWI or WWII, to the Wild West or "La Belle Epoque."

In my opening chapters, I asked how I became the 'Ultimate Hard-core, High-handed, Card-carrying Bibliophilist.' Qu'est-ce que c'est une 'Ultimate Hard-core, High-handed, Card-carrying Bibliophilist'? If it's someone who loves and collects books, and loves to not only read them, and talk about them, but also someone who loves to share them with others, then "Oui, C'est Moi!"

The New York Times Book Review (By The Book) always asks the author being interviewed, "What books are currently on your nightstand?" These are currently on mine:

1. *Book Club: How I Became the Ultimate Hard-core, High-handed, Card-carrying Bibliophilist*, by Donna J. Diamond
2. *War and Peace*, by Leo Tolstoy
4. *A Wrinkle in Time*, by Madeleine L'Engle
5. *Middlemarch*, by George Eliot
6. *Bossypants*, by Tina Fey

"Parting is such sweet sorrow," but it's time for me to go, off to my next great book, both my own, *Book Club II: The Smug Ultimate Hard-core, High-handed, Card-carrying Bibliophilist*, and some other bestseller. I have two more book clubs to write about, 'From Cover to Cover' at Harborfields Library, and 'Page Turners' at the Northport Library and still more stories and adventures to share. I look forward to reading with you again soon.

Best regards,

Donna

Oh, P.S. In 2015 Mark Zuckerberg started a book club. The world of books is alive and thriving, and so am I. "Quot Libros, Quam Breve Tempus!" ("So many books, so little time.")

"I cannot live without books."

~ Thomas Jefferson to John Adams, 1815.

~ Donna Diamond to whoever will listen.

"Je ne regrette rien."

~ Edith Piaf

« Je ne regrette rien jusqu' a maintenant, mais il y aura beaucoup de demain. Nous verrons...... »

~ Donna Diamond

MARK ZUCKERBERG'S YEAR OF BOOKS

1. *The End of Power: From Boardrooms to Battlefields and Churches to States, Why Being In Charge Isn't What It Used to Be*, by Moisés Naím
2. *The Better Angels of Our Nature: Why Violence Has Declined*, by Steven Pinker
3. *Gang Leader for a Day: A Rogue Sociologist Takes to the Streets*, by Sudhir Venkatesh
4. *On Immunity: An Innoculation*, by Eula Biss
5. *Creativity, Inc.: Overcoming the Unseen Forces That Stand in the Way of True Inspiration*, by Ed Catmull
6. *The Structure of Scientific Revolutions*, by Thomas Kuhn
7. *Rational Ritual: Culture, Coordination, and Common Knowledge*, by Michael Chwe
8. *Dealing With China: An Insider Unmasks the New Economic Superpower*, by Hank Paulson
9. *Orwell's Revenge: The 1984 Palimpsest*, by Peter Huber
10. *The New Jim Crow: Mass Incarceration in the Age of Colorblindness*, by Michelle Alexander

11. *Muqaddimah*, by Ibn Khaldun
12. *Sapiens: A Brief History of Humankind*, by Yuval Noah Harari
13. *The Player of Games*, by Iain Banks
14. *Energy: A Beginner's Guide*, by Vaclav Smil
15. *Genome: The Autobiography of a Species in 23 Chapters*, by Matt Ridley

THE HISTORY OF BOOK CLUBS

Dennis Adams, Information Services Coordinator at the Beaufort County Library, wrote: "A Brief History of Book Clubs" for the Book Club Corner. According to Adams, "book discussions are as old as books themselves, and certainly became more frequent with the invention of the printing press around 1455. The literary salons of Paris helped shape the cultural scene of the 17th and 18th centuries. The Encyclopedia Americana defined them as "fashionable assemblage(s), generally of literary, artistic, and political figures, held regularly in a private home." The hostesses were often authors in their own right, like Mlle de Scudery (1607-1701), Madame Francoise Scarron (1635-1719) and Madame de Stael, (1766-1817)."

Adams continues, "Coffee houses were a humbler, but no less vital, forum." Wherever men gathered to discuss the ideas circulated in print, " wrote Anthony J. La Vopa, ("The Birth of Public Opinion," in Wilson Quarterly, Winter 1991), "a network of enlightened communities peopled by only a few thousand souls, invented public opinion as a way of talking about and validating itself.

On September 28, 2008, Lisa Rufle in "A Brief History of Book Clubs/Suite 101", wrote: "Because literacy was initially reserved for only those members of society's upper classes, reading was not an activity that the general public could indulge in. This gave those who were literate, usually the wealthy and educated, an instant upper hand in society.

While there is some debate as to when the first book club was formed, (in part because the facts are vague,) Rachel Jacobsohn, author of *The Reading Group Handbook: Everything You Need to Know to Start Your Own Book Club*, recalls "a reading group comprised of "white glove-wearing, hat-wearing, tea-drinking, elitist old white women" from the late 1800s. This exclusive group was restricted to members who inherited a place among the coveted club."

Many book clubs started in the early 1900s are the foundation of our current obsession with reading. "In 1916, one Harry Sherman of Philadelphia – an advertising copywriter with expertise on mail-order promotion and a lover of books and reading – founded a mail-order book firm called the Little Leather Library with a couple of his colleagues." (18) Sherman's dream would grow and ultimately culminate in 1926 in a new company called Book-of-the–Month-Club. "Almost from the very beginning, Book-of-the-Month-Club was facing some serious competition. In 1927, another savvy marketer, Samuel W. Craig, developed a concept similar to European guilds and named the new company *The Literary Guild*. In 1930, *The Doubleday One Dollar Book Club* entered the scene; in 1934 its parent company, Doubleday and Co., acquired *The Literary Guild* and positioned itself as a strong alternative to BOMC: they offered their readers somewhat lighter reading, as opposed to Book-of-the-Month whose selections were deemed more literary." (19)

"In 1977 *Book-of-the-Month-Club* was acquired by publishing company *Time Inc.,* which later became *Time Warner Inc.* and later still *AOL Time Warner*, as a result of yet another merger, BOMC continued operating by and large independently under the new patronage." (20)

The 1980s were difficult times for the book club system as national bookstore chains made the purchase of books more readily accessible. Then the 1990s brought the eventual demise of the BOMC with the advent of the mega-bookstores such as Barnes & Noble.

In 1996, Oprah Winfrey's Book Club brought new life to books and reading, as heretofore unknown titles and authors were discovered, and talked about over coffee and the copy machine.

In 2002, the *Today Show*, the NBC morning talk and information series, launched a semi-regular national book club, which consisted primarily of works of fiction.

On April 11, 2002, the national newspaper, *USA Today*, created its own book club, with online chats, message boards and stories in the paper driving the discussion. Richard Russo's *Empire Falls*, which had just won the Pulitzer Prize for Fiction, was the first book selected by *USA Today*.

Oprah Winfrey ended the book club she had started in 1996 with two final selections in 2002, *Great Expectations*, and *A Tale of Two Cities*, by Charles Dickens. Oprah cited her reasons for ending her first "version" of the club: "It has become harder and harder to find books on a monthly basis that I feel absolutely compelled to share."

A newly revised digital "Oprah's Book Club 2.0" kicked off in July 2012 with *Wild: From Lost to Found on the Pacific Coast Trail*, by Cheryl Strayed.

The Women's National Book Association (WNBA) has designated October to be National Reading Group Month. Founded in 1917, WNBA promotes literacy, a love of reading, and women's roles in the community of the book.

Readers and reading groups today are fortunate to have many resources at their disposal to help them choose a book title and engage in lively discussions. From Great Group Reads (i.e., LongIslandReads.org to AllSeattleReads.org) to publisher's blogs and various book websites, my Tip #18 would be to recommend the following resources for book clubs:

Tip #18 -   Reading group resources and websites:

- www.BookBrowse.com
- www.BookRags.com
- www.BookPage.com
- www.BookReporter.com
- www.Offtheshelf.com
- www.ReadingGroupGuides.com
- www.NoveList.com
- www.Shelfari.com
- www.barnesandnoble.com
- www.simonandschuster.com
- www.LibraryThing.com
- www.ReadItForward.com
- www.hotatharper.com
- www.Amazon.com
- www.About.com/books
- www.BookChatter.com
- www.NextReads.com
- www.GoodReads.com
- www.BookTV.org (C-Span2)
- Random House Readers Circle
- HuffPostBooks
- AAKnopf
- Readmill (ebook reader for iPhone and iPad)
- DigiBookWorld (Twitter and Facebook)
- www.Youreadinggroup.co.uk

"A book is a device to ignite the imagination."

~ *Alan Bennett*

THE ADVENT OF THE eBOOK

The electronic book, e-book, eBook, ebook, digital book or e-edition is a book-length publication in digital form, consisting of text, images, or both, readable on computers or other electronic devices. (E-book, WIKIPEDIA, The Free Encyclopedia, 4/28/2015).

There is some discrepancy as to who invented the first e-book and when it first appeared. Perhaps, it was Bob Brown, who wrote 'The Readies' in 1930, after he had seen the first "talkies", (movies with sound,) or maybe it was Roberto Busa in 1940, who wrote a heavily annotated electronic index to the works of Thomas Aquinas, or Angela Ruiz Robles, a teacher from Spain, who patented the first electronic book in 1949. (E-book, WIKIPEDIA, The Free Encyclopedia, 4/28/2015).

The list of names goes on: Doug Engelbart and Andries van Dam, (1960s,) Michael S. Hart (1971). The dates range through 1971 with Project Gutenberg and the first digital library, and Marie Lebert's ten-year study, "A Short History of eBooks," NEF, University of Toronto, 2009.

Michael Kozlowski writing for goodreader.com, (May 17, 2010,) "A Brief History of eBooks,) claims that Stephen King's horror novel, Ride the Bullet, was released only as an eBook (initially) in 2000.

Amazon.com released the Kindle e-reader in 2007, followed by the Nook from Barnes & Noble in 2009.

Today it is possible to download an electronic book onto many different devices. To some, ebooks are the fast and easy way to read when you are traveling or on the go.

My nephew, Craig, my sister Diane's oldest son, who designed my website and is the techie genius who made this ebook possible, has opened up a whole new world to me, a world so different from the quiet sanctuary of my hardcover books. He brought me into the 21st century and introduced me to the benefits of the latest technology. And for that, I cannot thank him enough.

Craig lived with us, on and off for five or six years, from 1986-1992, before and while he was in college. Craig was the one who introduced his younger cousin, my son, Brett, to classic rock, to the pleasures of KISS and PINK FLOYD. He was the one who had smugly given me a copy of one of his favorite books, *The Know-it-All: One Man's Humble Quest to Become the Smartest Person in the World,* by A. J. Jacobs.

Before I experienced my second 'Miracle in Aruba' (2015), Ted bought a Kindle and downloaded *Dead Wake: The Last Crossing of the Lusitania.,* by Erik Larson. This time I did actually read the book digitally. It was a totally different experience that posed several questions for "The Ultimate Hard-core, High-handed, Card-carrying Bibliophilist." How would I sign my books out to family and friends? What about my marginalia? How would I know the number of pages that were left in each chapter? And what would I do now with all of the special bookmarks I have been collecting for years and years, the appropriate bookmark I would always select to coincide with the particular subject of the book I was currently reading, (i.e. the bookmark I had bought when I was in Turkey that was so fitting to use for my reading of Chris Bohjalian's, *The Sandcastle Girls,* or the Monet bookmark that I purchased at the artist's home in Giverny while enjoying *Claude and Camille: A Novel of Monet,* by Stephanie Cowell?)

Perhaps, it is time for me to open the door to a new reading experience. Perhaps it is time for me to consider the "other" (ebooks) point of view offered by author, journalist, satirist and critic, Joe Queenan:

"Electronic books are ideal for people who value the information contained in them, or who have vision problems, or who like to read on the subway, or who do not want other people to see how they are amusing themselves, or who have storage and clutter issues, but they are useless for people who are engaged in an intense, lifelong love affair with books. Books that we can touch; books that we can smell; books that we can depend on." (Queenan, Joe (2012). One for the books. Viking Adult. ISBN 97806700258214.

TIPS ON HOW TO START, LEAD AND ENHANCE YOUR BOOK DISCUSSION

(As prepared by 'The Ultimate Hard-core, High-handed, Card-carrying Bibliophilist)

Note: Of course, you can always ignore the aforesaid "Ultimate Hard-core, High-handed, Card-carrying Bibliophilist' and do and discuss whatever you want (preferably BEFORE and/or AFTER book club hours).

1. **Choose a venue for your book discussion**. Decide if you would like to meet in a bookstore, at one another's homes, at a restaurant or coffee shop or at your local library.

2. **Choose a time, day, month.** (Mornings/Afternoons/Evenings? Weekday or Weekend? Weekly? Monthly? Quarterly?)

3. **Choose a genre of book that you like to discuss.** (Fiction? Non-Fiction? Poetry? Short Stories? Classics? Alternating Genres?)

4. **Decide how you will choose the book.** Hostess Pick? Group designated facilitator pick? Members take turns? Random drawings?

5. **Begin each discussion by giving a brief biographical sketch of the author** and mention what may have inspired the book or the background behind it.

6. **NO POLITICS OR RELIGION** unless your members decide in advance that they would like to discuss these sensitive issues.

7. **NO PERSONAL DISCUSSIONS OF FAMILY OR HEALTH** unless your members decide in advance that they would like to discuss these sensitive issues.

8. **The Oprah Factor** - Make the most of Oprah's knowledge, choice of book titles and authors when making your selections for your book club.

9. **Contact an author** -Take the time to send an email, tweet, or contact an author by snail mail if you choose to let him/her know how you feel about his/her book. The author will either respond or ignore your message. What do you have to lose? It's a cathartic way for you to vent. Note re: Tip # 9 – Choose your own words wisely when writing. You know the old adage, "You can catch more flies with honey than you do with vinegar."

10. **TIMING IS EVERYTHING!** - Quite often "when" we read a book may be important – not the time of day or the month or year, but rather "what period" in our lives we may decide to start turning the pages. After a particularly bad or sad experience, we may have a negative view of a book. If we were to re-read that very same book months or even years later, at a happier time, our opinion would, undoubtedly, be different. So, I tell my book groups:

    TIMING IS EVERYTHING!!! Especially when it comes to reading.

11. **CELEBRATE!** - Even if your book club meets in a restaurant, once or twice a year gather for a special mid-summer or end of year celebration:

    Have a pool party with a literary theme, (i.e., The Paris Wife, by Paula McLain, The Great Gatsby, by F. Scott Fitzgerald, Rules of Civility, by Amor Towles, or Midnight in the Garden of Good and Evil, by John Berendt.

    OR

494

Celebrate your favorite author's birthday, the 25th, the 50th or 75th edition of a famous book, (i.e., To Kill a Mockingbird, by Harper Lee or Gone with the Wind, by Margaret Mitchell.

12. **Travel/Destination Book** - If your book selection deals with a particular place/location, ask if anyone has been there. Let that person describe his experience. (i.e., Hawaii or Texas or Poland, by James A. Michener or Under the Tuscan Sun: At Home In Italy, by Frances Mayes or Paris: The Novel or New York: The Novel, by Edward Rutherfurd.

OR

Call a travel expert or plan your own destination book tour. (i.e., Adriana Trigiani's tours to Italy to see the sites recorded in her VALENTINE series and The Shoemaker's Wife. Stroll the cobblestone streets of the West Village in New York City and enjoy the restaurants where Valentine Roncalli dined or the church where Lucia Santori prayed (Lucia, Lucia).

13. **Same Edition/Version** - Always make certain that everyone is reading the same edition or version of the book chosen for discussion AND IN THE SAME LANGUAGE! Those translations will get you every time.

14. **Give a name to your book club** - It can be based on your interests (i.e., The Wine Connoisseur's Book Club,) or a person's name, (Donna's Book Lovers). It can be funny or representative of its purpose, like The Guernsey Literary and Potato Peel Pie Society, by Mary Ann Schaffer and Annie Barrows.

15. **Series Books** - Read the first book in a series in order to introduce your readers to the author and the

subject contained therein. If the reader enjoyed the first book, he/she will continue reading Book # 2, or #3 or #4 in that particular series. If not, the reader will be able to determine whether or not this author appeals to him/her.

16. **Book to Movie** - Many of the books we read have been made into movies. Whenever possible, bring your lunch or some popcorn and watch the movie together after you have talked about the book. Oftentimes, especially if you loved the book, the movie will be disappointing or have a "Hollywood" ending, which is totally different from the book from which it has been adapted, (i.e., *Snowflower and the Secret Fan*, by Lisa See.) In many cases, an author will relinquish all book rights to a screenwriter maintaining that, while his book will always be his alone, the movie version will forever belong to Hollywood.

17. **Invite an Author** - Invite an author to join your group discussion if his/her schedule permits. Having the author talk about his work, and the inspiration for it always enhances the enjoyment and understanding of it.

18. **Reading Group Resources and Websites**
    o www.BookBrowse.com
    o www.BookRags.com
    o www.BookPage.com
    o www.BookReporter.com
    o www.Offtheshelf.com
    o www.ReadingGroupGuides.com
    o www.NoveList.com

- o www.Shelfari.com
- o www.barnesandnoble.com
- o www.simonandschuster.com
- o www.LibraryThing.com
- o www.ReadItForward.com
- o www.hotatharper.com
- o www.Amazon.com
- o www.About.com/books
- o www.BookChatter.com
- o www.NextReads.com
- o www.GoodReads.com
- o www.BookTV.org (C-Span2)
- o Random House Readers Circle
- o HuffPostBooks
- o AAKnopf
- o Readmill (ebook reader for iPhone and iPad)
- o DigiBookWorld (Twitter and Facebook)
- o www.Youreadinggroup.co.uk

19. **Choose a book from "The Calendar of Book Recommendations" (Jan.-Dec.)**

20. **Give each book a Rating - ***** - B**ased on a scale of 1-5 (with 5 being the best), have each member grade the book that you are currently reading based on the following criteria:

   a. Author's style of writing

   b. Plot/storyline

   c. Characters

      i. Were they likable? (Does that matter?)

      ii. Could you relate to them? (Does that matter?)

      iii. Did you care what happened to them?

    d. Would you recommend this book to someone else? Would you read another book by this author?

21. **Food/Beverage Themed Books** - Some books suggest certain foods or beverages. Make a specific food/drink your theme of the book party. (i.e., Coffee, as in Mario Puzo's, The Fortunate Pilgrim, or pretzels as in Charity Shumway's, Ten Girls to Watch, (for the Robert Rolland Pretzel Baron Family).

22. **Create a mood or "Sense of Time"** - Play the music of the era depicted in a particular book. (i.e. 'I'll Be Seeing You' as you read, String of Pearls, by Ben Baglio (July 2003) or The Girls of Atomic City: The Untold Story of the Women Who Helped Win WWII, by Denise Kiernan (Dec. 2013) - WWII songs, such as "The Boogie Woogie Bugle Boy From Company B," or music from "Psycho" or "Phantom of the Opera," as you discuss The Historian, by Elizabeth Kostova. It will surely take you back to that moment or memory of someone of a by-gone period.

23. **Bell or Noise-maker** - Bring a Bell or Noise-maker of some kind to your discussion in an effort to maintain order, stay on track, and avoid cross-chatting. (I always bring both a lovely Waterford crystal bell and my tough-looking cowbell, both compliments of my book club members.) Which bell I use is determined by how rowdy or raucous the conversation gets. Usually, I can 'silence the lambs' with a gentle threat of "Please don't make me have to use this bullhorn."

24. **Dual Titles** - If a book selected for discussion refers to another book, (for example, *Jane Eyre* in *The Eyre Affair* (- Jan., 2004), or if the chosen book is short and deals with the same subject or themes as another

relatively short book, then it is interesting and fun and informative to designate dual titles for that month's reading. (i.e., Making Toast: A Family Story, by Roger Rosenblatt and Room, by Emma Donoghue – Sept. 2011.)

25. **Deciphering the Title** - Try to decipher the title of the book that you are discussing. Do you think the title aptly describes the story contained therein? I say, YES! to The Devil in the White City: Murder, Magic and Madness at the Fair That Changed America, by Erik Larson and a resounding YES! to Dancing on Broken Glass, by Ka Hancock and Wait Till Next Year, by Doris Kearns Goodwin. Sometimes the title is appealing but quite misleading, for example, The Master Butcher's Singing Club, by Louise Erdrich. And sometimes you have to wait a long time until you discover the meaning or find a clue to the title, (i.e., Snow In August, by Pete Hamill).

26. **Draw Out The Timid** - You can have your timid or shy members write their questions or comments on a piece of paper and have it read aloud anonymously. OR For those members who may not be comfortable speaking in front of a group, ask them to take one question from 'The Reading Group Guide' and ask the person seated next to them to respond. You can then pass the 'Reading Group Guide' around the table, and the next person and the next will have the opportunity to be heard.

   Sometimes the timid or quiet would like to simply listen to what is being said by the group. It isn't always necessary to speak. (Refer to Quiet: The Power of Introverts in a World That Can't Stop Talking, by Susan Cain).

27. **"Light Reads" or "Comfort Reads"** - Select a book that is an easy read, unchallenging or fun, to be read either during the summer months or when the December holidays place more demands on your reading time.
28. **Favorite Quote or Passage** - Choose a favorite sentence, quote, or passage from the book being discussed and ask each book club member to share it with the group.
29. **What was the book about?** Ask the group what the book was about, the author's themes, the meaning of the story. (i.e., Beautiful Ruins, by Jess Walter, contained many "stories within the story").
30. **Acting/Playing the Story/Theatre** - For those with a theatrical bent or love of drama, try dressing up in the costume of the time period depicted in the book, and recite passages (in costume and make-up.)
31.

"What We Carry With Us"

One of the joys of being in a book club is the discussion of the book and how it impacts each of us individually. We all bring our own life experiences, memories and "baggage" with us. That will determine our enjoyment of a book and our subsequent critique of it. As we listen to the comments made by others in the book club, we may change our own minds in view of their different perspectives.

*Note: When asked to describe her ideal book club, actress, producer, and author, Mindy Kaling, replied: "My book club would be held on Sunday afternoons. Dress code: warm-weather black tie. Cocktails from 3-3:30. Chitchat from 3:30 to 4. Personal drama from 4 to 5. Book discussion from 5-5:30. Early dinner from 5:30 to 7. Then everyone goes home." (*The New York Times Book Review*, Sunday, Sept. 13, 2015, "By the Book," page 7.)

~ The Ultimate Hard-core, High-handed, Card-carrying Bibliophilist would approve of the above with the sole exception being: Book Discussion from 5 to 6:30 then dinner to follow.

CALENDAR OF BOOK RECOMMENDATIONS

In the book world, we have our own calendar from which to choose a timely or representative book. February, for example, is Black History Month. You and your group might elect to read *Roots: The Saga of an American Family*, by Alex Haley or *Striver's Row*, the third book in Kevin Baker's 'Dreamland Trilogy.' You might choose *The Invisible Man*, by Ralph Ellison or *Uncle Tom's Cabin*, by Harriet Beecher Stowe. Whatever book you choose to read that month, it might be fun to select a title which commemorates a group or event or celebrates something.

Tip #19 - Choose a book from the Calendar of Book Recommendations.

JANUARY - National Mentoring Month

1. E.R. Braithwaite, *To Sir With Love*
2. Laura Schroff and Alex Tresniowski, *An Invisible Thread: The True Story of an 11-Year-Old Panhandler, a Busy Sales Executive, and an Unlikely Meeting with Destiny*
3. John C. Maxwell, *Mentoring 101: What Every Leader Needs to Know*
4. Carson Pue, *Mentoring Leaders: Wisdom for Developing Character, Calling and Competency*

FEBRUARY - Black History Month

1. Isabel Wilkerson, *The Warmth of Other Suns: The Epic Story of America's Great Migration*
2. Kathryn Stockett, *The Help*
3. Barack Obama, *Dreams From My Father: A Story of Race and Inheritance*
4. Ernest Gaines, *A Lesson Before Dying*

MARCH - Irish American Heritage Month

1. Alice McDermott, *The Ninth Hour, Someone, Charming Bill*
2. Cormac McCarthy, *All the Pretty Horses, The Road, No Country for Old Men*
3. Dennis Lehane, *Shutter Island, Mystic River, Gone, Baby, Gone*
4. Frank McCourt, *Angela's Ashes, 'Tis, Teacher Man*

- National Women's History Month

1. Sonia Sotomayer, *My Beloved World*
2. Denise Kiernan, *The Girls of Atomic City: The Untold Story of the Women Who Helped Win World War II*
3. Leslie Sills, *Inspirations: Stories About Women Artists*
4. Rebecca Skloot, *The Immortal Life of Henrietta Lacks*

APRIL - National Poetry Month

1. Leon Bazelgette, *Walt Whitman: The Man and His Work, Translated from the French* by Ellen Fitzgerald
2. Gamaliel Bradford, *Portraits of American Women* (Emily Dickinson)
3. Elizabeth Barrett Browning, *Sonnets from the Portuguese*
4. Rainer Maria Rilke, *Letters to a Young Poet*

- National School Library Month

Encourage your children to make full use of their school library

MAY - South Asia Heritage Month

1. Jhumpa Lahiri, *The Lowland, Interpreter of Maladies, The Namesakei*
2. Abraham Verghese, *Cutting for Stone*
3. Rohinton Mistry, *A Fine Balance*
4. Arundhati Roy, *The God of Small Things*

- Haitian Heritage Month

1. Edwidge Danticat – *Claire of the Sealight, The Dew Breaker, Brother, I'm Dying*
2. Dany Laferrière – *L'Enigme du Retour*

- Asian Pacific American Heritage Month

1. Ha Jin – *Waiting, War Trash*
2. Chang-Rae Lee – *On Such a Full Sea, Native Speaker, Aloft, A Gesture Life*

3. Amy Tan – *The Valley of Amazement, The Joy Luck Club, The Kitchen God's Wife, The Bonesetter's Daughter*
4. Gail Tsukiyama – *The Samurai's Garden, Women of the Silk, The Language of Threads*
5. Lisa See – *China Dolls, Snowflower and the Secret Fan, Shanghai Girls, Dreams of Joy*

- Jewish American Heritage Month

1. Elie Wiesel – *Night, The Jews of Silence, A Beggar in Jerusalem, Passover Haggadah*
2. Saul Bellow - Herzog, *Humboldt's Gift, The Adventures of Augie March, Henderson the Rain King*
3. Alyson Richman – *The Garden of Letters, The Lost Wife*
4. Jodi Picoult – *The Storyteller*
5. Phillip Roth – *Portnoy's Complaint, The Human Stain, American Pastoral, The Plot Against America*
6. Isaac Bashevis Singer – *The Magician of Lublin, A Day of Pleasure: Stories of a Boy Growing Up In Warsaw*

JUNE - Caribbean American Heritage Month

1. Jamaica Kincaid (Elaine Potter Richardson) – (Antigua) – *At the Bottom of the River, Annie John, Lucy, The Autobiography of My Mother*
2. George Lamming - (Barbados) – *In the Castle of My Skin, The Pleasure of Exile*
3. Bernice L. McFadden (Barbados) – *Sugar, Nowhere Is a Place, Gathering of Waters*
4. V. S. Naipaul (Sir Vidiadhar Surajprasad) – (Trinidadian-British)- *Magic Seeds, The Masque of Africa: Glimpses of African Belief*
5. Elizabeth Nunez (Trinidad) – *Not For Everyday Use: A Memoir*
6. James Michener (American) – *Caribbean, a novel*

JULY – Dance Appreciation Month

In July you can find all kinds of books about dance and dancing, biographies about famous dancers and "How To" books on learning ballet, tap, jazz or ballroom dancing. You can read *Famous Dancers of Past and Present*, or *Top 10 Movies For Dance Lovers*, both by Treva Bedinghaus. Or you can find stories about choreographers like Twyla Tharp, Bob Fosse or George Balanchine. You can read non-fiction works detailing the life of:

1. Isadora Duncan
2. Mikhail Baryshnikov
3. Gregory Hines
4. Agnes DeMille
5. Rudolf Nureyev or Margot Fonteyn
6. Fred Astaire (and Ginger Rogers)
7. Gene Kelly
8. Savion Glover
9. Paula Abdul
10. Merce Cunningham
11. Martha Graham

My very personal favorite is to watch Sammy Davis, Jr. singing (and dancing) to MR. BOJANGLES. You can read a book about Bill "Bojangles" Robinson. And on my original "bucket list" was to have taken a dance class with Michael Jackson. What a "thriller" that would have been!

AUGUST - National Immunization Awareness Month

1. Mary Beth Keane - *Fever* (a novel about Mary Mallon, aka "Typhoid Mary")

2. Jennifer Rosenberg – *Typhoid Mary: The Sad Story of a Woman Responsible for Several Typhoid Outbreaks*
3. Victoria Sherrow - *Jonas Salk: Beyond The Microscope*
4. Robert W. Sears – *The Vaccine Book: Making the Right Decision for Your Child* (Sears Parenting Library)
5. J. D. Grabenstein - *Immunofacts*
6. Gay Salisbury and Laney Salisbury – *The Cruelest Miles: The Heroic Story of Dogs and Men in a Race Against an Epidemic*

SEPTEMBER - National Hispanic Heritage Month

1. Gabriel José de la Concordia Garcia Marquez – (Colombian) – *Love in the Time of Cholera, One Hundred Years of Solitude*
2. Julia Alvarez – (Dominican American) – *How the Garcia Girls Lost Their Accents*
3. Laura Esquivel - (Mexican) – *Like Water For Chocolate*
4. Isabel Allende – (Chilean) – *Ripper, The House of the Spirits, Daughter of Fortune, Maya's Notebook*
5. Paul Coelho – (Brazilian) – *The Alchemist, Aleph, The Book of Manuals*
6. Junot Diaz – (Dominican American) – *The Brief Wondrous Life of Oscar Wao, This is How You Lose Her*

YAHOO!!! ***** OCTOBER - NATIONAL BOOK CLUB MONTH

Go out and celebrate another year of **HAPPY READING** by reading **MY BOOK**, *Book Club: How I Became the Ultimate Hard-core, High-handed, Card-carrying Bibliophilist* with your book club.

- Filipino American History Month

1. Bob Ong – *Macarthur, Kapitan Sino, Lumayo Ka Nga Sa Akin*
2. F. H. Batacan – *Smaller and Smaller Circles*
3. Samantha Sotto - *Before Ever After*
4. Cecilia Manguerra - When *the Rainbow Goddess Wept*

- National Bullying Prevention Month

1. Jodi Picoult – *Nineteen Minutes*
2. Richard Russo – *Empire Falls*
3. Megan Kelly Hall – *Dear Bully: 70 Authors Tell Their Stories*

NOVEMBER - National American Indian & Alaska Native Heritage Month

1. Louise Erdrich – *The Plague of Doves, The Master Butcher's Singing Club, The Round House*
2. Joseph L. Coulombe – *Reading Native American Literature*
3. Dee Brown – *Bury My Heart At Wounded Knee: An Indian History of the American West*
4. Jim Fergus – *One Thousand White Women: The Journals of May Dodd* (a novel)
5. Mary Crow Dog – *Lakota Woman*
6. James Michener - *Alaska*
7. Sam Keith – *One Man's Wilderness: An Alaskan Odyssey* (from the Journals and Photographs of Richard Proenneke)
8. Gay and Laney Salisbury – *The Cruelest Miles: The Heroic Story of Dogs and Men in a Race Against an Epidemic*

DECEMBER - National Music Appreciation Month

Choose from a wealth of biographies of musicians, artists, and bands, from pop, rock, classical, blues, country,

Christian, hip hop, rap, R&B, folk, heavy metal, reggae, punk, alternative, grunge, Broadway tunes, opera and instrumental. From the Beatles, Michael Jackson, the Beach Boys, the Rolling Stones and Pink Floyd to Frank Sinatra, Michael Bublé, Dean Martin, Andy Williams, Harry Connick, Jr., Luciano Pavarotti, Rod Stewart, and Tony Bennett. From Garth Brooks, Blake Shelton, Carrie Underwood, Reba McEntire, and Sheryl Crow to Elvis Presley, Johnny Cash, (Carlos) Santana, Barry Manilow, Celine Dion, Bono, Neil Diamond (my make-believe cousin, of course!) Taylor Swift, Katie Perry, and Lady Gaga. From Pink or Madonna to John Legend, Maroon 5 and the Tommy Dorsey Band or the music of Rodgers and Hammerstein, biographies, memoirs, short stories and music appreciation études, from sheet music to piano concertos, books on music, artists and musicians abound.

In the meantime, you might want to check out:

1. Pete Hamill – *Why Sinatra Matters*
2. John Densmore – *Riders on the Storm: My Life with Jim Morrison and The Doors*
3. Keith Richards – *Life*
4. Billy Idol – *Dancing with Myself*

INDEX OF QUOTATIONS CITED

1. "Monday was the diving board…." – Jan Karon, At Home in Mitford, pg. 18
2. "Until I feared…." – Harper Lee, To Kill a Mockingbird, pg. 20
3. "A Man is known…." – Ralph Waldo Emerson, pg. 25
4. "All this happened…." – Beryl Markham, The Illustrated West With the Night, pg. 31
5. "Books were my pass …." – Oprah Winfrey, pg. 39
6. "We have our responsibilities…." – Virginia Woolf, pg. 45
7. "The reading of all good books …." – Rene Descartes, Discourse on Method, Pg. 55
8. "Choose an author…." – Christopher Wren, pg. 73
9. "I remember these moments…." – Anita Shreve, The Weight of Water, pg.82
10. "…half of memory is imagination anyway." – The Yellow Birds, pg.92
11. "I came to love grinding…." – Tracy Chevalier, Girl With a Pearl Earring, pg.96
12. "Beyond myself…." – Octavio Paz, "The Balcony," pg. 99
13. "Il n'y a pas de roses sans epines." – 'Every rose has its thorns.', pg. 118
14. "Lucky from the outside was an illusion." – Anna Quindlen, Still Life With Breadcrumbs, pg. 120
15. "To learn to read…." – Victor Hugo, pg. 130
16. "She is too fond of books…." – Louisa May Alcott
17. "Some memories remain close…." – Jess Walter, Beautiful Ruins, pg.155

TO BE CONTINUED

BIBLIOGRAPHY

1. Vintage Books, Reading Group Guide on David Guterson, 1995.
2. Vintage Books, Reading Group Guide on David Guterson, 1995.
3. Austin American – Statesman, Dec. 17, 1995, by Pam Lange, Special to the American – Statesman.
4. Ibid. (Same source as referenced above.)
5. *Newsweek*, Dec. 18, 1995.
6. *Primary Colors*, Newsday, Wed., Aug. 28, 1996.
7. *USA Today*, Fri., May 24, 1996, Melanie Wells, "Court Ruling Gives Tobacco Stocks a Boost" (Section B, MONEY, pg. 1A.)
8. *People Magazine*, Aug. 26, 1996, "Where There's Smoke…., Grady Carter's $750,000 Victory Has Tobacco Giants Doing a Slow Burn."
9. *Time*, April 29, 1996, BOOKS "A Long Way, Baby."
10. *USA Today*, Wed., May 29, 1996, LIFE Section D, pg. 9D.
11. *Time Inc.* Magazine, (July 19, 1937?), Copyright 1994, Compact Publishing Inc.
12. Current Biography Yearbook 1988, Jeffrey Archer, pg. 21.
13. Jeffrey Archer, WIKIPEDIA, the Free Encyclopedia, June 21, 2009, pg. 2, 1988 Current Biography Yearbook, pg. 21, Jeffrey Archer.
14. *The Fourth Estate*- Official Website for Jeffrey Archer, Books & Plays, July 23, 2012.
15. Dictionary of Literary Biography, Vol. 6: American Novelists Since WWII, Second Series, - (Mario Puzo,) ed. James E. Kibler, Jr., Gale Research Co., Detroit, 1980, pg. 268

16. *People Magazine*, "Picks & Pans," PAGES – The Last Don, by Mario Puzo, pg. 29, Aug. 12, 1996.

17. Jacquelyn Mitchard, Home Page Biography.

18. History of Book Clubs, Book Clubs-online.com/guides/history/The History of Book Clubs, pg. 1.

19. Ibid. (Same as above.)

20. Ibid. (Same as above.)

21. www.readitforward.com/you-never-really-know-the-hearts-and-minds-of-others, April 30, 2013, Interview with Nichole Bernier.

22. *New York*, Sept. 27, 1999: Books, Walter Kirn, GOODFELLA, 'Tis by Frank McCourt, pg. 82.

23. *Newsday*, Sun., Sept. 26, 1999, Currents & Books, pg. 1, Chang-Rae Lee, "Speaking in Tongues," by Bill Vourvoulias.

24. *Corelli's Mandolin*, a quote taken from Vintage Books Reading Group Guide Favorites, pg. 1, Corelli's Mandolin.

25. Chevalier, Tracy, Sept. 2005, *Girl With a Pearl Earring*, Deluxe Edition., Penguin Group, pg. ix – xvi, ISBN 0452287022.

26. *Newsday*, Thurs., Mar. 29, 2001, Maeve Binchy, "In a New Ireland, the Same Old Business," by Anna Mundow, pg. B2.

27. Picoult, Jodi, Reference from *Nineteen Minutes*, by Jodi Picoult, jodipicoult.com, retrieved 2011-05-10, WIKIPEDIA, the Free Encyclopedia.

28. *USA Today*, *Life* Section D, Wed., May 28, 2003, pg.1D, "National Spelling Bee Burrows in our Bonnet," High Drama is the Star in this Reality Show, by Greg Toppo.

29. *Newsday*, Section B, Mon., Nov. 8, 2004, Cover Story B2-3, Part II, "What Alice Munro Knows."

30. Tsukiyama, Gail, Mar. 29, 1998, Elisabeth Sherwin-gizmo@den.davis.ca.us, Printed Matter, Gail Tsukiyama page.

31. *USA Today*, Thurs., Dec. 19, 2002, Life Section, pg.9D.

32. *USA Today*, Thurs., Aug. 1, 2002, Life Section, pg. 6D.

33. *USA Today*, Aug. 1, 2002, Life Section, pg. 6D.

34. What Remains, *The Lovely Bones* by Alice Sebold, written by Katherine Bouton, The New York Times Book Review, Sun., July 14, 2002, pg. 14.

35. *USA Today*, Thurs., May 1, 2003, pg.2A, "Kidnap Victims Gather to Watch Bush Sign "Amber Alert" Law," by Richard Benedetto.

36. *Newsday*, Wed., May 3, 2006, "It Happened on Long Island," a feature produced by the Newsday Marketing Dept., pg. B13.

37. "Supplement to the Budget of Paradoxes," The Athenaeum no. 2017, pg. 836 col. 2 (and later reprints: e.g., 1872, 1915, 1956, 2000.)

38. Sack, John. The Butcher: The Ascent of Yerupaja epigraph (1952), reprinted in Shapiro, Fred R., ed., The Yale Book of Quotations 529, (2006).

39. Roe, Anne, "The Making of a Scientist," 46-47, (1952, 1953), "http:11listserv.linquistlist.org/cgi-bin/wa?A2-ind0712C&L=ADS-L&P=R3767&I=-3). Listserv.linquistlist.org. Retrieved 2012-04-19.

40. Murphy's Laws site – All the laws of Murphy in one place (/) www.murphys-laws.com, Murphy's Laws origin – article excerpted from "The Desert Wings," Mar. 3, 1978.

41. *USA Today*, May 6, 2003, 'Da Vinci Code' inspires fervent deciphering,' by Ayesha Court.

42. Dan Brown Website – Bio, www.danbrown.com/meet_dan/index.html, (5/7/2003.)

43. *The Good German* by, Joseph Kanon. Ted Zabel, The Book Bin. Northbrook, IL, wrote for Book Sense 76, Independent Book-seller Recommendations, July & August 2001.

44. Same as Dan Brown # 42 above.

45. *Gangs of New York* – (Paradise Alley, by Kevin Baker) by, Geoffrey C. Ward, The New York Times Book Review, Sun., Oct. 6, 2002, pg. 11.

46. *Newsday*, Tues., July 12, 2005, Part II, Section B, pg. B1

47. *USA Today*, Tues., June 14, 2005, Book Review by Carol Memmott. *The Historian*, by Elizabeth Kostova, Little Brown, 642 pg., $25.95

48. *The New York Times Book Review, The Historian*, by Elizabeth Kostova, Sun., July 10, 2005, "Stayin' Alive," by Henry Alford.

49. *The New York Times Book Review*, Sun., Aug. 14, 2005, pg. 5.

50. Long Island Reads 2006 Reader's Guide,Amagansett, a novel by Mark Mills, Plot Summary, pg. 3.

"THE LITERARY GALLERY"

Donna Diamond

Through the years .... (From 1996 – 2015)

May 1996 - SNOW FALLING ON CEDARS by, David Guterson

June 1996 - PRIMARY COLORS by, Anonymous

July 1996 - THE RUNAWAY JURY by, John Grisham

August 1996 - I WAS AMELIA EARHART by, Jane Mendelsohn

September 1996 - THE FOURTH ESTATE by, Jeffrey Archer

October 1996 - THE LAST DON by, Mario Puzo

November 1996 - THE DEEP END OF THE OCEAN by, Jacqueline Mitchard (My Oprah visit & her 1st book pick)

December 1996 - SNOW FALLING ON CEDARS by, David Guterson (Repeat)*

***

February 1997 - THE HORSE WHISPERER by, Nicolas Evans & THE THIRD TWIN by, Ken Follett (Dual Selection)

March 1997 - THE SHIPPPING NEWS by, E. Annie Proux

April 1997 - ANGELA'S ASHES by, Frank McCourt

May 1997 - MIDNIGHT IN THE GARDEN OF GOOD AND EVIL by, John Berendt

June 1997 - ALL THE PRETTY HORSES by, Cormac McCarthy

July 1997 - PLUM ISLAND by, Nelson DeMille

September 1997 - SONGS IN ORDINARY TIME by, Mary McGarry Morris

October 1997 - THE REEF by, Edith Wharton

November 1997 - UP ISLAND by, Anne Rivers Siddon

December 1997 - A CIVIL ACTION by, Jonathan Harr

***

January 1998 - LARRY'S PARTY by, Carol Shields

February 1998 - COLD MOUNTAIN by, Charles Frazier

March 1998 - THE COLOR OF WATER by, James McBride

April 1998 - A CERTAIN JUSTICE by, P.D. James

May 1998 - AT HOME IN MITFORD (The Mitford Series) by, Jan Karon

June 1998 - MEMOIRS OF A GEISHA by, Arthur Golden

July 1998 - A WIDOW FOR ONE YEAR by, John Irving

August 1998 - WAIT TILL NEXT YEAR by, Doris Kearns Goodwin & COLONY by, Anne Rivers Siddons

September 1998 - PHILISTINES AT THE HEDGEROW: Passion & Property In The Hamptons by, Stephen Gaines

October 1998 - SHE'S COME UNDONE by, Wally Lamb

December 1998 - FOR KINGS AND PLANETS by, Ethan Canin

***

January 1999 - A MAN IN FULL by, Tom Wolfe

February 1999 - THE LOOP by,Nicolas Evans

April 1999 - THE POISONWOOD BIBLE by, Barbara Kingsolver

May 1999 - AMSTERDAM by, Ian McEwan

June 1999 - THE READER by, Bernhard Schlink

July 1999 - THE EMPERORS OF CHOCOLATE by, Joel Glenn Brenner (Guest Author)

August 1999 - SUSPICION by, Barbara Rogan (Guest Author)

September 1999 - THE PILOT'S WIFE by, Anita Shreve

October 1999 - THE BEACH by, Alex Garland

November 1999 - MIDWIVES by, Chris Bohjalian

December 1999 - NO ORDINARY TIME: Franklin & Eleanor On The Home Front by, Doris Kearns Goodwin

***

January 2000 - 'TIS by, Frank McCourt

February 2000 - THE WEIGHT OF WATER by, Anita Shreve

March 2000 - A GESTURE LIFE by, Chang-rae Lee

April 2000 – THE HOURS by, Michael Cunningham

May 2000 - ALIAS GRACE by, Margaret Atwood

June 2000 - TUESDAYS WITH MORRIE by, Mitch Albom

July 2000 - HORSE HEAVEN by, Jane Smiley

August 2000 - HALF A HEART by, Rosellen Brown

September 2000 - FLAGS OF OUR FATHERS by, James Bradley

October 2000 - WINTER SOLSTICE by, Rosamunde Pilcher

November 2000 - CORELLI'S MANDOLIN by, Louis de Bernieres

December 2000 - THE SAMURAI'S GARDEN by, Gail Tsukiyama

***

January 2001 - TYRANNOSAURUS SUE: The Extraordinary Saga of the Largest, Most Fought Over T-Rex Ever Found by, Steve Fiffer

February 2001 - MORGAN'S RUN by, Colleen McCullough

March 2001 - PLAINSONG by, Kent Haruf

April 2001 - DROWNING RUTH by, Christina Schwarz

May 2001 - GIRL WITH A PEARL EARRING by, Tracy Chevalier

June 2001 - THE HOUSE OF SAND AND FOG by, Andre Dubus III

July 2001 - SCARLET FEATHER by, Maeve Binchy

August 2001 - SALEM FALLS by, Jodi Picoult

September 2001 - THE GATES OF THE ALAMO by, Stephen Harrigan

October 2001 - WHILE I WAS GONE by, Sue Miller

November 2001 - WAITING by, Ha Jin

December 2001 - JOHN ADAMS by, David McCullough

***

January 2002 - IN THE HEART OF THE SEA: The Tragedy of the Whaleship Essex by, Nathaniel Philbrick

February 2002 – THE BEE SEASON by, Myla Goldberg

March 2002 - THE AMAZING ADVENTURES OF KAVALIER AND CLAY by, Michael Chabon

April 2002 - HATESHIP, FRIENDSHIP, LOVESHIP, COURTSHIP, MARRIAGE by, Alice Munro

May 2002 - THE HEART IS A LONELY HUNTER by, Carson McCullers

June 2002 - PLAIN TRUTH by, Jodi Picoult

July 2002 - WOMEN OF THE SILK by, Gail Tsukiyama

Sept. 2002 - NINE PARTS OF DESIRE: The Hidden World of Islamic Women by, Geraldine Brooks

Oct. 2002 - THE TRUE SOURCES OF THE NILE by, Sarah Stone

Nov. 2002 - EMPIRE FALLS by, Richard Russo

Dec. 2002 - PEACE LIKE A RIVER BY, Leif Enger

***

January 2003 - STANDING IN THE RAINBOW by, Fannie Flagg

February 2003 - THE LOVELY BONES by, Alice Sebold

March 2003 - THE PIANO TUNER by, Daniel Mason

April 2003 - HOW THE GARCIA GIRLS LOST THEIR ACCENT by, Julia Alvarez (My 1st L.I. Reads)

May 2003 - SEABISCUIT by, Laura Hillenbrand

June 2003 - FIVE QUARTERS OF THE ORANGE by, Joanne Harris

July 2003 - STRING OF PEARLS by, Ben Baglio (Guest Author) *

August 2003 - BEL CANTO by, Ann Patchett

Sept. 2003 - THE VINEYARD: The Pleasures & Perils of Creating An American Family Winery by, Louisa Thomas Hargrave (Guest Author) *

Oct. 2003 - THE DA VINCI CODE by, Dan Brown

Nov. 2003 - ATONEMENT by, Ian McEwan

Dec. 2003 - THE SECRET LIFE OF BEES by, Sue Monk Kidd

***

Jan. 2004 - THE EYRE AFFAIR by, Jasper Fforde and JANE EYRE by, Charlotte Bronte

Feb. 2004 - THE PASSION OF ARTEMESIA by, Susan Vreeland

March 2004 - BENJAMIN FRANKLIN by, Walter Isaacson

April 2004 - SNOW IN AUGUST by, Pete Hamill (L.I. Reads)

May 2004 - THE AMATEUR MARRIAGE by, Anne Tyler

June 2004 - ALOFT by, Chang-rae Lee

July 2004 - ANGLE OF REPOSE by, Wallace Stegner

August 2004 - POMPEII by, Robert Harris

Sept. 2004 - THE OTHER BOLEYN GIRL by, Philippa Gregory

Oct. 2004 - THE NAMESAKE by, Jhumpa Lahiri

Nov. 2004 - THE GOOD GERMAN by, Joseph Kanon

Dec. 2004 - BEFORE YOU KNOW KINDNESS by, Chris Bohjalian (Tele-chat)

***

Jan. 2005 - THE KITE RUNNER by, Khaled Hosseini

Feb. 2005 - THE PLOT AGAINST AMERICA by, Phillip Roth

March 2005 - CROW LAKE by, Mary Lawson

April 2005 - TRAVELS WITH CHARLEY by, John Steinbeck (L.I. Reads)

May 2005 - THE DEVIL IN THE WHITE CITY: Murder, Magic & Madness at the Fair That Changed   America by, Erik Larson

June 2005 - PARADISE ALLEY by, Kevin Baker

July 2005 - VANISHING ACT by, Jodi Picoult

Aug. 2005 - NIGHTFALL by, Nelson DeMille

Sept. 2005 - McNALLY'S BLUFF by, Vince Lardo (Guest Author) *

Oct. 2005 - THE HISTORIAN by, Elizabeth Kostova

Nov. 2005 - THE CRUELEST MILES: The Heroic Story of Dogs and Men in a Race Against An Epidemic by, Gay and Laney Salisbury

Dec. 2005 - 1776 by, David McCullough

***

Jan. 2006 - SWEETWATER CREEK by, Anne Rivers Siddons

February 2006 – BLIZZARD (No Book Club)

March 2006 - THE MARCH by, E. L. Doctorow

April 2006 - AMAGANSETT by, Mark Mills (L.I. Reads)

May 2006 - SNOWFLOWER AND THE SECRET FAN by, Lisa See

June 2006 - LUCIA LUCIA by, Adriana Trigiani

July 2006 - THE BIRTH OF VENUS by, Sarah Dunant

August 2006 - THE TENDER BAR by, J.R. Moehringer

Sept. 2006 - TIME AND AGAIN by, Jack Finney

Oct. 2006 - FATE AND MS. FORTUNE by, Saralee Rosenberg (Guest Author)

Nov. 2006 - KRAKATOA:The Day The World Exploded by, Simon Winchester

Dec. 2006 - WATER FOR ELEPHANTS by, Sara Gruen

***

Jan. 2007 - FOR ONE MORE DAY by, Mitch Albom

Feb. 2007 - THE MEMORY KEEPER'S DAUGHTER by, Kim Edwards

March 2007 - THE DOUBLE BIND by, Chris Bohjalian

April 2007 - STRIVER'S ROW by, Kevin Baker

May 2007 - THE GEORGETOWN LADIES SOCIAL CLUB: Power, Passion & Politics In the Nation's Capital by, C. David Heymann

June 2007 - THE GLASS CASTLE by, Jeannette Walls

July 2007 - THE LAST VAN GOGH by, Alyson Richman (Guest Author) *

Aug. 2007 - 1,000 WHITE WOMEN: The Journals of May Dodd by, Jim Fergus

Sept. 2007 - THE GODS OF NEWPORT by, John Jakes

Oct. 2007 - NINETEEN MINUTES by, Jodi Picoult

Nov. 2007 - A THOUSAND SPLENDID SUNS by, Khaled Hosseini

Dec. 2007 - MAYFLOWER by, Nathaniel Philbrick

***

Jan. 2008 - LOVING FRANK by, Nancy Horan

Feb. 2008 - BRIDGE OF SIGHS by, Richard Russo

March 2008 - WHEN CRICKETS CRY by, Charles Martin

April 2008 - NATIVE SPEAKER by, Chang-rae Lee

May 2008 - THE CAMEL BOOKMOBILE by, Masha Hamilton

June 2008 - EAT, PRAY, LOVE by, Elizabeth Gilbert

July 2008 - THE PILLARS OF THE EARTH by, Ken Follett

Aug. 2008 - THE APPEAL by, John Grisham

Sept. 2008 - THE TEN YEAR NAP by, Meg Wolitzer (Guest Author) *

Oct. 2008 - MORE THAN IT HURTS YOU by, Darin Strauss (Author didn't show- miscommunication)

Nov. 2008 - DEAR NEIGHBOR, DROP DEAD by, Saralee Rosenberg (Guest Author) *

Dec. 2008 - MORE THAN IT HURTS YOU by, Darin Strauss (Guest Author) *

***

Jan. 2009 - SUITE FRANCAISE by, Irene Nemirovsky

Feb. 2009 - THE GUERNSEY LITERARY AND POTATO PEEL PIE SOCIETY by, Mary Ann Schaffer & Annie Barrows

March 2009 - VERY VALENTINE by, Adriana Trigiani

April 2009 - WAIT TILL NEXT YEAR by, Doris Kearns Goodwin

May 2009 - REVOLUTIONARY ROAD by, Richard Yates

June 2009 - THE STORY OF EDGAR SAWTELLE by, David Wroblewski

July 2009 - PATHS OF GLORY by, Jeffrey Archer

Aug. 2009 - HEART & SOUL by, Maeve Binchy

Sept. 2009 - SHANGHAI GIRLS by, Lisa See (Tele-chat)

Oct. 2009 - PEOPLE OF THE BOOK by, Geraldine Brooks

Nov. 2009 - OLIVE KITTERIDGE by, Elizabeth Strout

Dec. 2009 - THE LOST SYMBOL by, Dan Brown

***

Jan. 2010 - BREAKING THE BANK by, Yona Zeldis McDonough (Guest Author) *

Feb. 2010 - MANHUNT: The 12 Day Chase of Lincoln's Killer by, James L. Swanson

March 2010 - BRAVA VALENTINE by, Adriana Trigiani

April 2010 - THE RIVER OF DOUBT: Theodore Roosevelt's Darkest Journey by, Candace Millard (L.I.Reads)

May 2010 - THE HELP by, Kathryn Stockett

June 2010 - A RELIABLE WIFE by, Robert Goolrick

July 2010 - SECRETS OF EDEN by, Chris Bohjalian (Tele-chat)

Aug. 2010 - A SILENT OCEAN AWAY by, DeVa Gant (Guest Author)

Sept. 2010 - GIRL IN A BLUE DRESS by, Gaynor Arnold

Oct. 2010 - THE SURRENDERED by, Chang-rae Lee

Nov. 2010 - HALF A LIFE by, Darin Strauss (Guest Author)

Dec. 2010 - THE GIRL WITH THE DRAGON TATTOO by, Stieg Larson

***

Jan. 2011 - LET THE GREAT WORLD SPIN by, Colum McCann

Feb. 2011 - FREEDOM by, Jonathan Franzen

March 2011 - HOTEL ON THE CORNER OF BITTER AND SWEET by, Jamie Ford

April 2011 - SAG HARBOR by, Colson Whitehead

May 2011 - THE DISTANT HOURS by, Kate Morton

June 2011 - THE UNCOUPLING by, Meg Wolitzer (Guest Author)

July 2011 - CUTTING FOR STONE by, Abraham Verghese

Aug. 2011 - UNBROKEN: A World War II Story of Survival, Resilience & Redemption by, Laura Hillenbrand

Sept. 2011 – MAKING TOAST: A Family Story, by, Roger Rosenblatt & ROOM by, Emma Donoghue

Oct. 2011 - DIAMOND RUBY by, Joe Wallace (Guest Author) *

Nov. 2011 - DREAMS OF JOY by, Lisa See (Tele-chat)

Nov. 2011 – THE TIME IN BETWEEN by, Maria Duenas (Guest Author) *

Dec. 2011 - BOOKS, BOOKS, BOOKS, - 16 Year Recap Discussion & Anecdotes

***

Jan. 9, 2012 - ANOTHER PIECE OF MY HEART by, Jane Green (Author was disinvited)

Feb. 13, 2012 - THE GREATER JOURNEY: Americans in Paris by, David McCullough

March 19, 2012 - THE PARIS WIFE by, Paula McLain

April 9, 2012 - THE LOST WIFE by Alyson Richman *(A L.I. Reads Selection)

May 7, 2012 - RULES OF CIVILITY by, Amor Towles

June 11, 2012 - ISTANBUL PASSAGE by, Joe Kanon (Author Telephone Chat) * Wrote 'Reading Guide'

July 9, 2012 - DEFENDING JACOB by, William Landay

August 6, 2012 – THE SHOEMAKER'S WIFE by, Adriana Trigiani (Tele-chat with author) *

Sept. 10, 2012 – TEN GIRLS TO WATCH by, Charity Shumway (Guest Author) *

Oct. 15, 2012 - THE SANDCASTLE GIRLS by, Chris Bohjalian

Nov. 12, 2012 - THOSE WE LOVE MOST by, Lee Woodruff (Author Visit) *

Dec. 10, 2012 - THE PRESIDENT'S CLUB: Inside the World's Most Exclusive Fraternity by, Nancy Gibbs & Michael Duffy   Meeting at the John Engeman Theater in Northport – Holiday Luncheon @ Rockin' Fish

***

2013 – Elwood Library Book Discussion Group, "The Literary Gallery"

(2ND Monday of each month from `11:00AM-12:30PM

JANUARY 14, 2013 - A WEDDING IN GREAT NECK by, Yona Zelda McDonough (* Guest Author)

February 11, 2013 - THE LIGHT BETWEEN OCEANS by, M.L.Stedman

March 18, 2013 - GONE GIRL by, Gillian Flynn

April 8, 2013 - SUTTON by, J.R. Moehringer (** L.I. Reads Selection 2013)

May 13, 2013 - THE SECRET KEEPER by, Kate Morton

June 10, 2013 - A WEEK IN WINTER by, Maeve Binchy

NOTE: LAST BOOK DISCUSSION @ BARNES & NOBLE, EAST NORTHPORT (June 10, 2013)

July 8, 2013 - THE BURGESS BOYS by, Elizabeth Strout

NOTE: 1st Book Discussion @ Elwood Library (July 8, 2013)

August 12, 2013 - FEVER by, Mary Beth Keane (* SKYPE Chat w/ author)

September 9, 2013 - LIFE AFTER LIFE by, Kate Atkinson

October 7, 2013 - AND THE MOUNTAINS ECHOED by, Khaled Hosseini

November 4, 2013 - INFERNO by, Dan Brown

December 9, 2013 - THE GIRLS OF ATOMIC CITY: The Untold Story of the Women Who Helped Win WWII by, Denise Kiernan (* SKYPE Chat w/author)

18th Annual Holiday Luncheon @ RUVO'S (Broadway, Greenlawn)

***

January 13, 2014 - THE SUPREME MACARONI COMPANY by, Adriana Trigiani

February 10, 2014 - JACOB'S FOLLY by, Rebecca Miller

March 17, 2014 - THE ART FORGER by, B. A. Shapiro

April 7, 2014 - THE MANOR: Three Centuries At A Slave Plantation on Long Island by, Mac Griswold (**L.I.Reads Selection 2014)

May 12, 2014 - BEAUTIFUL RUINS by, Jess Walter

June 9, 2014 - ME BEFORE YOU by, JoJo Moyes

July 14, 2014 - THE HUSBAND'S SECRET by, Liane Moriarty

August 11, 2014 - SONGS OF WILLOW FROST by, Jamie Forde

September 8, 2014 - THE GOLDFINCH by, Donna Tartt (* Pulitzer Prize Winner 2014)

October 6, 2014 - DANCING ON BROKEN GLASS by, Ka Hancock (*SKYPE Chat w/author)

November 10, 2014 - STILL LIFE WITH BREAD CRUMBS by, Anna Quindlen

December 8, 2014 - I AM MALALA by, Malala Yousafzai and Christina Lamb

ANNUAL HOLIDAY LUNCHEON @ RUVO'S (Broadway, Greenlawn)

***

January 12, 2015 - SOME LUCK by, Jane Smiley

February 2, 2015 - LEAVING TIME by, Jodi Picoult (Snowstorm – Book Club canceled)

March 16, 2015 - GRAND CENTRAL: Original Stories of Postwar Love & Reunion by, Alyson Richman, Jenna Blum,

Melanie Benjamin, Amanda Hodgkinson, Pam Jenoff , Sarah Jio, Sarah McCoy, Kristina McMorris, Erika Robuck, Karen White (* SKYPE Chat with Alyson Richman)

April 13, 2015 - THE MUSEUM OF EXTRAORDINARY THINGS by, Alice Hoffman   (* L.I. Reads 2015 Selection)

May 11, 2015 - ALL THE LIGHT WE CANNOT SEE by, Anthony Doer

SUMMER BREAK: June, July, August 2015

ACKNOWLEDGMENTS

To my cherished "Mommy and Daddy," who I love so much, and who made me the Donna Jean Alicia Perlman Diamond, ("Ultimate Hard-core, High-handed, Card-carrying Bibliophilist"), that I am today.

To my sisters, Diane Perlman Posthauer and Renee Perlman D'Amico, you always believed I was meant to do this. And to my brother, Chris (Cubby). I love you all very much.

To my sister/cousin, Karyn Perlman Connolly, and my sister-in-law, Diane (DeDe) Barrett. You helped bring my story to life.

To Dimon and Dorothy Diamond, (my mother and father-in-law, YaYa and TaTa), who loved to read with me, and who believed someday I would get the attention of Oprah Winfrey. (From their lips to Oprah's ears!)

To my niece and Goddaughter, Kirsten Lamb O'Brien, for reading my story, and for laughing and crying when I hoped the reader would. Many thanks.

And last, but most importantly, to my nephew, Craig Lamb, with love and thanks for making my dream a reality. You designed my fabulous website, designed my book jacket cover, and brought me, kicking and screaming, into 21st Century technology. Mille fois merci!

Made in the USA
Middletown, DE
21 August 2019